The

BMW

Boxer Twins

All air-cooled models 1970-1996
(Except R45, R65, G/S & GS)

Bible

IAN FALLOON

Other great books from Veloce –

Speedpro Series
Harley-Davidson Evolution Engines, How to Build & Power Tune (Hammill)
Motorcycle-engined Racing Car, How to Build (Pashley)
Secrets of Speed – Today's techniques for 4-stroke engine blueprinting & tuning (Swager)

RAC handbooks
How your motorcycle works – Your guide to the components & systems of modern motorcycles (Henshaw)
Caring for your scooter – How to maintain & service your 49cc to 125cc twist & go scooter (Fry)
Motorcycles – A first-time-buyer's guide (Henshaw)

Enthusiast's Restoration Manual Series
Beginner's Guide to Classic Motorcycle Restoration YOUR step-by-step guide to setting up a workshop, choosing a project, dismantling, sourcing parts, renovating & rebuilding classic motorcycles from the 1970s & 1980s, The (Burns)
Classic Large Frame Vespa Scooters, How to Restore (Paxton)
Ducati Bevel Twins 1971 to 1986 (Falloon)
How to restore Honda Fours – YOUR step-by-step colour illustrated guide to complete restoration (Burns)
Yamaha FS1-E, How to Restore (Watts)

Essential Buyer's Guide Series
BMW GS (Henshaw)
BSA 350 & 500 Unit Construction Singles (Henshaw)
BSA 500 & 650 Twins (Henshaw)
BSA Bantam (Henshaw)
Ducati Bevel Twins (Falloon)
Ducati Desmodue Twins (Falloon)
Ducati Desmoquattro Twins - 851, 888, 916, 996, 998, ST4 1988 to 2004 (Falloon)
Harley-Davidson Big Twins (Henshaw)
Hinckley Triumph triples & fours 750, 900, 955, 1000, 1050, 1200 – 1991-2009 (Henshaw)
Honda CBR FireBlade (Henshaw)
Honda CBR600 Hurricane (Henshaw)
Honda SOHC Fours 1969-1984 (Henshaw)
Kawasaki Z1 & Z900 (Orritt)
Moto Guzzi 2-valve big twins (Falloon)
Norton Commando (Henshaw)
Triumph 350 & 500 Twins (Henshaw)
Triumph Bonneville (Henshaw)
Triumph Thunderbird, Trophy & Tiger (Henshaw)
Vespa Scooters – Classic 2-stroke models 1960-2008 (Paxton)

Those Were The Days ... Series
Alpine Trials & Rallies 1910-1973 (Pfundner)
Brighton National Speed Trials (Gardiner)
British Drag Racing – The early years (Pettitt)
Café Racer Phenomenon, The (Walker)
Drag Bike Racing in Britain – From the mid '60s to the mid '80s (Lee)

Biographies
Edward Turner – The Man Behind the Motorcycles (Clew)
Jim Redman – 6 Times World Motorcycle Champion: The Autobiography (Redman)

General
BMW Boxer Twins 1970-1995 Bible, The (Falloon)
BMW Cafe Racers (Cloesen)
BMW Custom Motorcycles – Choppers, Cruisers, Bobbers, Trikes & Quads (Cloesen)
Bonjour – Is this Italy? (Turner)
British 250cc Racing Motorcycles (Pereira)
BSA Bantam Bible, The (Henshaw)
BSA Motorcycles - the final evolution (Jones)
Ducati 750 Bible, The (Falloon)
Ducati 750 SS 'round-case' 1974, The Book of the (Falloon)
Ducati 860, 900 and Mille Bible, The (Falloon)
Ducati Monster Bible, The (Falloon)
Fine Art of the Motorcycle Engine, The (Peirce)
From Crystal Palace to Red Square – A Hapless Biker's Road to Russia (Turner)
Funky Mopeds (Skelton)
Italian Cafe Racers (Cloesen)
Italian Custom Motorcycles (Cloesen)
Kawasaki Triples Bible, The (Walker)
Lambretta Bible, The (Davies)
Laverda Twins & Triples Bible 1968-1986 (Falloon)
Moto Guzzi Sport & Le Mans Bible, The (Falloon)
Motorcycle Apprentice (Cakebread)
Motorcycle GP Racing in the 1960s (Pereira)
Motorcycle Road & Racing Chassis Designs (Noakes)
MV Agusta Fours, The book of the classic (Falloon)
Off-Road Giants! (Volume 1) – Heroes of 1960s Motorcycle Sport (Westlake)
Off-Road Giants! (Volume 2) – Heroes of 1960s Motorcycle Sport (Westlake)
Scooters & Microcars, The A-Z of Popular (Dan)
Scooter Lifestyle (Grainger)
SCOOTER MANIA! – - Recollections of the Isle of Man International Scooter Rally (Jackson)
Singer Story: Cars, Commercial Vehicles, Bicycles & Motorcycle (Atkinson)
Triumph Bonneville Bible (59-83) (Henshaw)
Triumph Bonneville!, Save the – The inside story of the Meriden Workers' Co-op (Rosamond)
Triumph Motorcycles & the Meriden Factory (Hancox)
Triumph Speed Twin & Thunderbird Bible (Woolridge)
Triumph Tiger Cub Bible (Estall)
Triumph Trophy Bible (Woolridge)
TT Talking - The TT's most exciting era – As seen by Manx Radio TT's lead commentator 2004-2012 (Lambert)
Velocette Motorcycles – MSS to Thruxton – New Third Edition (Burris)

For post publication news, updates and amendments relating to this book please visit www.veloce.co.uk/books/V4168

www.veloce.co.uk

First published in February 2009 by Veloce Publishing Limited, Veloce House, Parkway Farm Business Park, Middle Farm Way, Poundbury, Dorchester DT1 3AR, England. Fax 01305 268864 / e-mail info@veloce.co.uk / web www.veloce.co.uk or www.velocebooks.com.
Reprinted June 2014.

ISBN: 978-1-84584-168-3 /UPC: 6-36847-04168-7

THE

BMW

Boxer Twins

All models 1970-1995

BIBLE

VELOCE PUBLISHING
THE PUBLISHER OF FINE AUTOMOTIVE BOOKS

CONTENTS

INTRODUCTION & ACKNOWLEDGEMENTS

Since the release of the R32 in 1923, the boxer twin engine design and the BMW motorcycle have become synonymous. Other manufacturers have emulated, even copied, the design, and BMW has considered replacing the boxer with an alternative engine layout, but the boxer has endured. Max Friz chose the boxer layout because he felt it was ideally suited for a motorcycle application, and this remains relevant today. The two cylinders were out in the air stream for optimum cooling, the engine provided a low centre of gravity, was suited to shaft drive, and could be kept oil-tight. Later designs expanded these features, emphasising reliability and ease of service, BMW's boxer twin always setting the standard for all-round usability.

When the time came to replace the ageing and expensive /2-series it was no surprise that BMW continued its adherence to the boxer layout. While the new Type 246 was undoubtedly cheaper to produce than the /2, it continued to provide unparalleled quality and reliability. Gradually, the Type 246 evolved into the sporting R90S and sport touring R100RS – both landmark motorcycles. The R90S also provided BMW with racing success that had eluded it for decades. Although BMW planned to replace the venerable air-cooled boxer twin during the 1980s, consistent demand saw it remain in production until the mid-1990s. As BMW moved into a world of high technology, the uncomplicated air-cooled twins refused to die – providing pleasure to thousands of enthusiasts around the world. These owners value ease of maintenance and long-term reliability within an accessible technological framework. The air-cooled BMW boxer may no longer be at the cutting edge of high performance, but it remains relevant in a modern world with its open road speed limits and traffic congestion. Because it possesses a unique character and provides unparalleled competence over a wide variety of conditions, the air-cooled BMW boxer twin has, justifiably, earned a loyal following. This book endeavours to document the myriad developmental changes to these motorcycles during their long production run. The material is organised by model year, and only the larger capacity street boxers are included.

The preparation of this manuscript has only been possible with the assistance and enthusiasm of many friends and enthusiasts. Photographs were supplied by the BMW press department, Jeremy Bowdler, editor of *Two Wheels* magazine, Hans Crabbe, Helmut Dähne, Jeff Dean, Nico Georgeoglou, Ivar de Gier, Udo Gietl, Eric Heilveil, Mac Kirkpatrick, Jeff Whitlock and Nolan Woodbury. I must also thank my family, my wife Miriam and sons Ben and Tim, for their continued support of my dedication to such time consuming projects.

Ian Falloon
Melbourne, Australia

CHAPTER I

HISTORICAL BACKGROUND

BMW's first motorcycle was the R32, and it established the boxer twin layout with shaft final-drive that continues today.

The story of BMW motorcycles began during World War I, growing out of two struggling aircraft and aero-engine companies near Oberwiesenfeld airport, in the north-eastern outskirts of Munich. One was the Bayerische Flugzeug-Werke (Bavarian Aircraft Works), founded by Gustav Otto in 1910. The other, only a few hundred meters away, was Karl Rapp's Rapp Motor Works, a manufacturer of aircraft engines. By 1917, Bayerische Flugzeug-Werke was producing 200 aircraft a month, until a fire destroyed the factory and the company was reduced to building furniture. Things were little better for the Rapp Motor Works. Following a series of business disasters, it became a public company and, in 1917, the Bavarian Motor Works was established. The two companies continued to coexist until 1922 when a merger saw BMW move into the BFW premises at Neulerchenfelder Street, later known as Lerchenauer Street. This is still the site of the main BMW works.

In 1917, Rapp's BMW gained a new lease of life when Max Friz joined the company. Friz redesigned one of Rapp's problematic six-cylinder aero-engines, resulting in the BMW IIIa. This new engine allowed German flying ace, Ernst Udet, to down 30 enemy aircraft in his Fokker D VII during the final days of World War I.

Unfortunately for BMW, the 1919 Treaty of Versailles forbode any German company to be involved in aircraft manufacture. This provided the impetus for both BMW and the neighbouring BFW to seek salvation in other fields of manufacturing endeavour. BMW managed to survive after its director, Franz-Josef Popp, secured an order to produce railway pneumatic brakes. BFW decided to produce motorcycles, and its first effort was the Flink of 1920 with a 143cc Hanfland two-stroke engine. Coincidentally, BMW was also interested in motorcycles and in 1920

its foreman, Martin Stolle, stripped down his 1914 Douglas 500cc flat twin. Friz set about copying it, with a few modifications, and the BMW M2 B15 engine was born. This engine was then sold to several motorcycle manufacturers as a proprietary motor, including BFW for its Helios early in 1922. When BMW and BFW merged in June 1922, BMW inherited the Helios production line and some unsold stock. This encouraged Popp to engage Friz in motorcycle design, and Friz embarked on designing the first BMW motorcycle.

The R32 was first launched in Berlin in September 1923, heralding a long line of R-series BMW motorcycles. Although the engine specification was unremarkable, the R32 offered a new level of refinement compared to its contemporaries. Emphasising reliability with low maintenance, the R32 pioneered a formula that would distinguish all BMW motorcycles. While not revolutionary, Friz was the first to combine the features of a horizontal-transverse twin with shaft final-drive.

The R32's engine was based on the M2 B15, retaining the same 68x68mm bore and stroke, and one-piece, cast-iron, side-valve cylinder and head layout. With a 5.0:1 compression and single, small 22mm BMW special carburettor, the power was only 8.5 horsepower at 3200rpm. The clutch was a dry single disc type, and with the hand operated, three-speed, grease-filled gearbox, the R32 was years ahead of its time when it came to user-friendliness. The flat twin engine was housed in a closed-duplex tubular-steel frame, with a rigid rear end and short-swinging front fork. On early models, there was no front brake, and the block rear brake was an old-fashioned type, heel operated with a dummy-belt rim. The 122kg (268lb) R32 was capable of around 90km/h (56mph), and the second series of 1925 included a small (150mm) front drum brake. Although greeted with scepticism, the transverse-horizontal twin-cylinder engine layout proved ideally suited to a motorcycle. The two cylinders were

adequately cooled by the air stream, and the design provided a low centre of gravity, contributing to agile handling. Although the R32 was an expensive, premium quality, luxury product, it was a success and it paved the way for a succession of more sophisticated models.

By 1924, Friz was again working on aero-engines and motorcycle development was entrusted to Rudolf Schleicher. Schleicher was not only a fine engineer, but an outstanding motorcyclist, riding a prototype overhead-valve R32 to victory in the 1924 ADAC Winter Rally in Garmisch-Partenkirchen. This was BMW's first sporting success, and the overhead-valve R32 eventually became the R37. Although only 16 horsepower at 4000rpm, the R37 won nearly 100 races in Germany during 1925. Schleicher also took an R37 to England for the Six-Day race, winning a gold medal.

During 1926, the R32 evolved into the R42. The engine was still a side-valve 500, but with new detachable light alloy cylinder heads and circumferential cylinder cooling fins. The power was now 12 horsepower at 3400rpm, the engine located further rearwards to improve handling, and the braking updated with the introduction of a driveshaft rear brake with narrow brake shoes mounted on the gearbox case. Although only produced for two years, the R42 was the most popular BMW motorcycle of the 1920s and more than 6500 were sold.

By 1926 the R32 evolved into the side-valve R42, one of BMW's most successful motorcycles of the 1920s.

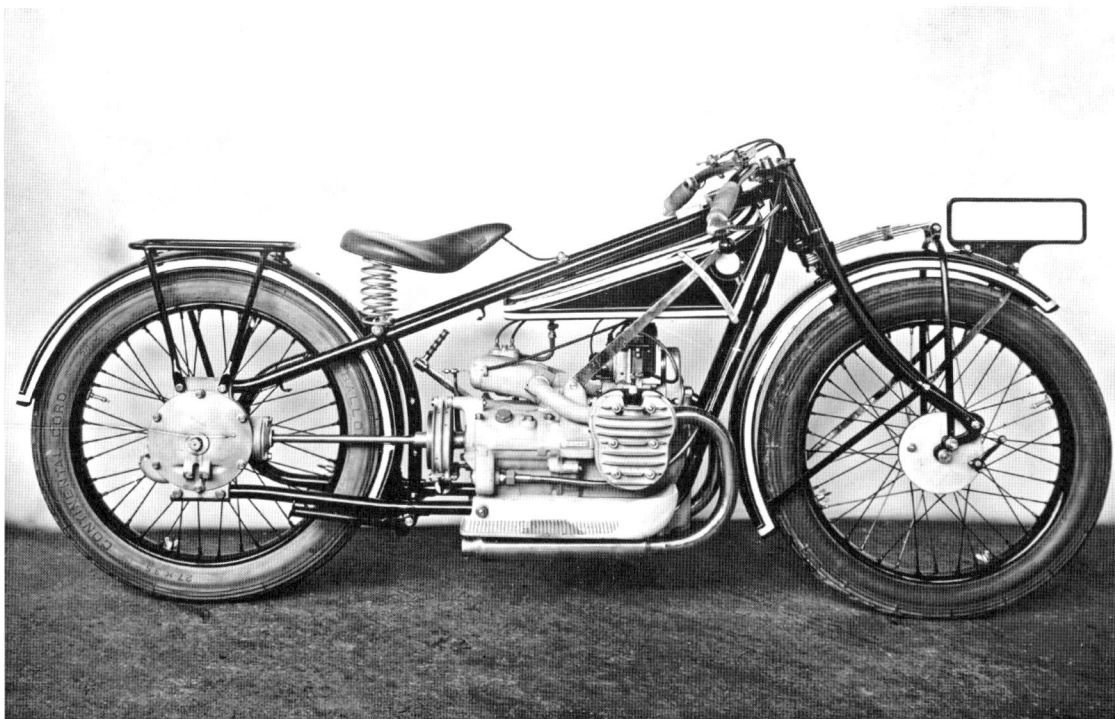

While BMW was earning a reputation for producing solid and reliable side-valve touring machines like the R32 and R42, it continued to develop the 500cc overhead-valve sporting model. In 1927, the R47 replaced the R37 and, while still an expensive sporting model, it shared the R42 chassis to keep costs down. The power was now 18 horsepower at 4000rpm.

Four new boxer twins were unveiled for 1928, including two 750cc models. The side-valve R52 and R62 shared a longer (78mm) stroke, while the overhead-valve R57 and R63 retained the 68mm stroke. Producing 24 horsepower at 4000rpm, and capable of 120km/h (75mph), the R63 was one of the fastest and most powerful motorcycles of its day. It also formed the basis of the next generation of racing machines, providing BMW with 91 victories through until 1930.

Problems with the frames cracking when fitted with a sidecar led to the replacement of the R62 and R63 with two new 750cc models in 1929. These were the side-valve R11, and overhead-valve R16, both with a pressed-steel frame. Ugly and heavy, the frame also included a pressed-steel trailing-link front fork and leaf-spring front suspension.

These new austere machines weren't particularly exciting, but the R11 found favour with the military and helped sustain the company through the difficult period of the early 1930s.

Germany was hit particularly hard by the 1929 world depression and, in the wake of falling sales, BMW decided to concentrate on world speed records instead of racing. Its first successful attempt was in September 1929, when Ernst Henne set a world record of 134.68mph (216.9km/h) on a short-stroke 750. Henne would set many more records over the next decade, culminating in November 1937 when he acheived 173.69mph (279.503km/h) on a supercharged 500. This record stood for fourteen years.

BMW's fortunes had improved by 1934, leading to the release of two new 750cc models for 1935. These were the side-valve R12, and overhead-valve R17, replacing the R11 and R16. The R12 proved even more popular with the military than the R11, and 36,000 were produced until 1942. Although it shared the utilitarian R12 chassis, the 33 horsepower R17 was sold as a high performance sporting machine, and was considerably more expensive.

Ernst Henne set many world speed records for BMW during the 1930s.

The R12 of 1935 was one of the first motorcycles to have a telescopic front fork.

Both the R12 and R17 were an amalgam of conservatism and radicalism. The engine and drivetrain were similar to those of their predecessors, as was the old-fashioned pressed-steel frame with a rigid rear end. But the front suspension was via a set of rudimentary oil-damped telescopic forks – the first hydraulic forks to appear on a production motorcycle. While the R12 found a ready market, during 1935 the 500 Kompressor established itself in the racing world and the time was right for a new sporting flagship. BMW responded with the R5, an all-time classic, and the most advanced motorcycle of its day.

Although the arc-welded tubular-steel frame and telescopic forks were similar to those of the racing Kompressor, the R5's engine was all-new, sharing little with the racer or earlier production models. Central to the design was the one-piece, tunnel-type, aluminium crankcase that would feature on all air-cooled twins through until 1996.

Instead of a single camshaft, the R5 had two chain-driven camshafts above the crankshaft, the long timing chain also driving the Bosch generator on top of the crankcase. The four-speed gearbox was now foot operated, and, while the power (24 horsepower at 5800rpm) was less than that of the R17, the 165kg (363lb) R5 was a much more sporting motorcycle. Despite the rigid frame, handling rivalled that of the best British singles, and a 600cc side-valve R6 joined it in 1937. The R6 featured a completely new engine design with a single gear-driven camshaft, but lasted just one year because the military still favoured the pressed-steel frame R12 for sidecar use.

The racing Kompressor gained rear-suspension for the 1937 season, and demonstrated its superiority by winning four Grand Prix races that year. In the wake of this success, rear suspension was added to four new production models for 1938. The R51 and R61 replaced the

9

One of the most outstanding pre-war BMW motorcycles, the R5 of 1936.

R5 and R6, while the side-valve 750cc R71 was introduced as another replacement for the R12. This time it was more successful, and the R71, BMW's final side-valve twin, lasted until 1941. But the most exciting new motorcycle for 1938 was the top-of-the-range sporting R66. Combining the overhead-valve cylinder heads of the R51, with the superior single gear-driven camshaft setup of the R6, R61, and R71, the 70x78mm 600cc twin produced an impressive 30 horsepower at 5300rpm. This was enough to provide a top speed of 90mph (145km/h), an impressive speed for a production motorcycle in 1938. BMW also offered racing versions of the R5 and R51 to well connected privateers. An R5SS and sprung frame R51SS appeared during 1937, but the most effective of these limited edition production racers was the R51RS (Rennsport). Although it retained pushrod operated overhead-valves, this was the closest production model to the works Kompressor. The single camshaft engine was based on the R66, and the power was 36 horsepower.

The side-valve twin remained popular throughout the 1930s; the most successful was the sprung frame R71, introduced in 1938.

Hungarian Champion Endre Kozma on an R51RS in 1939.

On the eve of World War II, Georg Meier won the Senior TT at the Isle of Man on the BMW Kompressor. (Courtesy Ivar de Gier)

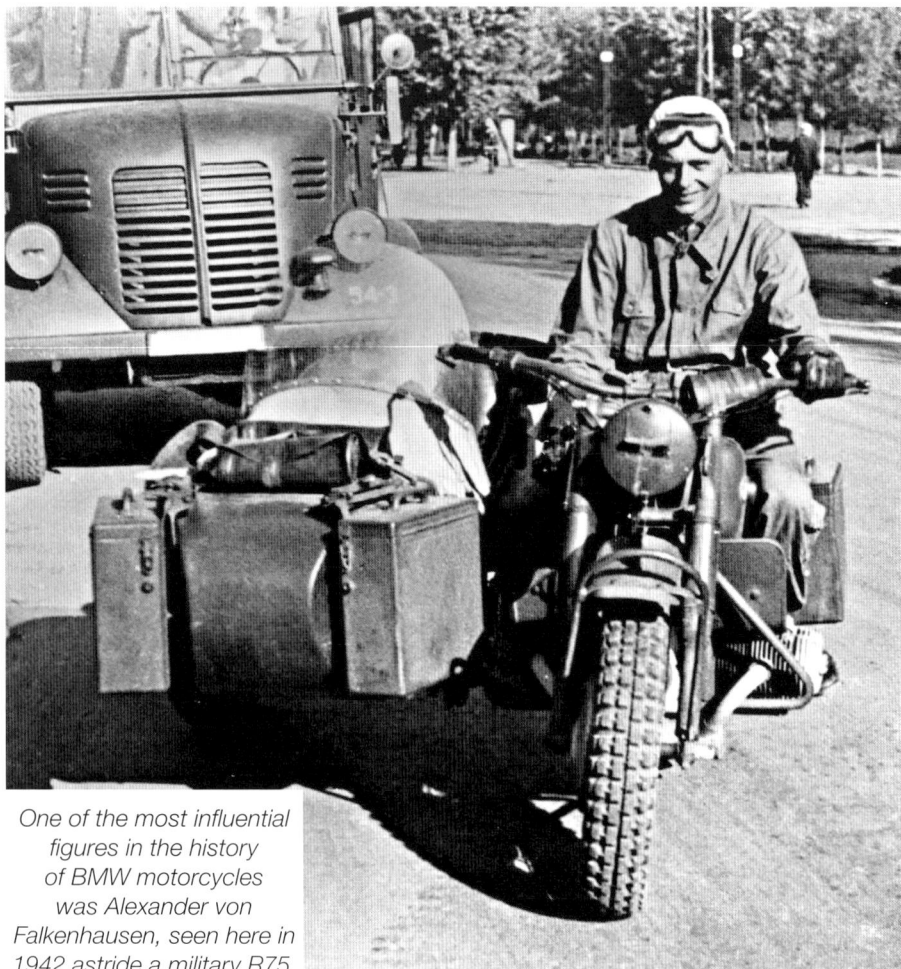

One of the most influential figures in the history of BMW motorcycles was Alexander von Falkenhausen, seen here in 1942 astride a military R75.

BMW's first post-war twin was the R51/2. This was very similar to the pre-war R51, and particularly suitable for sidecars.

BMW continued to develop the racing Kompressor, with Georg 'Schorsch' Meier winning the 1938 European Championship. This was a magnificent achievement, but his finest moment came at the Isle of Man in June 1939. Meier won the Senior TT, the first foreigner on a foreign machine, travelling an average speed of 89.38mph (143.8km/h). Jock West came second but BMW's victory was marred by the death of its other works rider, Karl Gall, after a crash during practice. Following the outbreak of World War II, military production assumed priority, including the venerable R12 and a new military motorcycle, the R75.

Although BMW's Munich-Milbertshofen plant was extensively bombed, by 1948 BMW was again producing motorcycles. Initially, this was restricted to 250cc and the first post-war motorcycle was the single cylinder R24, based on the pre-war R23. Capacity restrictions were lifted during 1949 but, with little money available for development, the 1938 R51 was resurrected as the R51/2. An updated R51/3 was introduced for 1951. Although similar to the R51/2, powering the R51/3 was a new engine with a gear-driven single camshaft above the crankshaft. This was joined soon afterwards by the 600cc R67 and higher performance R68. The R68 was marketed as an expensive lifestyle accessory, but was also one of the leading sporting motorcycles, available in 1952. With 35 horsepower at 7000rpm, the claimed top speed was 160km/h (100mph).

BMW's continued success in the early 1950s prompted a return to racing, and the creation of the RS54 Rennsport. With a bevel-gear-driven double overhead camshaft engine, derived from the pre-war Kompressor, the RS54 formed the basis of all factory racers for the rest of the decade. Fitted with an Earles leading-link front fork, the limited production RS54 was not particularly successful as a solo racer but, the engine subsequently powered sidecar world championship machines until the mid-1970s.

The RS54 racers had an Earles front fork but were not as successful a solo racer as envisaged.

with four new models being released in 1961.

Heading the new line up were two sporting models, the R50S and R69S, alongside new versions of the R50 and R60: the R50/2 and R60/2. The /2s looked outwardly similar to their predecessors but underneath there were a number of developments, primarily aimed at improving reliability. The R50S was short-lived due to its unreliability, but the R69S would become one of BMW's most successful twins. Now producing 42 horsepower at 7000rpm, the top speed was a claimed 109mph (175km/h).

Sidecars powered by the Rennsport engine were much more successful. Klaus Enders and Ralf Englehart won four World Championships between 1969 and 1974.

The production R50 of 1955 also had an Earles front fork.

Replacing the R51/3 and R68 in 1955 were two new twins, the R50 and R69. These featured front and rear swingarm suspension patterned on the RS54 racer. The driveshaft was now enclosed in the right-side of the swingarm, with the universal joint moved to the gearbox end. The next year saw a touring R60, but this coincided with a serious slump in motorcycle sales. During 1957, several German manufacturers (including Adler, DKW and Horex) disappeared, while BMW's motorcycle production slumped to less than 5500. There was virtually no motorcycle development for five years, and BMW faced bankruptcy in 1959. A rally of shareholders saw the company survive and, during 1960, the motorcycle range was developed and improved

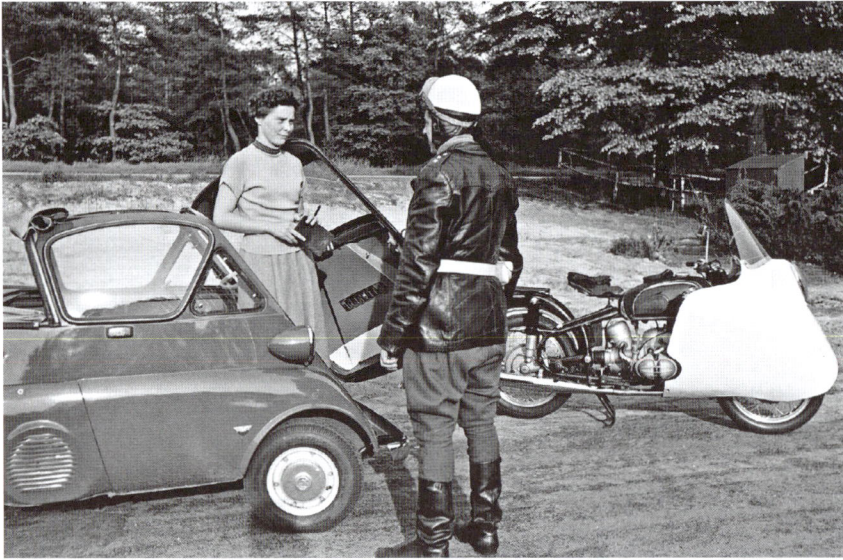

BMW motorcycles have always been popular with police forces.

Although production during the 1960s never managed to replicate the boom years of the early 1950s, the /2 twins sold solidly until 1967. As sales tapered, particularly in the US, specific US models were developed with a telescopic fork, replacing the idiosyncratic Earles fork. By this stage, car production was expanding and becoming increasingly profitable, and as a remnant of an earlier era, the /2 was expensive to produce. The /2 was built with lavish attention to detail and finish, and the engine – with its pressed together roller bearing crankshaft and gear camshaft drive – didn't lend itself to mass production. Even components such as the throttle control and the rear brake linkage were unnecessarily complex. As sales dwindled to around 5000 in 1968, it was becoming more difficult to justify the /2 existence. Fortunately, plans were in hand to introduce a new generation BMW motorcycle.

For 1961 BMW released the sporting R69S. This would head the motorcycle line up for the rest of the decade.

BMW motorcycle production moved to Berlin in 1967, and the first motorcycle to roll out of the new factory was an R60/2.

CHAPTER II

THE /5-SERIES (TYPE 246)

Times were tough for European motorcycle manufacturers during the 1960s. The Japanese already dominated the smaller capacity market but they gradually expanded their horizons. This threatened the survival of the British and European manufacturers that concentrated on motorcycles over 250cc. Built with up-to-date machinery, these new mass-produced Japanese motorcycles offered class-leading performance and were cheap and reliable. Although motorcycle sales sustained BMW early in the 1960s, by 1963 BMW's new range of cars was more successful and profitable. The increase in demand for cars was coupled with a reduction for motorcycles.

In spite of a threat to stop motorcycle production altogether, technical director Helmut Werner Bönsch remained firmly committed to motorcycles. Facing opposition during 1963, Bönsch managed to persuade BMW's directors to sanction a pilot scheme, to develop a replacement for the /2 with an internal designation of Type 246. Under the supervision of Claus von Rücker a new chassis was fabricated for the R69S. Von Rücker came from Porsche in 1964, bringing with him Hans-Günther von der Marwitz to head the Test Department. Hailing from a distinguished family, von der Marwitz was born in 1927 (he died in 2002), and had also worked with Kreidler and Henkel. Like Friz and Schleicher before him, he was an avid motorcyclist, used to racing around on an AJS 7R. He was dismayed at the handling of the Earles fork R69S and wanted the new BMW to handle as well as a Manx Norton. It was no coincidence that the prototype frame for the new boxer twin

The impetus behind the /5 design was Hans-Günther von der Marwitz.

was a full cradle duplex type, that bore more than a passing resemblance to the Rex McCandless Manx Norton 'featherbed.'

Replacing the Earles fork of the /2 on the 246 prototype was a set of telescopic forks. Initially, these were rather rudimentary with small diameter fork tubes, but already included a leading axle mount to reduce the trail. The first version was

built in off-road guise, with a high-rise single muffler exhaust on the right and minimal street equipment. Its debut was at an off-road event in Eschwege, in April 1964.

During 1964, the 246 prototype evolved into a street model. As a test rider, von der Marwitz had a strong influence on the design, ensuring the new bike handled well. There was no longer a requirement for sidecar capability and the prototype was considerably lighter than the R69S. A 19-inch front wheel and stronger front fork were fitted, and the styling of the fuel tank and seat began to assume the proportions of the eventual production version. The telescopic front fork soon found its way on the US /2, while chassis development of the 246 continued throughout 1965 and 1966. A new engine was required if overall development was to proceed further.

By 1965, the specifications for a more

modern boxer twin were being considered by Engine Development head Alex von Falkenhausen and Ferdinand Jardin. To improve reliability and reduce costs they decided to introduce many features of the recently developed, smaller capacity BMW automobiles, in particular, a plain-bearing crankshaft. While the four-speed gearbox, single-plate dry clutch and driveshaft through the swingarm was similar to the /2, a Bosch electric start and three-phase generator were new additions. By 1967, the prototype was close to the eventual production version.

Despite a recession in Germany during 1967, demand for BMW's new range of compact cars from 1500 to 2000cc continued unabated. It was decided to move motorcycle production to Berlin to provide additional capacity in Munich. BMW already owned a repair and machine work factory in the West Berlin suburb of Spandau, and

The /5 broke with the traditional BMW motorcycle mould, establishing a formula that would last 25 years.

THE /5-SERIES (TYPE 246)

during 1967, this was converted into a motorcycle production facility. Originally set up as an aircraft engine factory by Siemens & Halske in 1928, in 1936 it became Brandenburgische Motorenwerke (Bramo). Bramo merged with BMW to become BMW Flugmotoren-Gesellschaft in 1939, and after World War II, the works became BMW Maschinenfabrik Spandau. It initially produced scythe and sickle hand tools for agricultural use, and from 1958, was involved in the manufacture of vehicle components. While the motorcycle development and administration remained in Munich, the first motorcycles left the Spandau factory in 1967. Gradually, the plant was prepared for the release of the /5 for the 1970 model year, and when it was released at Hockenheim on August 28, 1969, even the sceptics were impressed.

R75/5, R60/5, R50/5 1970 model year

Although a small number of all types were built for press and dealer evaluation in August 1969, production of the R60/5 commenced in September 1969, the R75/5 in October, and the R50/5 in November. The R75/5 was also the first official 750cc twin since the military R75 of 1942-44, but even as the 750 was first rolling off the production line, BMW was testing 900cc versions. 1970 model year frame numbers for the R50/5 began at 2900001, through to 2901810. The R60/5 frame numbers began at 2930001, finishing at 2932774, while the R75/5 began at 2970001, ending at 2973761. Each model received a new code from BMW, R75/5 (0260), R60/5 (0250), and R50/5 (0240).

/5 engine

The air-cooled boxer engine in the /5-series and subsequent developments was known as the M04*. The design differed significantly in detail and execution to the /2. Reliability rather than outright power was emphasised in the design, and the crankshaft now a one-piece forged type running in plain main bearings. The single camshaft was also located below the crankshaft, as originally proposed by Leonhard Ischinger in the prototype M205-M208 500-800cc twins of 1932. These extremely advanced designs also featured a one-piece tunnel crankcase and forged crankshaft with plain bearings, but never reached the production line.

As the camshaft was now underneath the crankshaft, the pushrods were also below the cylinders, tidying the look of the engine. The pushrod tubes also provided an oil return to the crankcase. Unlike the /2 engine that featured a gear camshaft drive, the camshaft was driven by a duplex chain. Also improving the engine aesthetics, was the extension of the crankcase to the fuel tank, with aluminium covers for the new electric start and air filter on top of the engine. Considerable effort was spent in minimising weight and, instead of the earlier pressed steel sump, the /5 had a cast aluminium sump cover.

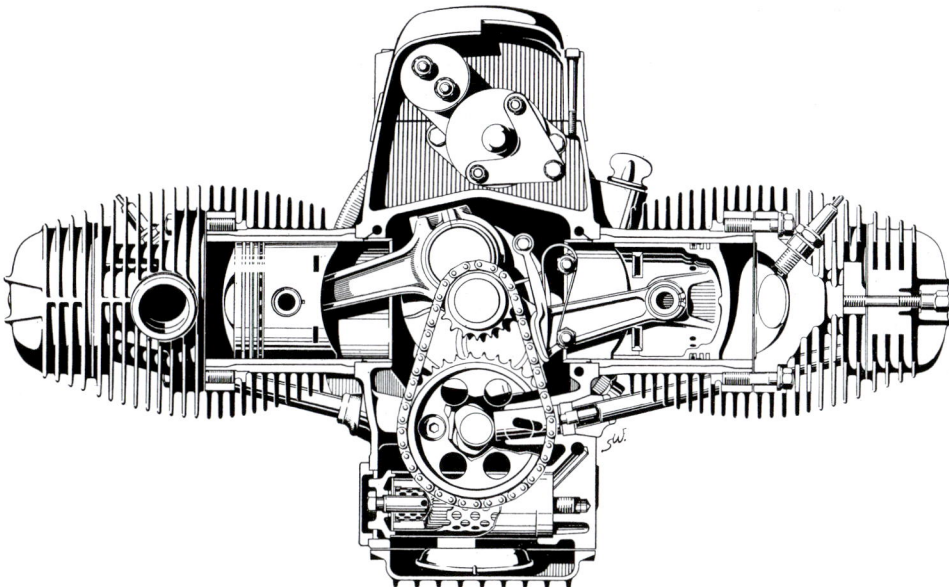

The /5 camshaft was chain-driven and situated below the crankshaft.

Ostensibly the three /5 variants were identical, sharing the same stroke but with different bores. With carburettors and oil, but without ignition coils and an induction system, the R50/5 engine weighed 58.5kg, the R60/6 engine 63.5kg, and the R75/5 engine 64.9kg. Typical of BMW's methodical development, the basic engine design was so sound that it survived through until 1996 with only minimal updates.

As on all boxer twins since the R5, the /5 engine housing was a one-piece tunnel type, however, because it incorporated an electric starter motor and air filter above the crankcase, it was bulkier than its predecessor. Internal gussets reinforced the cast aluminium housing, and the engine number was located on the engine block, on the left, above the oil filler. There was also a BMW logo stamped after the seven-digit number. The very earliest crankcase housing (July 1969) featured 'BMW' lettering, cast above the cylinder like on the /2 series (and carried a different part number), although, during 1970, the crankcase was standardised. The three models were differentiated through identification plates on either side of the upper crankcase, the earliest plates without a black background. Instead of the /2's pressed-steel sump cover, the /5 had a cast aluminium cover, retained by 14 instead of 12 bolts. The aluminium housing for the timing chain was two-piece and smooth cast, without any air vents.

While maintaining a design without a centre main bearing to minimise offset, the crankshaft was now a one-piece drop-forged steel type. Rigidity was achieved by increasing the main bearing journal diameter to 60mm (from 35mm on the R69S), with three-layer (bronze, tin, and indium) plain bearings shared with the newly developed six-cylinder M06* 2500cc BMW car engine. These bearings were pressed into a die-forged alloy bearing bush inserted in the front and rear of the crankcase. Also increased, was the big-end journal diameter (to 48mm), while the die-forged steel conrods were two-piece (with a 22mm off-centre gudgeon pin). The conrods, also shared with the M06* six-cylinder car engine, ran in three-layer plain bearings, while the gudgeon pins ran in bronze bushes. With an eye-to-eye length of 135mm the stroke to conrod length ratio was 1.91:1, close to the optimum 2:1. An automotive-type flywheel was bolted onto the end of the crankshaft and included a ring gear for the electric start.

Three-ring convex, rising oval, forged aluminium pistons were fitted to the /5. These were almost flat topped, with very little valve cutaway. The top piston ring (compression) was hard chrome-plated and quite thin to avoid flutter and loss of compression at higher rpm. The second ring was an L-shaped Dykes pattern compression ring, with a third, oil-scraper ring. There was also a higher compression competition piston available for the R75/5.

Unlike the R69S that had cast-iron cylinders, the /5 cylinders were aluminium with bonded cast-iron sleeves. The sleeves were molecularly bonded to the cylinders, through a process known as Al-Fin, and provided the benefits of less weight and improved heat dissipation. Because of the more uniform expansion rates between the piston and cylinder, closer tolerances were specified (0.0035-0.0045mm). Two pushrod tubes were pressed into the bottom of the cylinder, also providing an oil return to the crankcase. The 0.5mm cylinder base gasket was aluminium fibre, with the cylinder head gasket being metal-asbestos.

There was a new cylinder head design for the /5, with the two overhead-valves set at a shallower, 65-degree included angle. The finned cylinder head was constructed

An electric start motor was situated above the large crankcase. A four-speed gearbox was available on the /5.

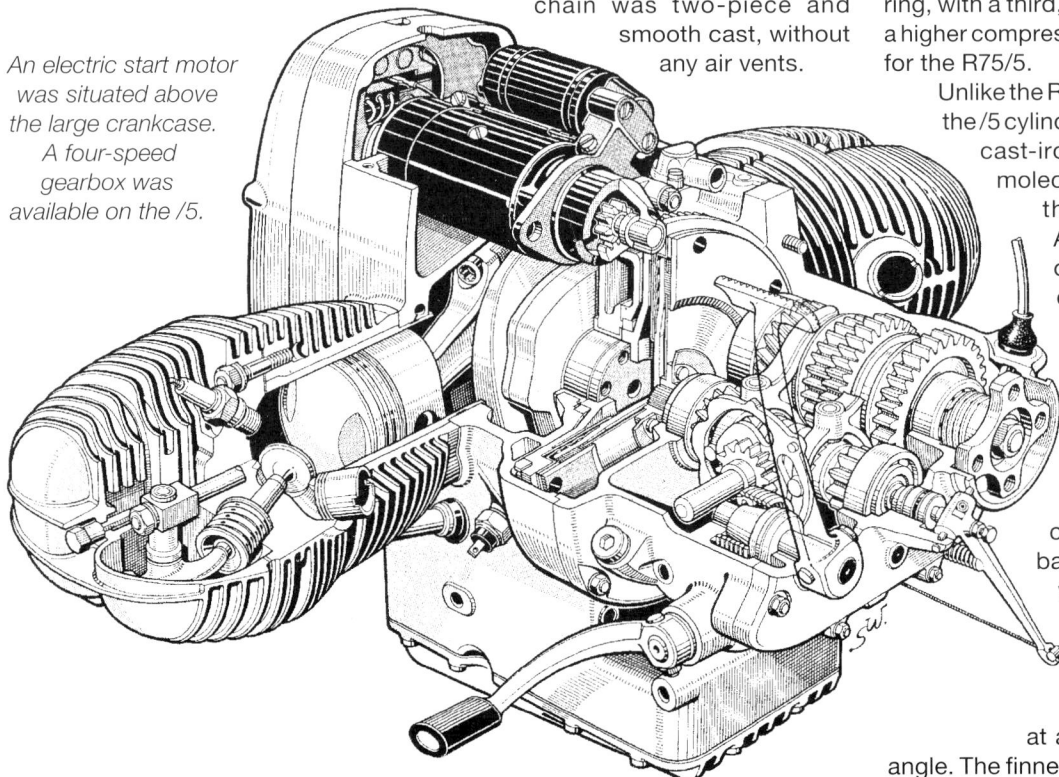

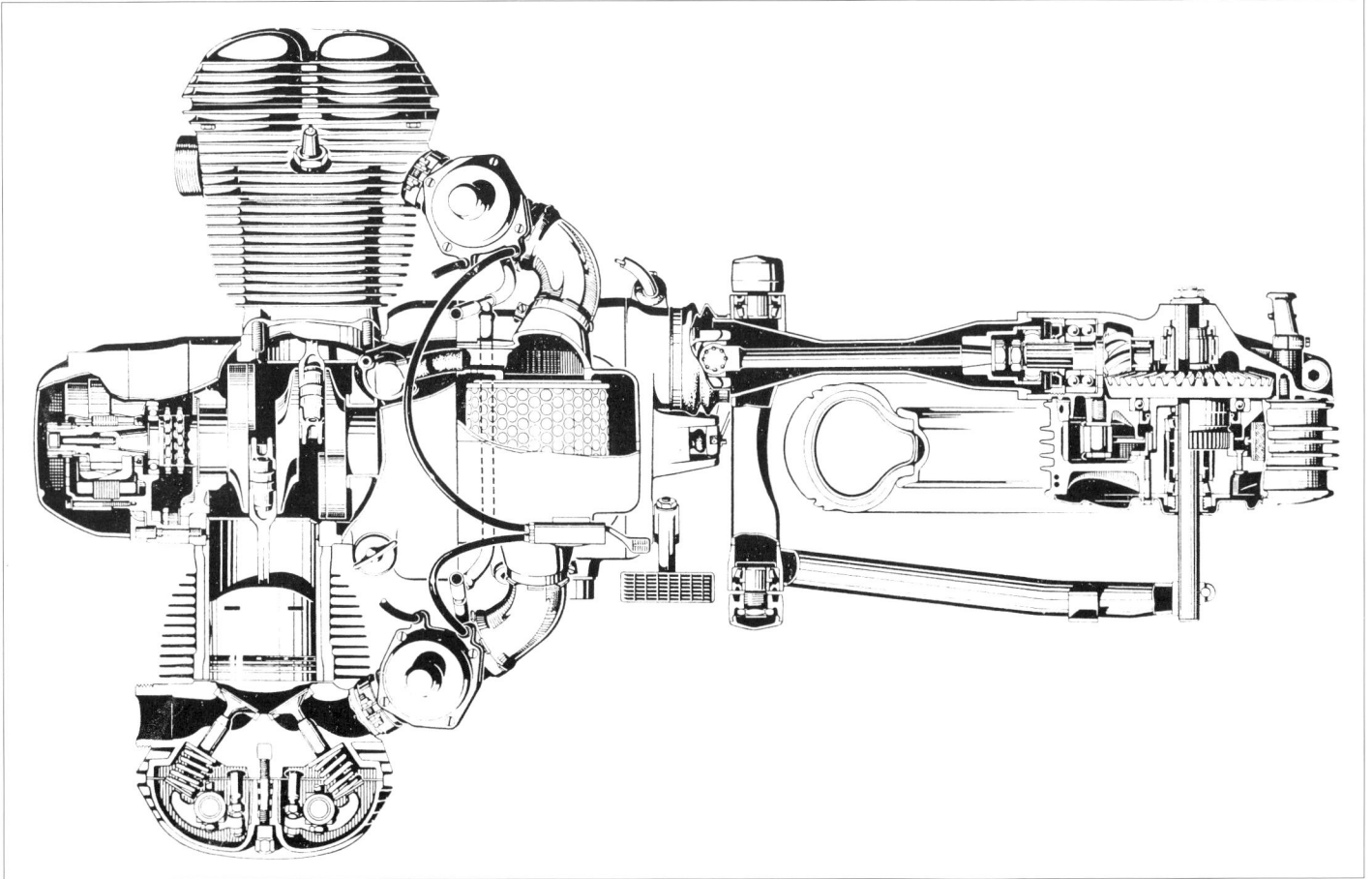

of aluminium alloy, with shrunk-in valve seats, fine pearlitic grey iron for the intake, and high alloy grey iron for the exhaust. Each version of the /5 came with different valves, the R75/5 with 42mm intake and 38mm exhaust (both 98.8mm long). On the R60/5, the valves were 38mm intake (98.5mm long) and 34mm exhaust (97.5mm long), with the R50/5 receiving 34mm and 32mm valves (103mm and 102.5mm long). All valve stems were hard chrome-plated and 8mm in diameter, while the exhaust valves had a heat conductive ferrite stem, and an austenitic head. The valves were actuated through 22mm hardened followers, pushrods, and rocker arms, with the pushrod having a similar coefficient of expansion to the cylinder to maintain a consistent valve clearance. The valve springs were a single coil-type, and the valve guides 54mm long.

The threaded intake manifold was 26mm in diameter for the R50/5 and R60/5, and 36mm in diameter for the R75/5. The R75/5 manifold was 30mm long, though this was later reduced to 25mm. Von der Marwitz insisted on longer and sturdier cylinder bolts and, for the first time on

a BMW motorcycle engine, the cylinders and cylinder head were retained by four long studs (10x275mm). Two additional bolts (10x30mm and 10x50mm) connected the cylinder head with the cylinder. Rocker arm blocks were attached to these through-bolts, with the rocker arms pivoting on 18mm floating bronze bushings. The rocker arm ratio was 1:1.39. Soon after production commenced, sealing of the top end locating dowels was improved, with 15x2x3mm O-rings and spacers (from R50/5 2900602, R60/5 2930965, and R75/5 2970980).

The case-hardened die-cast camshaft ran directly into the crankcase at the rear, and into a flanged aluminium bearing support at the front. It was phosphated for lower friction, and an oil pump rotor for the Eaton oil pump was incorporated at the rear. Located on the front of the camshaft were the ignition advance unit and the tachometer drive gear. While the R50/5 and R60/5 shared the same camshaft, the R75/5 used a sporting camshaft with greater overlap and a 110-degree lobe centre (compared to the 90-degree lobe centre for the R50 and R60/5). The R75/5 camshaft also provided

The cylinder head design was new, with a narrower included valve angle. An alternator was also fitted to the front of the engine.

6.756mm of valve lift, compared to 6.198mm for the R50/5 and R60/5.

The duplex chain camshaft drive was similar to that on the overhead camshaft BMW car engines. The 50-link double roller 3/8x7/32in chain incorporated an automatic leaf spring tensioner, and the lower sprocket ran in a 35x62x9mm bearing in the housing. A 5x6.5mm woodruff key located the sprocket on the camshaft.

The plain bearings inside the engine required copious amounts of filtered high pressure oil, and this was supplied by an Eaton hypo trochoidal pump – essentially a four-bladed impeller revolving inside a five-chamfered housing, it was capable of delivering 1400 litres per hour at 6000rpm. On the early /5 a very small 2.5x3.7mm woodruff key connected the inner rotor to the camshaft. The oil pump sucked oil from the oil pan through a suction bell with a perforated screen, pumped it through the main lubricating passages and into the automotive type disposable full flow oil filter. This was retained by a plain cover on the /5.

Oil was then pressure fed to passages in the camshaft bearing flange and the main bearing cover, through the left-side of the crankcase to the rear main bearing. It then went upward, through the two upper through-bolt holes in the cylinder, to the tappet bearing blocks and shafts, lubricating the valve mechanism. The connecting rods were lubricated through holes in the crankshaft, receiving their oil from the annular groove of the front or rear main bearing sleeve, with the rear camshaft bearing lubricated directly by the oil pump. The timing chain was splash lubricated from the sump and a venting dome on top of the crankcase separated the oil mist from crankcase pressure, through a check ball valve. This was then fed back into the intake. Undoubtedly, the efficiency of the lubrication system contributed to the outstanding reliability of the M04* engine throughout its long production lifespan.

A new air intake system was designed for the /5. Instead of the air filter being situated in a separate housing above the transmission, it was now incorporated inside the engine cases, also at the rear above the gearbox. At the top of the housing, underneath the fuel tank, was a rear facing air intake grill. As the air intake faced rearward there was no ram air effect but the air filter volume was 60 percent larger than that of the R69S. A small amount of air went to cool the electrical components on the front of the engine, before the filtered air entered a common chamber, under the large 'Micro Star' disposable dry paper air filter element. Air then proceeded to two individual carburettor ducts and, while this

The R75/5 had new Bing constant vacuum carburettors. Early models had sliver plastic intakes that changed colour over time. (Courtesy Eric Heilveil)

convoluted intake system didn't contribute to horsepower, it successfully quelled intake noise as well as providing excellent air filtration. To prevent oil from the engine breather contaminating the air filter, an improved engine breather tube was fitted after R50/5 2901704, R60/5 2932473, and R75/5 2973142.

After considering Japanese Keihin carburettors, the Nuremburg company Bing eventually gained the contract to supply the /5. Two types of carburettor were fitted. The R50/5 and R60/5 received Bing 26mm concentric carburettors, and the R75/5 received a new vacuum type Bing 32mm carburettor. The vacuum carburettors were initially built in the BMW development shop to very fine tolerances. Unfortunately, the first batch of Bing vacuum carburettors suffered from inadequate tolerances, delaying the introduction of the R75/5 until after the two smaller versions. The R75 carburettors were also attached to the cylinder heads through short rubber sleeves and 52mm diameter clamps to isolate them from vibration. There was no choke provided on the concentric carburettor, only an enriching float plunger, while an accelerator pump supplied additional fuel. The plastic intake tubes were silver on 1970 models. After R50/5 number 2900441, a 135 main jet replaced the 145 main jet and the needle position was changed from 2 to 3. A kit to improve the accelerator pump action was also installed on the R60/5, from number 2930530. Eventually, BMW provided an updated carburettor for the R75/5, from number 2972061, the carburettor receiving a reinforced 0.4mm diaphragm and a 'C' on the top of the carburettor body.

All /5s shared the chrome-plated steel 38x1.5mm exhaust headers and distinctive 100mm diameter cigar-shaped muffler. This large capacity exhaust system included a crossover pipe in front of the engine and was designed to minimise backpressure over a wide rpm range, accentuating quietness over performance.

The /5 received an up-to-date 12 volt electrical system, including an automotive-type three-phase alternator positioned on the end of the crankshaft. Designed by BMW and built by Bosch, this G1 14V 13A19 alternator provided 180 watts and a maximum current strength of 13 amps. There was a diode plate mounted above the alternator and a Bosch AD 1/14V regulator controlled the voltage. A small Varta 15 Ah battery completed the electrical system, and the first modification to the /5 was during the autumn of 1970, when a new, more flexible battery cable was installed (from number R50/5 2900921, R60/5 2931336, and R75/5 2971545) to minimise damage from vibration. At about the same time, there was an improved alternator rotor (R50/5 2901772, R60/5 2932606, and R75/5 2973649), claimed to be more stable and with a blue or white marking.

The battery and points ignition system included a single contact breaker opened by a cam incorporated on the end of the camshaft. Common to all three /5 models was the Bosch centrifugal ignition advance unit sitting on the end of the camshaft. Ignition advance began at 800rpm, ending at approximately 2500rpm. The dwell angle for 1970 was 110 degrees or 61 per cent. Right at the end of the 1970 model year, in July (R75/5) and August (R50/5, R60/5), a new centrifugal advance unit was fitted (from R50/5 2901787, R60/5 2932689 and R75/5 9273307). It provided maximum advance at 3000rpm with 43 per cent dwell, but can really be considered a 1971 model year update. Twin Bosch 6 volt coils were mounted in series and the high tension leads were 550mm, with metal shrouded (with resistor) Bosch or Beru sparkplug caps.

The R50/5 and R60/5 retained the earlier Bing slide-type carburettor with plunger enrichment for cold starting.

The sparkplug caps on the /5 were metal shrouded Bosch or Beru.

on early examples, with the starter inadvertently engaged while the engine was running.

A 180mm single disc dry clutch connected the crankshaft and the transmission input shaft, with a diaphragm spring compressing a pressure plate and bonded friction lining clutch plate. The R50/5 and R60/5 spring was 2.4mm thick and 17.5mm high, while the stronger R75/5 spring was 2.6mm thick and 19.0mm high. A diaphragm was spot-welded to the pressure plate, between the flywheel and pressure ring, allowing the pressure plate to move axially and to transmit some engine torque. The 6mm clutch plate was mounted on the splines of the transmission input shaft and was disengaged by a pushrod inside the input shaft, activated by a lever.

Hidden underneath a removable alloy cover and located above the crankcase was a Bosch DF 12V 0.5-horsepower series wound D.C. electric start motor and transistor-controlled relay. The electric start was standard on the R75/5 and R60/5, and optional on the R50/5. Although the /5 was the first BMW motorcycle to feature an electric start, there was still the traditional kick start incorporated at the back of the gearbox and connected to the input shaft. Starting was generally reliable, although, despite the small battery, the penalty was weight because the electric start assembly weighed more than 20kg. There was some solenoid problems

Designed by Development Team member Rüdiger Gutsche, the gearbox was similar to that of the /2 but with wider gears, and a lighter, stronger housing. Gutsche was not only an engineer, he was a leading competition rider. He would later achieve notable success in the ISDT on his specially-developed R75/5 and, after a few years, would be responsible for the R80 G/S. Gutsche was instructed to retain the earlier gearbox drilling equipment. The all-indirect four-speed transmission mounted directly to the engine housing, the three-shaft design comprising an input shaft,

The US /5 had higher handlebars than European versions.

countershaft, and output shaft. The countershaft and output shafts incorporated four gears, each in constant mesh, with a spring and cam-type shock absorber also on the output shaft. The transmission shafts were supported in ball bearings and, although the gearbox shifted more smoothly than earlier BMW twins, it still wasn't flawless. There were to be many modifications to the shifting mechanism over the next few years. A close-ratio competition gearbox was an option.

Drive from the gearbox was through an enclosed driveshaft running in an oil bath on the right-side of the swingarm. There was a needle bearing universal joint at the gearbox end, bolted to a drive flange mounted to the taper of the transmission output shaft, with a hypoid gear coupling at the input end. To facilitate ease of wheel removal, an internally-splined 1:6 coupling was at the rear of the driveshaft. Rear drive was through a set of Klingelnberg Palloid helical-tooth spiral bevel-gears, already well proven on the /2 series. To provide the optimum performance, each version of the /5 received a different set of final drive ratios. After number 2973204, in July 1970, to improve acceleration the R75/5 final drive ratio was lowered to 1:3.2 (10:32). The final drive ratios for the R50/5 and R60/5 were unchanged.

/5 chassis

The two-piece frame of the /5 was constructed of variable section conical tubing that included changes in taper and ovality in accordance with the anticipated stress. Unlike the Norton 'featherbed' frame that inspired it, the /5 had a single backbone tube instead of two. This 45x3mm diameter dual-walled backbone was attached to double loops that varied from 28x1.5mm diameter to 32x3mm. Weighing 13kg (4.5kg less than the /2) the frame was argon-welded and weighed 13kg. 4mm gussets allowed longitudinal elasticity without affecting torsional rigidity while bracing the forged one-piece 46x4.5mm diameter steering head. On the very first frames these gussets were butt-welded. The tunnel for the fuel tank was very shallow, the engine located with two bolts, and the light triangular rear subframe bolted to the main frame with four 8mm bolts. The swingarm pivoted in the frame on adjustable tapered roller bearings, but the short swingarm favoured by von der Marwitz was criticised for impeding stability. Some of these deficiencies were overcome through fitting tyres with increased lateral stiffness in the tyre sidewall construction. Von der Marwitz believed too much frame stiffness was detrimental for a street motorcycle and, although the strength of the structure was questioned, it remained

essentially unchanged through until 1996. Unlike earlier /2 twins with a removable aluminium VIN plate attached to the steering head, the /5 came with a paper VIN identification. The frame number was stamped to the right of the steering head.

The Sachs-manufactured (to BMW specification) telescopic fork first appeared on the R50, R60, and R69 US of 1968. With long travel and progressive springs they weighed 11.7kg (down from the 14.5kg Earles fork) with a 57 per cent reduction in the moment of inertia. Unlike earlier US models with ball steering head bearings, on the /5 they were supported by two tapered roller bearings in the steering head. The upper fork triple clamp was steel and the lower triple clamp forged aluminium. With 36mm hard-chromed fork tubes, this leading axle design provided trail of 93mm and 208mm of spring travel. The damper tubes were conically-tapered and the fork was one of the best available on a motorcycle in 1970.

The /5 had a telescopic leading axle front fork and light alloy wheel rims.

A 13-rib rubber gaiter protected the fork tubes from stone damage, and a tubular-steel brace provided additional rigidity. There was a friction steering damper, with a knob adjuster on top of the upper triple clamp, but a more effective hydraulic steering damper was available as an option. The early forks suffered from stiction caused by the one-piece bush held by a snap ring inside the fork tubes. The soft fork springs also dived under braking, and there was an option of a stiffer fork spring and damping ring.

Twin 316mm Boge shock absorbers were fitted on the rear, providing 125mm of spring travel. There was an alloy cover over the top of the spring, and spring pre-load adjustment was made through a lever incorporated at the bottom of the shock absorber. The springs were black, and the shock absorber pressure was 240-310 Kilo-Pascal.

High quality aluminium wheel rims graced the /5, a 1.85Bx19in on the front and 1.85Bx18in on the rear. These included 40x4mm straight pull spokes on each wheel, and were a new design compared to the /2 that sometimes failed as a result of the spoke head breaking off. Instead of a rim lock to prevent the tyre bead leaving the rim if the tyre deflated, BMW wheel rims were stamped with five dents opposite the valve stem. This prevented the tyre bead from moving into the centre well allowing the other side to climb off the rim. The wheel bearings were a sealed taper roller type, and the front axle was 14mm. Because of problems with stability on early /5 models, certain Continental or Metzeler tyres were specified: a rib 3.25x19in on the front and 4.00x18in Universal on the rear. Metzeler introduced the Block 66 Touring Special rear tyre specifically for the /5.

BMW had no experience of disc brakes on motorcycles, so the /5 had drum brakes. Although there was some experimentation with a radially vented, four leading shoe brake, ultimately, the double leading shoe remained. Compared to the /2, the brake drums offered increased rigidity with deep stiffening and cooling ridges in the alloy

The /5 front brake was a double leading shoe.

Levers were forged aluminium with finger indents.

housing. The front brake was a 200x30mm Duplex (double leading shoe), with a 200x30mm Simplex (single leading shoe) on the rear. The left plates were chrome-plated. Although narrower than those of the /2, the brakes were considerably more effective due to the new bonded brake linings developed for Porsche cars earlier in the 1960s. Instead of an adjustable rod between the two front brake pivot arms, with both arms pulling in the same direction, the single brake cable attached directly to the arms, moving them together when the front brake lever was pulled. The system worked well and, when properly adjusted, the front brake was perfectly adequate. Rear brake actuation was by a rod, and both brakes also featured chrome-plated covers on the left side. During 1970 (from R50/5 2900689, R60/5 2931055 and R75/5 2971013) a new brake light switch was fitted to the rear foot lever. This featured improved insulation between the plastic and metal case.

Two types of chrome-plated tubular-steel handlebar were initially available for the /5: a 600mm and optional higher 680mm handlebar. The handlebars attached to the top fork crown with two-piece aluminium risers, similar to those of the 1968-69 US telescopic forks R50, R60, and R69. The handlebar controls were also similar to the final /2, Magura-forged aluminium levers with finger indentations. Each lever had Teflon bushings at the pivots, with spring washers between the lever and body to ensure a smooth action. The throttle control incorporated a cam and chain, similar in design to the previous R50/R60/R69-type but providing a quicker and more progressive action. Unlike the earlier twins, there was a rubber boot where the cables entered the throttle.

Generally, only one handlebar-mounted rear vision mirror was fitted to the /5, the chrome-plated round mirror screwing into threaded holes in the lever mounts. There were mirror mounts on both lever assemblies, and both short- and long-stemmed mirrors were specified. The short-stemmed were intended for the higher handlebars, but there was considerable inconsistency as to which type was fitted. Neither type of mirror was very satisfactory, especially above 125km/h.

Rüdiger Gutsche was entrusted to design the distinctive large fuel tank. The shape would become representative of the /5-series, and the first tanks were 24-litres, rubber mounted at the front with a single rubber pad, and two rubber blocks at the rear. The tank was retained by two wing nuts at the rear. The paint quality was extremely high, with fastidiously accurate hand-painted pinstripes. The tank incorporated rubber knee pads on each side, but the early tanks didn't include ribs to retain the rubbers. The shape at the rear was also slightly different on earlier tanks. There were the traditional fired cloisonné enamel BMW emblems with rubber washers, screwed into the tank with two 4x8mm oval-headed screws.

silver with blue pinstripes (559) and white with black pinstripes (084/584) /5s were produced. All versions (R50/5, R60/5, and R75/5) were available in these three colours.

Von der Marwitz was determined to reduce weight, and eventually persuaded the Construction Department (after some reluctance) to incorporate fibreglass mudguards. These were painted to match the fuel tank (with pinstripes). Generally, the pinstripe colour matched that of the fuel tank but not always, and this inconsistency accentuated the hand-crafted aspect of the /5. A fuel tank that incorporated a lockable tool box in the top, similar to that of some earlier BMW motorcycles, was an option.

The Everbest fuel petcocks were carried over from the /2.

The dual Denfeld seat, without model identification badge on the rear, hinged from the right to reveal a storage tray. The seat was lockable, utilising the same Neiman key as the steering lock, while on each side was a chrome passenger grab rail. A solo seat with lockable rear compartment was an option. The round footpeg rubbers were also Denfeld, and both a centre and side stand were fitted – the side stand was manually retractable on 1970 versions. A chrome-plated lifting handle was positioned near the seat lock, and a factory engine protection bar was available as an option. Other options included a luggage rack, leather saddlebags, hard plastic bags, and a black rear mudflap with a BMW logo.

Each /5 came with a specific handbook encased in a plastic envelope and the usual comprehensive 22-piece BMW toolkit: with embroidered towel, tyre repair kit, and tyre pump. The tyre pump was located under the seat, on

The large fuel tank incorporated rubber knee pads and screwed-on badges.

The fuel filler cap was not lockable although a locking filler cap was an option, and initially opened towards the rider. The fuel cap was aluminium. As the fuel tank was constructed in two sections to clear the frame backbone there were two fuel petcocks. These screwed directly into the tank, and the one-piece metal Everbest petcocks were carried over from the /2. The Everbest petcocks weren't easily rebuilt, and featured cork seals that could block the fuel flow. Initially only black with white pinstripes (086/590), metallic

The left Hella handlebar switch was for the horn and high beam.

On the right were the electric start and turn signals.

The instrument layout was basic, and ignition controlled by a plunger.

the left of the rear subframe. An even more comprehensive 33-piece toolkit was available as an option until 1984. One of von der Marwitz' innovations was to include a removable plastic tool tray, a very useful and practical feature.

On the left handlebar was a three-way Hella horn/high beam and head light flasher switch, with the turn signals and starter switch on the right. The hard rubber handgrips were Magura, and the plunger ignition switch in the head light was the universal type, as on the /2. This also operated the lights. The plunger was not really an ignition key, more of a kill switch in reverse, but it did have some advantages as it could be operated with gloves and easily snapped into position. The plunger receptacle had a spring-loaded cover that provided effective water protection. A Bosch 0320 123013 horn was fitted on 1970 models, with an optional heavy-duty low tone horn available.

The /5 instrument cluster was incorporated into the headlamp. A single 3½in glass contained the mechanical speedometer and tachometer, along with four warning lights. These were for high beam (blue), neutral (green), oil pressure (orange), and alternator (red). An odometer was included but there was no room for a trip meter. The MotoMeter instruments featured white numbers on a black background, but the numbers were quite small and difficult to read. The speedometer read from 10-120mph or 20-200km/h, the tachometer to 8000rpm and a redline at 6800rpm. Not all tachometers included a redline and the instruments differed between the various /5 models, as the speedometer drive was from the gearbox and the speedometer was matched to a specific final drive ratio.

The Bosch 0 303 550 002 headlamp was a 160mm 45/40 watt unit, encased in a metal shell – a H4 headlamp conversion was an option. From R50/5 2901379, R60/5 2932142 and R75/5 2972388, the head light shell incorporated a single turn signal indicator light. This fifth warning light, on the left of the ignition switch, was mostly green, but orange on some examples. The tail light was a rectangular Hella, with US models

receiving a specific tail light lens that differed from European versions in that there was no circle in the centre. The rectangular turn signal indicators had aluminium bodies, and US models (for 1970 and 1971) included reflectors on the front and rear turn signals.

/5 distinguishing features 1970 model year

Early crankcase housing included 'BMW' lettering cast above the cylinder
Plain oil filter cover
61 per cent ignition dwell angle and maximum advance at 2500rpm
Top end locating dowels with O-rings and spacers (from R50/5 2900602, R60/5 2930965 and R75/5 2970980)
Improved engine breather tube fitted after R50/5 2901704, R60/5 2932473 and R75/5 2973142
Butt-welded steering head gussets without outer welds
Early fuel tanks 24-litres without ribs to retain the knee rubbers
Fuel cap opened in the opposite direction
Everbest fuel petcocks
Seat with two side grab rails

Seat without rear badge
Four warning lights in speedometer
From R50/5 2901379, R60/5 2932142 and R75/5 2972388 indicator light in the head light shell
R75/5 higher final drive ratio until July 1970 (2973203)
After R50/5 2900441 main jet changed to 135 and needle to position 3
Accelerator pump carb kit from R60/5 2930530
From R50/5 2900689, R60/5 2931055 and R75/5 2971013 new brake light switch with improved insulation
R75/5 from number 2972061 carburettor with 0.4mm diaphragm and 'C' marking
New alternator rotor from R50/5 2901772, R60/5 2932606 and R75/5 2973649)

R75/5, R60/5, R50/5 1971 model year

As /5 development lasted nearly six years and was extremely exhaustive, there were few updates for the 1971 model year. Visually, there was little to distinguish the 1971 model year from 1970. Frame numbers for the 1971 model year R50/5 were 2901811-2903660, the R60/5 2932775-2938932 and the R75/5 2973762-2982998.

Gradually, BMW ironed out the few small problems that afflicted the earliest bikes. Early in the model year, on the R75/5 from number 2977321, new 32mm Bing 64/32/9 and 64/32/10 vacuum carburettors were fitted. Despite a modification during 1970 the first series remained troublesome, and the new carburettors featured a revised throttle slide with a greater wall clearance, a different needle jet, stronger neoprene diaphragm and a domed carburettor cover. The result was an improved idle, and with the new carburettors came a new Magura choke lever assembly with stronger cables. Other updates introduced during 1971 included slightly reshaped exhaust silencers and an optional close-ratio gearbox.

The R60/5 was little changed for 1971.

1971 model year bikes featured the new centrifugal advance unit, with maximum advance at 3000rpm and 43 per cent dwell. The gremlin in the starter-solenoid circuit that sometimes allowed the starter to engage whilst the engine was running was sorted out. The R75/5 now included a lower final drive ratio and the plastic and rubber components improved to resist premature ageing. To alleviate criticism of head shaking and wobbles, updates included more careful assembly of the long travel front fork, with closer tolerances so it would react to bumps more immediately. To further improve stability, the steering head angle was extended to 28 degrees. In the spring of 1971 (from R50/5 2902093, R60/5 2933525 and R75/5 2975253), the battery carrier was modified to include five rubber buffers. The fuel tank was slightly reshaped, the tank cap opened in the opposite direction and it now held 22-litres. From R50/5 2903008, R60/5 2937402 and R75/5 2981006 there was a new leak-free oil pump cover, without a releasing slot. Other updates included a shim on the tachometer drive to reduce oil leakage (from R50/5 2903617, R60/5 2938592 and R75/5 2982663). Just before the end of the 1971 model year, the side stand was changed to be self-retracting (from R50/5 2903624, R60/5 2938705 and R75/5 2982738) – this feature continued for 1972. The choice of three colours for the /5 range was unchanged for the 1971 model year.

/5 distinguishing features 1971 model year

R75/5 from number 2977321 with 32mm Bing 64/32/9 and 64/32/10 carburettors

R75/5 included a lower final drive ratio (10:32)

R75/5 new Magura choke lever assembly with stronger cables

New centrifugal advance unit, maximum advance at 3000rpm and 43 per cent dwell

New silencers

Steering head angle 28 degrees to further improve stability

Fuel tank reshaped and held 22-litres, cap opened in opposite direction

From R50/5 2902093, R60/5 2933525 and R75/5 2975253 battery carrier included five rubber buffers

From R50/5 2903008, R60/5 2937402 and R75/5 2981006 new oil pump cover

From R50/5 2903617, R60/5 2938592 and R75/5 2982663 shim on tacho drive

From R50/5 2903624, R60/5 2938705 and R75/5 2982738 side stand self-retracting

R75/5, R60/5, R50/5 1972 model year

The /5 received many more updates for the 1972 model year and most were stylistic. With the

ntention of making the /5 more appealing for he US market, the fuel tank was downsized with chrome side panels and accompanied by matching chrome-plated side battery covers. It soon earned he nickname 'Toaster' tank because of its similarity in appearance to the kitchen appliance. The previous 22-litre tank was still available as an option. Frame numbers for the 1972 model year were: R50/5 2903661-2905718, R60/5 2938933-2945721 and R75/5 2982999-2984790.

Bob Lutz joined BMW in 1972, and was influential in the subsequent development of the /5 and /6. (Courtesy Two Wheels)

Engine (1972)

Updates to the /5 engine were minimal for the 1972 model year, but improvements were gradually implemented when necessary. Early in the model year, in September 1971 (from R50/5 2903693, R60/5 2938962 and R75/5 2982820), a 2mm thrust washer and new bush were added to the gearbox output shaft. A stronger crankshaft with new bearing shells was installed during February 1972 (from R50/5 2904190, R60/5 2940740 and R75/5 2985208). The crankshaft material was changed from CK 45 to 41 CR 4 V 80, and the crankpin to crank web radius enlarged from 1.6mm to 2.2mm.

The engine housing was also modified, and this would run through until the /6 (1976 model year). Complaints about excessive noise meant new slotted rocker shaft supporting brackets and hardened steel shims were fitted from March 1972 (R50/5 2904721, R60/5 2942632 and R75/5 2989472). One update the R75/5 (from 2993256 in June 1972) received that the smaller models didn't – until a few months later – was new cylinder heads with cast dowels, eliminating the O-rings and spacers introduced in 1970.

The R75/5 from 2992320 (June 1972) also received vacuum ports on the carburettors. Some later 1972 model year R75/5s featured black carburettor air intakes instead of silver. These black intakes were a precursor for the 1973 model year, providing more legroom, but only a few 1972 R75/5s had them. The model identification badges on the engine cases were now on a black background, and the exhaust header pipes were slightly thinner (38x1mm). Some US examples featured additional vented heat shields over the header pipes.

Chassis (1972)

The most noticeable styling features for 1972 were the inclusion of a smaller 17-litre fuel tank, chrome-plated side panels, and matching chrome-plated battery covers. Nicknamed the 'Toaster' because of its similarity to this household electrical appliance, the tank incorporated three

The 'Toaster' tank was intended to appeal to the US market, but wasn't as successful as anticipated. A black R75/5 is reflected in the chrome panel. (Courtesy Jeff Dean)

painted stripes, and the side panels four stripes. Another feature of the 'Toaster' tank was that the underside was already designed for the impending /6 under tank front brake master cylinder, but the optional larger tank was not modified until mid-1973. Not all markets greeted the 'Toaster' fuel tank with unequivocal acclaim: in Australia the /5 was sold with the earlier-style larger tank as standard and BMW (GB) followed suit later in the year.

A wider selection of colours was also available for 1972. Alongside the existing black, silver or white were metallic blue with white pinstripes (033/533) and metallic curry gold with black stripes (029/529). Black, blue, or silver bikes came with black or blue stripes on the chromed panels, but there was some inconsistency in the colour of these stripes although they were obviously intended to match the tank. Along with the smaller fuel tank, there was a new seat with a single handrail running across and behind the passenger. This included a model-type black highlighted emblem on the rear, a white bead following the line of the handrail and longitudinal pleating on the upholstery.

Along with slightly wider 650mm handlebars, some 1972 /5s had two mirrors. An extra mirror on the right was sometimes fitted to balance the left handlebar and alleviate weaving. US models had a 680mm handlebar, and this was also blamed for high speed weaving, especially when combined with the US propensity for strapping luggage to a rear rack. US and European /5s shared the same aluminium-bodied turn signal indicators, with the large, round US-required reflectors located on

Chrome side panels complemented the chrome tank panels. (Courtesy Jeff Dean)

the head light brackets at the front and license plate bracket at the rear. There were new head light brackets for 1972, and many 1972 models had a Hella B31 horn. This large round horn had a chrome-plated grill, as did the equivalent Bosch horn. One small practical improvement was the rerouting of the cables, allowing easier reading of the small tachometer.

One of the more significant updates during 1972 was to the front fork. To further improve fork action, from R50/5 2904276, R60/5 2941811 and R75/5 2987432, a three-piece floating damper nozzle replaced the one-piece bush held by a snap ring inside the fork tubes. The aluminium centre damper ring was now supported by two outer threaded rings that allowed the piston to move more freely, also altering the rebound damping slightly. From R50/5 2904276, R60/5 2940990 and

R75/5 2985890, three types of fork springs were available: 538x4mm, 567x4mm and 543x4.5mm. A third fork modification occurred at the very end of the 1972 model year (R50/5 2905654, R60/5 2945479 and R75/5 2994494), when a copper asbestos sealing ring was fitted at the bottom of the front fork. The Boge shock absorbers also gained heavier damping and the springs were now chrome-plated. Although the tyre sizes remained unchanged, from October 1971 all /5s received a wider WM3 2.15Bx18in rear wheel rim (from R50/5 2903756, R60/5 2939207 and R75/5 2983280).

During 1972, BMW expanded the range of luggage and accessories available. In addition to the larger fuel tank, traditional leather panniers were first offered, followed by plastic cases – produced initially by Claus Wilcke and later 'Gigi' Krauser (a Munich dealer).

/5 distinguishing features 1972 model year

From R50/5 2903693, R60/5 2938962 and R75/5 2982820, 2mm thrust washer and new bush was added to the gearbox output shaft

From R50/5 2904190, R60/5 2940740 and R75/5 2985208, stronger crankshaft

Modified engine housing

From R50/5 2904721, R60/5 2942632 and R75/5 2989472, new rocker shaft supporting brackets

R75/5 (from 2993256) cylinder heads with cast dowels

From June 1972, R75/5 featured carburettor vacuum ports

Later in the 1972 model year, R75/5s featured black carburettor air intakes

Engine case model identification badges with a black background

Thinner exhaust header pipes (38x1mm)

17-litre fuel tank, with chrome side panels and chrome battery covers

New seat with a single rear handrail and identification badge

Slightly wider, 650mm handlebars, some with two mirrors

New head light brackets

Some with Hella B31 horn

From R50/5 2904276, R60/5 2941811 and R75/5 2987432, fork included a three-piece floating damper nozzle

From R50/5 2904276, R60/5 2940990 and R75/5 2985890, three types of fork springs were available

From R50/5 2905654, R60/5 2945479 and R75/5 2994494, a copper asbestos sealing ring fitted to the bottom of the front fork

Shock absorbers with more damping and chrome-plated springs

From October 1971, a wider WM3 2.15Bx18in rear wheel rim fitted

R75/5, R60/5, R50/5 1973 model year

Market resistance to the gaudy 'Toaster' tank in Europe led to BMW returning to their more traditional, conservative styling during 1973. The 22-litre tank was standard and 17-litre tank was optional, both with rubber knee pads. The chrome 'Toaster' tank was still fitted to many US models. Frame numbers for the 1973 model year were R50/5 2905719-2907865, R60/5 2945722-295272 and R75/5 in three series, 2984791-3000000 4000001-4008371 (from January 1973) and 4009001-4010000 (the final series in August 1973) There was some overlap between model years with the fitting of the 'Toaster' tank, even for Europe the 'Toaster' finishing at R50/5 2906304, R60/5 2947966, and R75/5 2997986.

In response to continual complaints regarding the high speed stability, a longer swingarm was fitted from January 1973. This lengthened the wheelbase and also allowed for a larger battery and longer seat. Two longer wheelbase R75/5s were selected at random from the production line by the West German Motorcycling Federation, and shipped in sealed cases to the Isle of Man in May 1973. In an attempt to win the coveted Maudes Trophy, awarded to manufacturers for extremely commendable performance and run under strict ACU control, fourteen riders rode the two R75/5s

The 'Toaster' tank was also offered on some 1973 /5s. (Courtesy Hans Crabbe)

continuously for a week. Despite heavy rain and two crashes, the machines covered 16,658 miles (26,808.5km) and won the Trophy. Towards the end of 1973, in addition to the normal US specification machines imported by Butler and Smith, a number of European specification /5s from the Italian distributor ended up in the US. These bikes had different reflectors, with the rear ones glued to the fender because the license plate bracket was flat.

Engine (1973)

Engine updates were minor for 1973. The R50/5 (from 2905756) and R60/5 (from 2946787) received the new cylinder heads with cast dowels. A new inner rotor for the oil pump included a larger 3x5mm woodruff key connecting it to the camshaft. As the

camshaft drive sprocket woodruff key was also reduced to the same 3x5mm, the camshaft was new. Another centrifugal advance unit was fitted from November 1972 (from R50/5 2905857, R60/5 2946096 and R75/5 2996220). Ignition advance now commenced at 1550rpm, with full advance at 3000rpm.

Chassis (1973)

While the tanks with rubber kneepads made a return during 1973, the earlier battery covers were optional. These were now painted black or blue but many were also chrome-plated as before. US examples with 'Toaster' tanks also had chrome battery covers. From October 1972 (R50/5 2905828, R60/5 2946037 and R75/5 2995073), the steering head bearing adjuster was

During 1973 the /5 gained a longer swingarm to lengthen the wheelbase. (Courtesy Hans Crabbe)

Most 1973 /5s had the earlier-style fuel tank and no battery covers.

changed from the round indented nut to a large hexagonal nut. 1973 /5s also received a new top throttle cam cover, and US examples a new Hella tail light lens. During 1973, the earlier Everbest fuel petcocks were replaced by Karcoma or Germa, depending on supply at the time of manufacture. Eight colours were available for the /5 for 1973. In addition to the five existing colours, were red with white stripes (023/523), green metallic with white stripes (074/574) and metallic silver with blue stripes (559).

To further improve stability, a longer swingarm was fitted after R50/5 2906304, R60/5 2947966 and R75/5 2997986. The splined coupling ratio was now 1:7 (instead of 1:6). The new swingarm lengthened the wheelbase 50mm, and was also claimed to provide increased clearance between the riders' shins and the carburettors. The footpegs were actually in the same position, and the improved clearance was achieved through the new

shape of the black intakes. These were 36mm in diameter, and 25mm long. On the first examples of long wheelbase /5s, the extra swingarm length was rather crudely achieved through an inserted welded sleeve with a temporary mudguard mount. Eventually, a specific, longer swingarm appeared, fitted on most final /5s and still including a welded seam, but also a larger diameter transverse tube to increase stiffness. From June 1973, the R75/5 also incorporated a 108mm spacer tube at the rear crankcase mount – this continuing on all later models from the /6 onwards. Accompanying the longer swingarm were a longer seat, longer rear subframe, longer rear brake rod and longer rear mudguard mounting bolts. A breathing hole was also included in the gearbox cover to prevent the rubber gaiter inflating. The rear axle oil capacity was also increased to 150cc (from 100cc) of SAE 90 hypoid gear oil. The long wheelbase significantly improved the straight-line stability of the /5,

1973 was the final year for the R50 boxer, shown here with the optional 17-litre fuel tank.

This 1973 /5 was sold with the 22-litre fuel tank and chrome battery covers.

reducing wobbles, and also enhancing cornering ability through better weight distribution. It also allowed more room in the frame for a larger 16Ah battery.

To overcome problems with the spoke heads disintegrating on the rear wheel, from September 1972 the rear wheel spokes were moved 1.5mm to the left to provide more swingarm clearance, and there was a new spoke type. This featured from R50/5 2905646, R60/5 2945366 and R75/5 2994445. The spoke now had a small shoulder that kept it from spinning if the tension was correct. From R50/5 2905828, R60/5 2946097 and R75/5 2995037, the high US handlebar was reshaped for improved ergonomics.

Over its four-year lifespan the /5-series more than lived up to its expectations. With nearly 69,000

/5 distinguishing features 1973 model year

New camshaft, inner oil pump rotor and centrifugal advance unit

R50/5 (from 2905756) and R60/5 (from 2946787) with the new cylinder heads and cast dowels

Fuel tanks with rubber kneepads (17- or 22-litres) during 1973

Battery covers optional

US bikes retained the 'toaster' tank and chrome battery covers

From R50/5 2905828, R60/5 2946037 and R75/5 2995073, steering head bearing adjuster changed to a large hexagonal nut

New top throttle cam cover

US models with a new Hella tail light lens

During 1973, the Everbest fuel petcocks replaced by Karcoma or Germa

Longer swingarm with welded seam

was fitted after R50/5 2906304, R60/5 2947966 and R75/5 2997986

Splined coupling ratio 1:7 with longer swingarm

With the longer swingarm were a longer seat, longer rear subframe, longer rear brake rod and longer rear mudguard mounting bolts

With longer swingarm breathing hole included in the gearbox cover

From R50/5 2905646, R60/5 2945366 and R75/5 2994445, the rear wheel spokes were moved 1.5 mm to the left

From R50/5 2905828, R60/5 2946097 and R75/5 2995037, US handlebar reshaped

produced, the /5 almost matched the entire production run of the R50, R60 and /2-series from 1955, through until 1969. It continued the BMW motorcycle tradition of offering unparalleled touring comfort and reliability, whilst (particularly the R75/5) providing acceptable performance. But in some respects the /5 was outdated. By 1973, the single face combined speedometer and tachometer and the plunger ignition switch was old fashioned. The era of the disc brake had also arrived, as had closer ratio five-speed gearboxes. On July 28th 1973, only three days after the 500,000th BMW motorcycle (an R75/5) came off the production line, the last /5 left Spandau. The end of the /5 also saw the demise of the 500cc boxer twin, initiated with the R32 back in 1923. By 1973, the demand for a 32 horsepower 205kg motorcycle was virtually nonexistent.

/5 frame numbers

Type	Numbers	Model year	Production dates
R50/5	2900001-2901810	1970	11/69-08/70
	2901811-2903660	1971	09/70-08/71
	2903661-2905718	1972	09/71-08/72
	2905719-2907865	1973	09/72-07/73
R60/5	2930001-2932774	1970	09/69-08/70
	2932775-2938932	1971	09/70-08/71
	2938933-2945721	1972	09/71-08/72
	2945722-2952721	1973	09/72-08/73
R75/5	2970001-2973761	1970	10/69-08/70
	2973762-2982998	1971	09/70-08/71
	2982999-2984790	1972	09/71-08/72
	2984791-3000000	1973	09/72-01/73
	4000001-4008371	1973	01/73-07/73
	4009001-4010000	1973	08/73

CHAPTER III

THE /6-SERIES (TYPE 247)

Although the /5 can be credited with saving the BMW motorcycle from extinction, even when it was released in 1969 the market for motorcycles was changing. During the /5 production run a new wave of 'superbikes' evolved: from Honda's 750 Four to the Kawasaki Z1 900 and Laverda's 1000cc triple. Motorcyclists now demanded more performance, and this inevitably meant an increase in engine capacity.

BMW was reluctant to follow this trend. While Dr Helmut Bönsch encouraged the development of the R75/5, he declared that it would be unfortunate if BMW followed the path of producing larger and more powerful motorcycles. Bönsch retired in 1972, but even after that there was an unwillingness to embrace a displacement increase to 900cc.

As a result, the development of the /6-series initially proceeded along similar lines to the /5. The team responsible included Rudolf Graf von der Schulenburg (later to head the motorcycle department) and Ferdinand Jardin, in charge of engine development. Jardin was assisted by Gerd Wirth and Wolfgang Wurst (engine testing). Hardy Müller was in charge of motorcycle strategy, Günther von der Marwitz coordinated the overall design while Rüdiger Gutsche was responsible for the updated chassis and five-speed gearbox.

Without the intervention of Bob Lutz, is it unlikely the /6 would ever have evolved into 900cc or the R90S. Lutz joined BMW as executive vice president of BMW Sales during 1972. The American educated but Swiss-born Lutz came to BMW from General Motors in Europe, and was a member of the BMW Board. An ex-US Marine fighter pilot and motorcycle enthusiast, Lutz was troubled by the state of the motorcycle division when he arrived at BMW. Lutz grew up with Hondas and told the author: "I had just arrived at the company, had to sell my almost-new Honda CB 750 Four, and was dismayed at what I found. There was no 'bike division.' There was a symbolic, small bike group in each of the main departments – sales, engineering, design, etc – but they all reported to their various functional bosses. Nobody was in charge of the overall motorcycle business." Soon after arriving at BMW Lutz ordered a special R75/5, but he saw the future in high performance motorcycles, saying in 1972, "I admit that what attracted me to the big Honda was brute power and the sex appeal of four cylinders. The growth market is in big bikes and that is why we are taking a look at a motorcycle which might be more exciting for the high performance man. A bigger BMW would be another harmonious synthesis of all things or we won't build it."

Lutz approached BMW's CEO, Von Kuenheim, about contributing to motorcycle development and, at a meeting of the motorcycle department, it was agreed to increase the engine displacement to 900cc. This initially went against the wishes of the engineering department and von der Marwitz, who was happy with a 750. Von der Marwitz envisaged an S variant of the R75/5, believing an increase to 900cc would compromise BMW's traditional reliability. Von der Marwitz thought 50 horsepower was enough for the average rider but Lutz wanted to match the 67-horsepower of the Honda 750. In the end Lutz was more influential, but, while

he was the chief protagonist for more capacity, Rüdiger Gutsche had already successfully built his own 900 in 1970, boring an R75/5 to 90mm. Celebrating the 50th anniversary of the BMW boxer twin, the /6-series was released for the 1974 model year. The R60/6 was now the base model, with the R90S the spearhead. The /6s (including US versions) also received new production codes, now changed with each new model year.

R90S, R90/6, R75/6, R60/6
1974 model year

Creating a Superbike out of the R75/5 was not an easy proposition but, from experience gained with Helmut Dähne's racing R75/5, BMW knew a well-balanced machine with a wide power band was extremely effective on road circuits such as the Isle of Man. Knowing a twin-cylinder motor could never match a four-cylinder for outright horsepower, BMW chose to emphasise all-round performance instead of pursuing high revs and high horsepower. Although the R90S would spearhead the BMW range for 1974, the /6 included many important updates, notably a five-speed gearbox, disc front brake (except the R60/6), and revised instrument panel. Numbers for the 1974 model year were R60/6 (code 0251) 2910001-2911677.

But for a front disc brake, the 1974 R75/6 was very similar to the R75/5. This example has the larger fuel tank with rubber knee pads.

US versions received a specific number sequence for the first time: 4900001-4900827 (code 0253), R75/6 (code 0261) 4010001-4012831 and US versions 4910001-4911097 (code 0263). The R90/6 for 1974 (code 0271) were numbered 4040001-4044971, the US versions (code 0273) 4930001-4932218, the R90S (code 0272) were 4070001-4075054 and the US versions (code 0274) 4950001-4951005.

/6 engine

Considering the performance differential between the four models, the similarity in engine specification was striking and an example of clever model rationalisation. The quoted weight of the /6 engines (including starter and carburettors but without ignition) was also similar. The R90/6 engine weighed the same as the R90S (62.5kg), while the R75/6 was the heaviest, at 64.9kg. The R60/6 engine weighed 63.5kg.

Designated the Type 247, the essential tunnel-style engine housing was carried over from the final series R75/5, but was strengthened around the front crankcase aperture. The front crankshaft bearing was now in a closed seat and there was a new outer alternator and ignition cover. This included three air vents and vertical ribbing instead of the earlier smooth cast type, and was

slightly different for the R90S. Inside the engine there were only minor updates, the Eaton type oil pump including a new inner rotor and the engine breather check valve was modified slightly to accommodate the larger piston pulses from the 180-degree twin. At the time, 90mm pistons were amongst the largest diameter fitted to a production motorcycle, and the R90/6 check valve was in the same position as that of the R90S, lower than for R60/6 and R75/6.

The drop-forged, three-bearing crankshaft with 70.6mm stroke was similar in all the /6s, although for the high performance R90S with 9.5:1 pistons, 90 per cent tungsten plugs were inserted in the crank webs. This was to reduce the crank web diameter to 130mm because the strengthened front crankcase tunnel aperture was too small to allow a large, fully counterweighted crankshaft to pass through. Even with the smaller crank weights and tungsten plugs, the crankshaft was a very tight fit through the front crankcase opening and required tilting for removal and installation. Only the R60/6 crankshaft could pass easily through the smaller aperture of the new crankcase. As the R75/6 crankshaft was identical to that of the R90/6 (and R90S), it was a relatively easy operation to convert an R75/6 to 898cc. The forged I-section connecting rods for the 900cc models were also constructed of a higher tensile steel, while the conrod bearings were now four-layer instead of three-layer as on the 750. The automotive-like eight-pound flywheel was bolted to the crankshaft with the same five small 10x1mm bolts as the /5. Some of the early R90 engines vibrated excessively, particularly between 4100 and 4500rpm.

Along with the capacity, the cylinder heads of all models varied. The R60/6 cylinder head was identical to that of the R60/5, and the R75/6 the same as the R75/5. The R60/6 retained the 38mm and 34mm valves (98.5mm and 97.5mm long) and the R75/6 the 42mm and 38mm valves (98.8mm long). The R90/6 valves were the same 42mm and 40mm as for the R90S. The valve lengths were 98.8mm, with an 8mm stem, and the valves were constructed of a high tensile Nimonic steel alloy. The valves were manufactured in two pieces, with the head fusion-welded to the stem. R90S valve guides (48mm) were shorter than the /6 (54mm), and the rocker arms on all /6s pivoted in needle roller bearings instead of bronze bushes, with new, wider, rocker support blocks. The R90S also had larger (38mm) intake manifolds, but the 308-degree camshaft was shared with the R90/6 and R75/6. The cam lift was 6.756mm and a more sporting 336-degree camshaft was available as an option. The R60/6 retained the 284-degree camshaft. While the pistons for the R60/6 and R75/6 were identical to those on the /5, the 90mm R90/6 pistons had a flatter dome than the R90S, and a lower 9.0:1 compression ratio. The cylinders on /6s were plain aluminium, and painted black on the R90S.

All models featured a Micro Star dry air filter, but the carburetion differed. Like the R50/5 and R60/5, the R60/6 included two slide-type Bing

Dell'Orto carburettors were new for the R90S. The kick start lever was retained for 1974. (Courtesy Jeff Whitlock/Mac Kirkpatrick)

26mm carburettors, with accelerator pumps, initially without a choke. From number 2911378 and US 4900617, a choke was incorporated with the usual Magura choke lever attached to the air filter housing. The earliest R90/6 featured constant vacuum Bing carburettors (64/32/13-14), identical to those on the R75/5 except for a 150 main jet, 2.68 needle jet, and needle in the first position.

Although some R90S prototypes were fitted with Bing carburettors, the production R90S received a pair of Italian 38mm Dell'Orto PHM 38BS and BD concentric carburettors. The PHM Dell'Orto was relatively new in 1973, incorporating an accelerator pump, and hence was nicknamed 'pumper.' Every time the throttle was wound open 0.4cc of fuel squirted into the cylinder. On the first R90S the carburettor bodies were smooth cast PHM 38AS and AD, without any provision for a choke attachment. Starting enrichment was by a float depressor, but these carburettors were fitted to only the very earliest examples. Most production models incorporated a choke, with the Magura lever in the usual position on the left-side of the aluminium air filter cover. The early Dell'Orto carburettors featured polished aluminium float bowls, aluminium banjo fittings and a 14mm float bowl nut. The aluminium cable guide at the carburettor top was also sharply bent (almost 90 degrees). There were a number of variations to the carburettors during 1974, some early examples coming without a plugged hole for connecting a vacuum gauge. The inconsistency in Dell'Orto specification was typical of Italian manufacture, especially during this period, and there were also variations in the choke setup on the carburettor bodies.

The intake manifolds were 26mm in diameter on the R60/6, and 36mm (25mm long) on the R90/6 and R75/6. While the R90S featured a new air filter housing with larger intakes suitable for the larger carburettors, the R60/6, R75/6, and R90/6 aluminium housing was shared with the /5 series. The /6 exhaust system included double radius 38x1.5mm exhaust headers coupled with 87mm (3.39in) diameter mufflers. The R90/6 was also offered a specific US muffler (California, Florida, and Oregon).

/6 gearbox

In addition to the earlier /5 gearbox, Rüdiger Gutsche was responsible for the /6 five-speed gearbox on the Type 247. The die-cast housing was new, lighter and smaller than the previous four-speed unit, while the three-shaft design included an input shaft (supported by caged ball bearings) in constant mesh with a helical-gear driven gear

on the lay shaft. Also included on the input shaft was a kick start engagement gear and spring-loaded shock absorber cam to provide a cushion between the engine and final drive. Shifting was achieved with two cam plates rotating, one sliding two shift forks and two gears on the main shaft, with the other sliding one shifting fork and gear on the lay shaft. While shifting was improved over the /5, there was still room for improvement and the 1974 transmissions were problematic. A design fault led to pawl spring breakage – resulting in no shifting – while the kick start pinion gears were very soft. Sometimes loose metal destroyed the bearings, while neutral was often difficult to find on early models. The R90S clutch featured a new forged pressure ring, with ribbed supports, and a stronger (2.8mm) diaphragm spring. The clutch throw out bearing was now a needle instead of ball type, and the clutch cable lined to improve clutch action. While the driveshaft was the longer type, introduced on the final /5, there was a new type of DNTP bearing for the ring gear. The R90/6 shared the 2.8mm clutch diaphragm spring of the R90S, but both the R75/6 and R60/6 used the 2.6 mm R75/5 clutch spring. As with the /5, each model of the /6 had a different final drive ratio, with the R90S having the highest final drive ratio of the range and the option of an even higher (1:2.91).

/6 electrical system

All /6 models received an updated electrical system, with a larger 25-Ah battery and G1 14V 20A 21/280W (14 volt, 20 amp) three-phase Bosch alternator for the R60/6, R75/6 and R90/6. The R90S featured a 240 watt (14 volt, 17 amp) alternator with a smaller diameter to provide more clearance at higher rpm, when crankshaft whip was more evident. Another electrical improvement was the colour-coded wiring system which included a Bosch printed circuit diode board in the head light shell. The head light was a 180mm Bosch 60/55 watt H4 quartz iodine and the head light shell also housed a new key-type ignition on the left mounting bracket, with five positions on the 1974 models to also combine the head light low beam switch. Three ignition keys were supplied: a flat metal key, a hinged key with a plastic upper and a barrel-shaped, plastic key.

1974 model year /6 retained the older style /5 Hella handlebar switches, the left switch operating the head light high beam, flasher and horn. The right switch operated turn signals and starter. There was no engine stop switch, and the 1974 /6 included aluminium-bodied turn signals. New for the R90S and R90/6 was an updated ignition advance, with the dwell angle increased

overcome some high speed instability, caused by the handlebar-mounted cockpit fairing. The bolt-on rear subframe on all /6s was new, but the strength of the entire structure remained questionable due to little rigidity provided by triangulation. The Fichtel & Sachs leading axle 36mm telescopic fork was internally identical to that of the R75/5, with soft springs and generous wheel travel, but the R60/6 fork legs were new and specific for that model. The forged aluminium lower triple clamp on all /6s and the R90S was also new, but the /5 steel upper triple clamp remained. The R90S had a specific upper triple clamp, and the forks distinguished by fork cups instead of the traditional ribbed gaiters. Inside the fork cups were oil-soaked felt rings to maintain a smooth action. Like the /5 there was only a single axle pinch bolt (on the right), this changing to two pinch bolts sometime during 1974. The front axle was still 14mm in diameter for 1974.

to 110 degrees. The ignition advance unit for the R60/6 and R75/6 was the same as the /5. The sparkplug caps were still metal shrouded Beru, and the starter motor a Bosch 0.5-horsepower.

/6 chassis

The Type 247 frame was a development based the Type 246 (/5). With 34mm outer diameter steel tubing, and an internal cylindrical tube on the R90S, there were some additional gussets around the steering head. The R90S received the additional frame strengthening in an attempt to

An early publicity photo of the 1974 R90/6. The side cover decals are missing and the fuel tank badges are still the screw-on type. There are no rubber knee pads on the tanks, and early examples like this had rear view mirrors with curved stalks.

The /6 fork springs were initially shorter than those of the R90S, at 538mm. After R60/6 2910998, R75/6 4012043 and R90/6 404461, the fork springs were changed to the longer (567x4mm) R90S type. A shorter and stronger section (543x4.25mm) fork spring was available when the bike was fitted with a full fairing. On early /6s the fork spring locator bush was too wide at 16mm, and was subsequently reduced to 15.5mm to prevent fork spring breakage.

As on the /5, the /6 swingarm pivoted in taper-roller bearings, and the earliest examples had a welded seam. The 316mm Boge shock absorbers were new for the R90S and /6 series. Although some early publicity photos showed /6 rear shock absorbers without aluminium spring covers, production shock absorbers had covers. Providing a plush ride, the rider was well insulated from road irregularity but the soft suspension and extra long travel did compromise ultimate sporting ability. Acknowledging that high speed stability wasn't perfect, BMW fitted a three-way adjustable double-acting Stabilus hydraulic steering damper under the steering head. The steering damper knob turned a shaft inside the steering head tube, moving the damper away from the steering head axis. This provided a very effective damping adjustment, although the damper unit was prone to oil leakage.

One of the /6's main updates was to the braking system, the R90S, R90/6 and R75/6 all receiving a front disc brake. The R60/6 retained the earlier Duplex drum front brake, similar to the previous /5 unit, but with a new ribbed casting and no chrome cover. In cooperation with Alfred Tewes GmbH (ATE) of Frankfurt, BMW developed a floating piston brake caliper. The floating piston meant the front wheel could then be removed without unbolting the caliper.

The caliper was black anodized (for improved heat dispersion), and piston size was 38mm. The caliper was mounted on the left behind the fork leg to minimise angular momentum in turning. Brake pad adjustment was by an eccentric pin underneath the fork leg, and the ATE master cylinder was located underneath the fuel tank – crudely attached to the top frame tube with a hose clamp on the earliest versions. A Bowden cable connected the master cylinder to the handlebar-mounted brake lever and, while this seemed excessively complicated, the front brakes worked adequately if set up correctly. The master cylinder size was 14.29mm, with the dual disc R90S receiving a larger 15.87mm master cylinder. The master cylinder location was again, one of practicality, under the fuel tank where it was well protected in the event of an accident.

The disc rotors were solid for 1974, and the R90S received dual front disc brakes. (Courtesy Jeff Whitlock/Mac Kirkpatrick)

The solid stainless steel brake disc was 260mm, the R90S receiving dual front discs. The rod-operated rear brake was the 200x30mm Simplex of the/5, but with a stronger hub casting and US DOT-required inspection windows to check brake lining wear without removing the wheel. The wheels included Weinmann light alloy wheel rims (1.85Bx19in and 2.15Bx18in) and the finned front hub featured 40 stainless steel straight pull spokes, to provide maximum strength for the front wheel with disc brakes.

The /6 instrument layout with a separate 85mm MotoMeter speedometer and tachometer and five warning lights was shared with the R90S, but each speedometer was geared for a specific final drive. The new instruments featured black faces with white numbers, and the 1974 instruments incorporated a white outer ring. The speedometer also included a trip meter for the first time on a BMW. The speedometer read to 140mph or 220km/h, and the 8500rpm tachometer was redlined at 7000rpm (or 6750rpm in early brochures). Some early R90Ss were inadvertently fitted with an R90/6 speedometer designed for a lower final drive ratio, resulting in optimistic speedometer and odometer readings.

The R90S also received a clock and voltmeter, mounted in the small Muth-designed fairing. In 1974, a clock as standard was revolutionary – the first as standard equipment on a motorcycle since the wind-up eight-day clock on the Ariel Square Four, thirty years earlier. The black anodized aluminium Magura handlebar levers incorporated finger grooves, and the cam and chain throttle assembly was matched to the Bing carburettors. On the R90S the throttle was very slow acting.

The R90S established a new style; a landmark motorcycle for BMW.

The standard /6s had a smaller (18-litre) fuel tank and a larger 22-litre tank was optional. Only the larger tank now featured rubber kneepads. Most tanks for 1974 included glued thin metal BMW badges, but some /6s and R90Ss received the older-style enamelled (cloisonné) gas tank badges. Some early /6 badges were screwed, as on the /5, but on the R90S even the enamelled badges were glued. There was a range of six colours for the /6: Black with White pinstripes (086/590); White with Black pinstripes (084/584); Metallic Blue with White pinstripes (033/533); Red with White pinstripes (026/526); Metallic Curry with Black pinstripes (029/529) and Green Metallic with White pinstripes (077/577). The hand-painted pinstripes fully encircled the side of the smaller tank. A 22-litre police specification fuel tank, with lockable built in toolbox, was available as an option. Some early /6s and R90Ss had the older style Everbest petcocks, but these were gradually replaced by Karcoma or Germa during 1974.

On the /6 the dual Denfeld seat was similar to the 1973 /5, with longitudinal pleats on the upholstery, a white plastic bead and a single chrome-plated handrail at the rear. The seat also had a black model emblem on the tail and a shorter solo seat was an option through until the 1976 model year. The /6 fibreglass front mudguard wasn't shaped as deeply as that of the R90S but a deeper police mudguard was an option. In addition to the pressed steel brace between the fork legs, /6s also included a chrome-plated tubular stay that connected the rear of the mudguard to the lower fork leg. The fibreglass side covers were painted to match the tank and fenders. Some early brochures showed side covers without decals, but production models came with a decal indicating the capacity, '900cc', '750cc' or '600cc'.

The R90S seat was also different to that of the /6. For 1974, the seat covering was smoother. (Courtesy Jeff Whitlock/ Mac Kirkpatrick)

Unlike the /6 that featured a fuel tank and seat similar to the /5, the R90S had a new shape 24-litre tank and seat with fibreglass base. In a ground-breaking move for motorcycle design, BMW enlisted the services of an industrial designer and stylist, Hans A Muth. Educated as a toolmaker, Muth went on to study design and graphics in Wuppertal, in the Ruhr valley, before becoming a freelance automotive designer. From 1965 he worked at Ford, moving to BMW in 1971 as the chief designer of car interiors. Muth was a motorcycle enthusiast, riding an MV Agusta 750 at that time, and approached von der Marwitz regarding motorcycle design. The /6 and R90S was his first motorcycle project, and he had to fit it in with his automotive work.

Hans Muth was responsible for the design of the R90S, and also the later R100RS.

45

As many European sporting motorcycles were beginning to incorporate standard fairings, in 1972 it was decided this should also feature on the R90S. The production fibreglass fairing was beautifully finished, and many early examples featured two holes underneath the head light. Muth's styling makeover not only included the fairing, but extended to the steel 24-litre fuel tank and Denfeld saddle. The saddle had a fibreglass base and incorporated a sporting rear cowling. Underneath were two storage trays, one removable and slightly different to that of the /6. The seat pad was thinner than the other /6s, with denser foam, but was just as comfortable. The 1974 seat covering was without pleats and the tank cap was aluminium.

Only one colour was available on the R90S for 1974, Silver Smoke with Gold pinstripes (561). The Silver Smoke was hand painted and air brushed, with a clear lacquer over the paint. The paint was supplied by Herbol of Würzburg and the dual colours had to be applied within 20 minutes of each other. Muth felt the R90S needed a special colour scheme that wasn't shared with other BMW motorcycles. The pinstriping was initially by gold tape instead of the usual hand-painting because a suitable paint providing a uniform finish wasn't available in 1974. The fuel tank was also located by wing nuts for 1974. The fibreglass front mudguard of the R90S differed to the /6 as it didn't incorporate a lower stay. Front mudguards had pinstripes, but not the rear mudguard of the R90S. The 1974 R90S front mudguard had a longer centre section than later front guards, where it angled in to clear the fork. Completing the specification of the /6 and R90S was an extremely

1974 models had many individual features, one of which was an aluminium fuel tank cap. (Courtesy Jeff Whitlock/Mac Kirkpatrick)

Another distinguishing feature of the 1974 R90S was a number of chrome-plated bolts. (Courtesy Jeff Whitlock/Mac Kirkpatrick)

comprehensive toolkit, including a BMW towel, tyre patches and tyre pump.

While the R90S was envisaged as a sporting model, BMW didn't follow the strict café racer route, the low 600mm handlebar providing a semi-sporting riding position. The other /6s included new head light support brackets and a new tubular-steel handlebar: a standard 600mm and a broader 680mm for the US. The handlebars were connected to the top triple clamp with polished aluminium clamps and the twin round mirrors were chrome-plated, rather than black as on the R90S. While all R90S had black mirrors, the mirror stalks on the 1974s (and some early 1975s) were curved, and not straight as on later models. BMW also installed reflectors on the sides of the forks and at the rear on each side for those markets that required them, in particular the US. Most fibreglass components were coded for the year of manufacture, including the fairing, battery side covers and mudguards.

/6 options included the R90S fairing, with voltmeter and clock, or a touring fairing with high windshield provided by Avon in England. The voltmeter and clock were also available as accessory pods mounted on top of the forks. In addition, there was the usual lockable fuel filler cap, engine protection bars, soft and hard luggage and additional driving lights.

The R90S was sold as an expensive luxury model and exceeded BMW's expectations. Bob Lutz said: "We made more out of each R90S than a 1600cc car." Apart from the additional horsepower, extra front disc brake, larger tank, cockpit fairing and special Silver Smoke paint, a number of detail touches set the R90S apart.

Besides the lower output alternator and Dell'Orto carburettors, the R90S also received black painted cylinders for improved heat dissipation. The handlebars on the R90S were clamped with black highlighted aluminium brackets to the black top triple clamp and many bolts (including the shock absorber bolts) were chrome-plated. There were special R90S emblems on the motor and seat, and only the R90S received 16 supplemental breather holes in the back of the air filter housing to assist induction at higher engine speeds. The high price ensured the R90S earned celebrity status, finding a place in the garages of racing car champions Emerson Fittipaldi and Hans Joachim Stuck, and motorcycle enthusiast King Hussein of Jordan.

All BMW motorcycles of this period were characterized by superb quality control. Each bike was assembled by one technician and 86 inspectors checked various components and the motorcycles before they left the factory in Spandau. Many inspectors stamped their initials in an inconspicuous place and 28 paint spots throughout the machine indicated bolts had been correctly torqued. Every engine and transmission was run for 15 minutes on a dyno, before its final assembly and a road test.

Not just a high-priced luxury motorcycle, the R90S provided performance to match the style. (Courtesy Jeff Whitlock/ Mac Kirkpatrick)

/6 distinguishing features
1974 model year

Stronger crankcases with closed seat front crankshaft bearing

Alternator and ignition cover with three air vents and vertical ribbing

New inner oil pump rotor and the engine breather check valve

Five-speed gearbox with new die-cast housing

Larger 25-Ah battery and 280 Watt three-phase Bosch alternator

180mm Bosch 60/55-Watt H4 quartz iodine head light incorporating five positions ignition key

No engine stop switch

Older style /5 Hella handlebar switches retained

R90S and R90/6 with updated ignition advance, the dwell angle increased to 110 degrees

Aluminium-bodied turn signals

Frame received additional steering head gussets and new bolt-on rear subframe

New forged aluminium lower triple clamp

Early fork with single axle pinch bolt with two bolts during 1974

Early /6 fork springs shorter at 538mm

New Boge shock absorbers

Adjustable Stabilus hydraulic steering damper

Solid 260mm single disc brake with 38mm floating piston ATE caliper for R90/6 and R75/6

14.29mm master cylinder underneath fuel tank

Stronger rear hub casting with brake lining inspection window

Finned front hub with 40 stainless steel straight pull spokes

Separate speedometer and tachometer with five warning lights and white outer ring

Black Magura handlebar levers incorporated finger grooves

18-litre fuel tank standard without rubber kneepads, most with glued thin metal badges

New head light support brackets, and a new tubular-steel handlebar

Handlebars clamped with polished aluminium clamps

Twin round mirrors chrome-plated with curved stalks

R90S distinguishing features
1974 model year

Tungsten plugs inserted in the crank webs

Cylinders painted black

Dell'Orto PHM 38BS and BD concentric carburettors, the earliest 38As without chokes. Sharply bent aluminium cable guide

Air filter housing with larger intakes and 16 breather holes

Clutch with a 2.8mm diaphragm spring

Smaller diameter 240 watt alternator

Specific upper triple clamp, the forks without ribbed gaiters

Top frame tube with additional reinforcing tube

Dual 260mm discs with 15.87mm master cylinder

Clock and voltmeter mounted in fairing

Only colour was Silver Smoke

Gold pinstripes initially by gold tape

24-litre fuel tank with aluminium fuel cap located at the rear with wing nuts

Early examples with Everbest fuel taps

Seat with fibreglass base and seat covering unpleated

Front fibreglass mudguard not as deeply shaped as /6 and didn't include lower stay. 1974 front mudguard with longer centre section

Rear mudguard without pinstripes

Black mirrors with curved stalks

Handlebars clamps black highlighted aluminium brackets

Many bolts (including the shock absorber bolts) chrome-plated

Chrome acorn-shaped nut on the right lower shock mount

R90S emblems on the motor and seat

First R90Ss with a different instrument support bracket

R90S, R90/6, R75/6, R60/6
1975 model year

BMW continued its policy of gradual evolution of the R90S and /6 during 1974, and, in June and July that year, several 1975 model year pre-production examples of the R90S and /6 were prepared. There were new production codes and a new number sequence for 1975: R90S (0276) 4080001-4084675, US examples (0278) 4980001-4981738; R90/6 (0275) 4050001-4053311, US (0277) 4960001-4963602; R75/5 (0265)

4020001-4023688, US (0267) 4940001-4942087; R60/6 (0255) 2920001-2923868, US (0257) 4920001-4921103.

There was some overlap with the end of the 1974 series, but general 1975 model year production commenced in September after the summer holiday break, as was customary. The early 1975 model year bikes were essentially similar to the final 1974 bikes, except for updated cosmetic and electrical equipment. As was evident during 1974, there was no definitive date for the implementation of all the 1975 model year updates. The R90S and /6 continued to evolve through the production cycle.

The R60/6 retained a front drum brake and was similar to the earlier R60/5.

Evolution of the R90/6 saw a number of updates for 1975, though the general style was unchanged.

Engine

The basic engine for 1975 was carried over from 1974, but BMW installed new jet production equipment that provided smoother alloy engine castings, and while the rear gearbox cover still provided for a kick start, this was now optional. Several updates were incorporated gradually, after: R90S 4080438 and US version 4980305; R90/6 4050187 and US 4960791; R75/6 4020453 and US 4940407; R60/6 2921611 and US 4920663. The motor was updated with a new crankshaft, front main bearing, flywheel and stronger (11x1.5mm) flywheel retaining bolts. These bolts replaced the previous M10x1mm ones that were known to fail on the larger engines. The ignition advance unit also received new springs to eliminate the shudder that existed at around 2800rpm, the smaller R60/6 and R75/6 now shared the centrifugal ignition unit with the 900cc models. The ignition timing was also reduced from 9/34 degrees to 6/22 degrees to suit lower octane fuel.

There were new 15mm 41CR4 cylinder head nuts after numbers: R90S 4081381 and US version 4980678; R90/6 4050895 and US 4961838; R75/6 4021199 and US 4940956; R60/6 2921572 and US 4920637. At around the same time, the flywheel oil seal was updated: R90S 4081381 and US version 4980678; R90/6 4050895 and US 4961958, R75/6 4021205 and US 4940987; R60/6 2921627 and US 4920738. Now made of silicon, this included a stronger sealing lip.

The weakest component, the 5-speed transmission, also came in for some updates with new 1st and 2nd gear shifting forks from: R90S 4081390 and US version 4980430; and R90/6 4050991, US 4961904. A larger, 26x7x16mm, oil seal prevented oil leaks from the gearshift lever. As the kick start was now optional, a slightly more powerful Bosch 0.6-horsepower

starter motor was fitted. This increased the short circuit starting current to 320 amps (from 290 amps), ensuring reliable starting in even the most adverse conditions. A change in the starter ratio from 8.93 to 9.111 further improved starting efficiency. The R90S regulator was also fitted to the rest of the /6 range for 1975. While ostensibly the carburettors were unchanged, there were new mixture chambers for the Bing constant vacuum carburettors on the R90/6 and R75/6 this year. 900cc models also received updated cylinder head centring during 1975. From R90S 4081080 and R90/6 4050544 the clamping dowels and countersunk nuts were discontinued. These were accompanied by new cylinder base gaskets. The sharply angled Dell'Orto carburettor cable guides on the R90S were discontinued during 1975.

The kick start was an option on the R90S and /6 from 1975. (Courtesy Jeff Whitlock/Mac Kirkpatrick)

Chassis

For 1975, the frame on the touring /6 models received the reinforced top frame tube of the R90S. All 1975 models received new fork legs, a new front

hub and a larger diameter (17mm) axle to tighten the handling. The front fork included pinch bolts on both fork legs, as on the final 1974 model year bikes. There were some gradual updates during the production cycle: From R90S 4081154 (US 4980521), and as an option for the R90/6 4050984 (US 4960803); R75/6 4020748 (US 4940641); and R60/6 2921589 (US 4920637) there were new fork damping tubes, and a stronger damping ring. Primarily to accommodate the double disc front brake, these new dampers provided more compression damping. They not only stiffened the suspension, but reduced the fork travel to 200mm. While the brake calipers and under tank master cylinder were unchanged, the stainless steel disc rotors were now drilled (100 holes in each). Although unsprung weight was reduced slightly, the primary reason for the holes was to

improve wet weather braking performance – the perforations aiding the dissipation of water more quickly. The R60/6 retained the drum front brake, but with new front brake plate.

The /6 also received updated handlebar controls, with black dogleg Magura levers and new Hella handlebar switches. The new clutch lever provided an improved ratio for clutch actuation and was joined by an improved throttle assembly. The R90S throttle included a faster action 40-stroke bevel-gear and chain specifically for the larger Dell'Orto carburettors. The other /6s retained the 33-stroke throttle. The throttle cam provided a more progressive action, shortening the throttle throw to a quarter of a

The front discs were drilled from 1975. (Courtesy Jeff Whitlock/Mac Kirkpatrick)

turn, improving throttle response. During the year, the R90S Dell'Orto carburettors received ports for vacuum balancing. There was also an additional cable adjuster incorporated at the top of the carburettor, facilitating carburettor synchronization.

The integrated Hella handlebar switches included the horn and light buttons on the left, with engine start and turn signals on the right. As the ignition key no longer switched on the head light, this now included only three positions. On US models the lights were always on with the ignition. Other running updates, some installed gradually throughout the model year as the supply of earlier components was used, included straight stalks for the black mirrors on the R90S, and a chrome-plated steel fuel filler cap. By now, all the fuel petcocks were Karcoma. The MotoMeter speedometer and tachometer had smaller graduation marks and no white outer ring, with the tachometer including a

Pinstripes were still painted by hand during the 1970s.

The instruments and switches were new for 1975. (Courtesy Jeff Whitlock/Mac Kirkpatrick)

51

An additional colour for the 1975 R90S was Daytona Orange. (Courtesy Jeff Whitlock/Mac Kirkpatrick)

larger redline band and high beam light. The Hella turn signal indicators now featured low reflective black plastic bodies rather than aluminium.

The R90S received a new seat cover for 1975, with transverse grooves rather than smooth. This was introduced in response to complaints that the earlier smooth seat allowed the rider to slip backwards under full-throttle acceleration. Also new that year, was an additional colour to Silver Smoke: Daytona Orange (510), known in house as 'egg yolk.' Officially, colours were named after racetracks in 1975: Daytona Orange (after Daytona Beach, Florida) joining TT (Isle of Man Tourist Trophy) Silver Smoke. There are many stories in circulation regarding how exactly the Daytona Orange colour came about, which at the time seemed out of character for such a conservative company as BMW. One 1975 brochure describes the colour as 'Daytona Orange-Safety Colour,' and this could make sense within the context of BMW's philosophy. Although Sales Director Bob Lutz wasn't enamoured with the bright Daytona Orange, during the 1980s he claimed responsibility for the colour, saying the inspiration was a sunrise at Daytona Beach.

The pinstripes were now individually hand painted, Red for the Daytona Orange (still without a rear fender pinstripe) and Gold for the TT Silver Smoke. The initials of the pinstripe painter were often under the seat, tank or to the right of the fairing inside it. Two plastic knobs, rather than wing nuts, now retained the fuel tank and the centre of the horn went from chrome to black during 1975. There were also fewer chrome-plated nuts and bolts, the lower right shock mount changing from a chromed acorn to a plain nut.

A number of updates also flowed onto the /6 for 1975. Following the success of Helmut Dähne and Hans Otto Butenuth in production racing and production-based racing in Europe, colours for 1975 were named after racetracks. Five colours were available and included: Monza Blue with White stripes (038/538); Nürburg Green metallic with White stripes (077/577); Bol d'Or Red with White stripes (026/526); Imola Silver with Black pinstripes (559); and Avus Black with White stripes (590). There was a new seat cover with transverse grooves for the 1975 /6, also without white beading. Instead of a specific model emblem on the tail, there was now a round BMW emblem. Other equipment was shared with the R90S, including the MotoMeter speedometer and tachometer, ignition key and handlebar switches, but the new twist-grip was a 33 cam. In the same year, the /6 was offered with an optional touring package that included a windshield and the larger fuel tank or a touring luxury package – with this came a full range of accessories.

/6 distinguishing features 1975 model year (some introduced gradually)

New crankshaft, front main bearing, flywheel and flywheel retaining bolts

New ignition advance springs, all /6s sharing the centrifugal ignition unit

15mm cylinder head nuts fitted

Updated flywheel oil seal

New 1st and 2nd gear shifting forks for R90S and R90/6

Larger 26x7x16mm gearshift lever oil seal

More powerful Bosch 0.6-horsepower starter motor

R90S regulator fitted to all /6s

New mixture chambers for R90/6 and R75/6 Bing carburettors

New 900cc cylinder base gaskets and clamping dowels discontinued

Frame on /6 models with R90S reinforced top frame tube

New fork legs with twin pinch bolts, new front hub and a 17mm axle

New fork damping tubes and stronger damping ring

Stainless steel front disc rotor drilled (twin discs an option)

R60/6 with new front brake plate

New handlebar controls with black dogleg Magura levers

New Hella handlebar switches

Three position ignition key

New clutch lever and 33-stroke throttle assembly

Speedometer and tachometer with smaller graduations, no white outer ring, and larger redline band

Chrome-plated steel fuel filler cap

Hella turn signals with black plastic bodies

Fuel tank retained by two plastic knobs

Horn centre black instead of chrome

New seat cover with transverse grooves, no white beading, and a rear round BMW emblem

R90S distinguishing features 1975 model year

Faster action 40-stroke throttle

Dell'Orto carburettors received ports for vacuum balancing and an additional cable adjuster

Dell'Orto cable guides discontinued

Black mirrors had straight stalks

New seat cover with transverse grooves rather than smooth

Daytona Orange available alongside Silver Smoke

Fewer chrome-plated nuts and bolts

R90S, R90/6, R75/6, R60/6 1976 model year

As BMW prepared for the introduction of the 1000cc boxer twin and the /7 series, many interim updates appeared on the R90S and /6 for 1976. There was another new number sequence: R90S (0284) 4090001-4093724 and US versions (0294) 4990001-4991260; R90/6 (0283) 4060001-4063018 and US (0293) 4970001-4973316; R75/6 (0282) 4030001-4035306 and US (0292) 4945001-4947578; R60/6 (0281) 2960001-2965122 and US (0291) 4925001-4925914. As usual, there was some overlap between model years and the introduction of all updates gradual, as the parts supply for earlier versions was exhausted.

There was nothing subtle about the Daytona Orange R90S ...

The R90S epitomised 1970s style. This is from a period advertisement for women's clothing.

Engine (Type 247/76)

While the 1976 R90S and /6s looked visually similar to 1975, there were many unseen updates, particularly to the motor – most a precursor to the new /7. The updates were officially incorporated from February 1976, with the proviso that these "modifications were subject to alteration without notice." The Type 247/76 engine included new crankcases, cylinders, pistons and cylinder heads. The reinforced crankcases accepted larger cylinder spigots and were strengthened around the front main bearing. There was also a 10mm deeper oil sump pan (and longer dip stick), although the engine oil capacity of 2.25-litres was unchanged. The new sump pan moved the oil further from the crankshaft and camshaft to reduce internal friction, stabilize oil consumption, and lower oil temperature. In October 1975, a 59x3mm O-ring was inserted between the crankshaft and flywheel after numbers: R90S 4090352 and US 4990308; R90/6 4060267 and US 4970610; R75/6 4030398 and US 4945030; R60/6 2960660 and US 495289. Also new for 1976, was the timing chain case and inner and outer cover, with larger bushes and oil seals for the timing advance mechanism. All /6s now shared the R90S alternator cover.

The cylinder heads were also new, with modified valve guide positions to provide a greater clearance between the rocker and valve spring plate. All models shared valve guides with the R90S and the inlet valve guides were longer, at 54mm, while the exhaust valve guide remained at 48mm. There were wider rocker arm support blocks and a spacer was included in the cylinder head pushrod supports. These updates were aimed at reducing valve clatter. The shorter rocker arms, centred in the cylinder head with special fitted rings instead of sleeves, were re-angled to increase stiffness and striking angle efficiency. The rocker arm ratio was unchanged, but incorporated self-aligning needle bearings. This had a practical benefit in that the valves didn't require readjustment every time the cylinder head was re-torqued. The 275mm pushrods were 20 per cent lighter, hollow

Although the 1976 R90S looked very similar to that of 1975, inside the engine were a number of updates.

three-part aluminium/steel/aluminium, similar to those used on the V8 automobile engines, with new lower rubber grommets. These pushrods expanded more consistently with the aluminium cylinders and provided quieter running from cold to full operating temperature. Instead of an aluminium base gasket to seal the new cylinders, 'Hylomar' sealing compound was used, with O-ring seals on the cylinder studs. The Hylomar compound needed to be applied sparingly so as not to block the small O-rings. The new cylinders also included new pushrod tubes.

Although the camshaft valve lift and timing were as before, the camshaft spindle diameter was increased from 12mm to 20mm. The larger diameter spindle was intended to reduce camshaft flex, with a reduction in oil seal wear and improved valve operation. The front cam bearing flange was cast-iron, instead of aluminium, with a bronze bush – resulting in closer tolerances and cam timing accuracy. The reduced bearing play was also claimed to reduce load on the sealing ring, which was now larger. Inside the oil pump was a new inner rotor and the clearance between the oil pump rotor and pump housing, as well as the gap between the inner and outer rotor, was tightened. The woodruff key locating the oil pump rotor on the camshaft was increased to 5.0x6.5mm, although the sprocket key remained the same as before. During 1976, a new engine breather cover was also introduced. The R75/6 engine breather check valve was now in the same position as that of the R90/6, and all models were fitted with the same front alternator cover as the R90S. The R60/6 and R75/6 also received the R90/6 automatic ignition advance unit.

Gearbox updates included strengthened transmission cases and a new gearshift cam plate and detent spring to improve the gearshift. The neutral indicator was also revised, with a redesigned spring-loaded neutral indicator switch detent plunger in the gearbox, and the recess in the shift cam replaced by a raised projection. The other gearbox update was a new torsion spring for the switch pawl, with five turns instead of three. The US R60/6 and R75/6 received a lower final drive to improve top gear acceleration, and featured revised speedometers.

Except for a new Bosch diode carrier and slightly higher rated Bosch alternator, the electrical system was largely unchanged. The maximum output was now 250 watts with 18 amps of current. The starter included a wider chamfer on the starter gear ring, and a modified starter pinion for easier starting and pinion engagement. Updates to the Dell'Orto carburettors on the R90S saw the carburettor slides activating the accelerator pumps earlier, to improve low speed engine pickup.

Chassis

There were also a number of chassis updates for 1976. The swingarm was more conventional than before, and instead of the single transverse bracing tube welded across the extreme closed end of the arm, BMW now adopted a pressed out box section, welded in place, and reinforcing the swingarm so the bearing pivot couldn't twist torsionally as before. The cross strut on the centre stand was repositioned to provide clearance for the deeper sump.

There were also updates to the braking system, with larger piston (40mm) ATE black anodized front brake calipers and new brake pads. The calipers were marked '40' to indicate their piston size. Accompanying the larger calipers on the R90S (and the twin disc option for the /6) was a new master cylinder with a larger (17.46mm) piston, considerably reducing hand lever effort. The R75/6 and R90/6 also featured a 40mm brake caliper, along with a new master cylinder, but unlike the R90S, this wasn't correspondingly larger with the piston size remaining at 14.29mm. A coil clip replaced the hose clamp retaining the master cylinder to the frame, and there was a new Bowden brake cable connecting the handlebar lever to master cylinder, with a larger (12mm instead of 10mm) cable nipple.

The suspension also included some updates.

To improve the handling there was less clearance between the fork tube and fork leg (0.1mm instead of 0.24mm). The brake caliper mounts were wider (72.5mm from 72.2mm) for the larger brake calipers, and the rear shock absorbers had dual rate springs. Not all 1976 R90Ss and /6s were identical, and some 1976 examples had a cut-away for the rear subframe bolt in the right side cover. The clutch lever featured a repositioned pivot point and, when combined with the reduction in clutch spring pressure, made for a lighter clutch pull and improved clutch engagement.

The 1976 /6 and R90S looked similar to the 1975 examples as the colour range was unchanged. By June 1976, production of the R90S and /6 was scaled down, as BMW prepared for the /7, R100S, and R100RS, and some R90Ss appeared with /7 features. Some of these features included: a /7-style flush gas cap; black rear grab rail and black left lift handle instead of chrome; matte black finish on the rear mudguard and side covers; and a matt black tyre pump. The valve covers were also black and the cylinder fins unpainted on some of the final R90Ss. To move excess stock in the US, BMW also offered the R90/6 Limited Edition. This included a standard clock and voltmeter rubber mounted on brackets from the top triple clamp, four-way emergency flasher and stiffer fork springs so the LE could be fitted with a fairing.

Chassis upgrades for 1976 included brake calipers with larger pistons. (Courtesy Jeff Whitlock/Mac Kirkpatrick)

Daytona Orange (R90S only)

Monza Blue (/6 versions only)

Bol d'Or Red (/6 versions only)

*Metallic paintwork
at extra charge

Nürburg Green (/6 versions only)

TT Silver Smoke (R90S only)

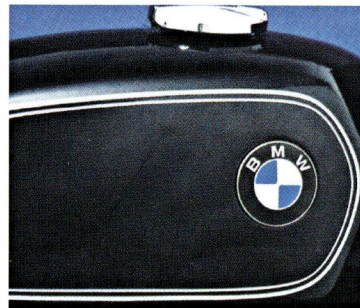

Avus Black (/6 versions only)

Imola Silver (/6 versions only)

*The range of colours
available for the R90S and
/6 for 1975 and 1976.*

R90S and /6 distinguishing features 1976 model year (some introduced gradually during the model year)

New crankcases, cylinders and pistons, and cylinder heads

10mm deeper oil sump pan and longer dip stick

O-ring inserted between the crankshaft and flywheel

New timing chain case and inner and outer cover shared with the R90S

Modified valve guide positions, longer inlet valve guides, wider rocker arm support blocks, shorter rocker arms with special rings and needle bearings

Lighter pushrods with new lower rubber grommets

Sealing compound on the cylinder base and O-rings on the cylinder studs

Camshaft spindle 20mm

Cast-iron front cam bearing flange with a bronze bush

New inner oil pump rotor

Oil pump rotor Woodruff key on the camshaft now 5.0x6.5mm

New engine breather cover introduced

R75/6 engine breather check valve now the same position as R90/6

R60/6 and R75/6 with R90/6 automatic ignition advance unit

Strengthened transmission cases, and new gearshift cam plate and detent spring

Revised neutral indicator

New torsion spring for the gearbox switch pawl

US R60/6 and R75/6 with lower final drive and revised speedometers

New Bosch diode carrier and alternator

Modified starter pinion

New swingarm

Centre stand altered to provide clearance for the deeper sump

Front brake caliper with 40mm piston and new master cylinder

12mm brake cable nipple

New front fork with wider brake caliper mounts

Clutch lever pivot point repositioned

R90S Dell'Orto carburettor slides activated accelerator pumps earlier

R90S 40mm brake calipers with larger (17.46mm) master cylinder

Some final R90Ss with /7-style flush gas cap and miscellaneous /7 black parts

/6 frame numbers

Type	Numbers	Model year	Production dates
R60/6	2910001-2911677	1974	07/73-08/74
	2920001–2923868	1975	08/74-08/75
	2960001-2965122	1976	08/75-06/76
	4900001-4900827	1974 (US)	01/74-07/74
	4920001-4921103	1975 (US)	08/74-07/75
	4925001-4925914	1976 (US)	09/75-05/76
R75/6	4010001-4012831	1974	09/73-08/74
	4020001-4023688	1975	09/74-08/75
	4030001-4035306	1976	09/75-08/76
	4910001-4911097	1974 (US)	09/73-08/74
	4940001-4942087	1975 (US)	09/74-08/75
	4945001-4947578	1976 (US)	09/75-08/76
R90/6	4040001-4044971	1974	09/73-08/74
	4050001-4053311	1975	06/74-08/75
	4060001-4063018	1976	08/75-06/76
	4930001-4932218	1974 (US)	01/74-06/74
	4960001-4964263	1975 (US)	08/74-08/75
	4970001-4973316	1976 (US)	09/75-06/76
R90S	4070001-4075054	1974	09/73-08/74
	4080001-4084675	1975	06/74-09/75
	4090001-4093408	1976	08/75-06/76
	4950001-4951005	1974 (US)	01/74-07/74
	4980001-4981738	1975 (US)	07/74-08/75
	4990001-4991260	1976 (US)	08/75-06/76

CHAPTER IV

THE /7-SERIES (TYPE 247)

The R100RS was the new range leader for 1977; it was a superb riding machine.

The success of the /6-series, particularly the R90S and R90/6 during 1974 and 1975, resulted in the establishment of BMW Motorrad GmbH in January 1976. Although engine development was as before, the production and sales of motorcycles were now separate from the car division. Under the control of Hans Koch, with Horst Spintler in charge of sales, the development team of von der Marwitz, Muth, Dr Dietrich Reister and Gerd Wirth were encouraged to produce an innovative design, more functional than the flawed R90S.

Following the success of the R90S, Hans Muth was asked to style a motorcycle emphasising rider protection and aerodynamic function. Again he was successful, and the R100RS was the first production motorcycle to offer a fully integrated fairing that not only provided outstanding weather protection, but also contributed to the stability of the motorcycle. Sharing the RS abbreviation with the legendary bevel-gear racing 500 of the 1950s, instead of Rennsport RS, now indicated a more appropriate Reise Sport or Touring Sport. The new fairing improved aerodynamics but, because the frontal area was increased, the top speed was less than that of the R90S. High speed handling was superior though, as was rider comfort.

Alongside the R100RS for 1977 was a completely new range, the /7-series. Now comprising five models, replacing the successful four model range of the R90S and /6, displacement jumped up to 980cc with the R100RS. The 900cc models were discontinued, and the 750cc and 600cc versions were initially much as before, in updated form. Although the R90S continued as the R100S, this model was relegated down the line-up as the R100RS established itself as the range leader. It was also an improved motorcycle, even if it lacked the R90S mystique. Despite a slightly lower power output, it was arguably the strongest performer in the 1977 line-up. The other /7s also incorporated many of the improvements introduced on the R100RS. As in the past, there was a high degree of model uniformity and parts interchangeability, with all /7s sharing much with the more expensive R100RS.

R100RS, R100S, R100/7, R75/7, R60/7 1977 model year

As usual, there was some overlap between the final 1976 and early 1977 model years, with all 1977 variants receiving a new frame number sequence: R100RS (code 0306) 6080001-6085159 and US (code 0316) 6180001-6181263; R100S (0305) 6060001-6063149 and US (0315) 6160001-6161385;

R100/7 (0304) 6040001-6043414 and US (0314) 6140001-6142451; R75/7 (0302) 6020001-6024507 and US (0312) 6120001-6121474; R60/7 (0301) 6000001-6005517 and US (0311) 6100001-6100407.

Engine (Type 247/76)

Despite the success of the /6-series, BMW's board wouldn't agree to the development of a new engine for the /7, so the engine remained very similar. Many of the engine updates for the R100RS, and its /7-series stablemates, were introduced on the R90S and /6 for the 1976 model year. But while the R100RS engine carried the same 247/76 internal engine designation, the new engine type was known as the M65*. The deeper oil pan introduced during 1976 featured on all /7s except the R100RS for California, Florida and Oregon, where it was optional. As was typical of BMW, the engine continually evolved. Although the silumin crankcases were further reinforced to withstand the increased horsepower, engine weight was identical to that of the earlier R90S at 62.5kg. The quoted weight of other /7 engines was also identical to their respective /6 variants.

The most noticeable development for 1977 was the increase in capacity for the R100RS, R100S and R100/7, achieved with 94mm pistons and cylinders. Constructed of a new lightweight aluminium alloy by either Mahle or Kolben Schmidt, the pistons weighed the same as the previous 90mm type. The cylinders had thicker and shorter cooling fins to reduce noise, and no longer were there any black-painted cylinders (as on the R90S). The piston clearances were also tighter on all /7s, with a maximum wear limit of 0.08mm instead of 0.12mm. The crankcase ventilation system was improved and, along with a small baffle chamber cast into the crankcase starter cavity, there was a new breather

An R100/7 replaced the R90/6, although the style was similar. This example has many optional accessories.

The R75/7 was short-lived and only produced for 1977. (Courtesy Two Wheels)

housing that included a small rectangular top hat and new outlet. A longer hose and new intake bell accompanied the housing, and it still ventilated into the right carburettor intake. The engine breather system on the R75/7, R100/7 and R100S was the updated setup of the R100RS, while the R60/7 retained the /6 engine breather housing.

Inside the 980cc cylinder head were larger inlet valves, now 44mm (98.8mm long) with 48mm inlet and exhaust valve guides. The R100S cylinder head was identical to the R100RS, while the R100/7 valves were the 42mm and 40mm of the R90/6. Inside the cylinder head of the R60/7, the 38mm and 34mm valves were the same as the R60/6 (and R60/5). The 42mm and 38mm valves of the R75/7 were unchanged from the earlier 750.

There were still only two camshafts, the R60/7 receiving the milder 284-degree camshaft and all other models the 308-degree camshaft. The camshaft drive system was also unchanged, but longer (8x45mm and 8x55mm) studs retained the camshaft drive housing. Although lighter aluminium pushrods featured on the 1976 R90S and /6, it wasn't until 1977 that tighter valve clearances of 0.10mm for the inlet and 0.15mm for the exhaust were specified to reduce noise. The one-piece forged crankshaft was unchanged but the conrods exhibited more resistance to cracking due to improved forging.

Changes to the lubrication system included a gasket for the oil pump pick-up in the sump, and a new oil filter outer cover plate. The oil filter included a steel shim and O-ring and, as already mentioned, the deeper oil pan from 1976 featured on all /7s except the R100RS where it was optional in some US states until 1979 (number 6183254).

Towards the end of the 1977 model year, the rocker arms were strengthened by widening the bridge between the hub and thread from 7mm to 11mm. These were fitted from: R100RS 6084553 and US 6181262; R100S 6062884 and US 6161323; R100/7 6043219 and US 6142340; R75/7 6024207 and US 6121470; R60/7 6005190 and US 6100407. At the very end of the model year, the R100RS (from 6085018) received new Seeger pattern gudgeon circlips and a redesigned piston crown for improved combustion and oil debris reduction. These would feature on all 1978 model year engines.

As with the /6 series, each model of the /7

All /7s had new angular rocker covers and Bing carburettors. The covers were black on the R100RS. (Courtesy Two Wheels)

series represented a slightly different variation or the engine type 247/76 theme. Inside, the engine of the R60/7 and the R75/7 differed very little from their respective /6 variants, while the R100/7 was also similar to the R90/6. The R100S engine was identical in specification to the R100RS, although the power output was slightly less due to a more restrictive exhaust system.

Setting all the new engines apart from earlier versions were new angular rocker covers. Compared to the older round rocker covers that first appeared on the R68 of 1952, the new covers were larger and heavier, increasing engine width slightly. 'L' and 'R' marks were cast inside the covers to represent left and right. Both the R100RS and R100S featured black anodized rocker covers with polished fins. The R100RS special engine emblems were black with silver and blue highlighting, while the R100S emblem was highlighted in red to match the bodywork.

Rather than the concentric Dell'Orto carburettors of the R90S, the R100RS and R100S both received Bing 40mm Type 94 constant vacuum carburettors. With these carburettors came 40mm intake manifolds, a new airbox and a revised intake bell on the top of the air filter box. With larger 40x1.5mm exhaust header pipes, new star exhaust pipe nuts and an 87mm muffler, the R100RS was the most powerful boxer twin to date. The larger exhausts came with 42mm clamps, although the smaller 38mm exhaust header pipes (with 40mm clamps) were listed as an option for 1977. All California, Oregon and Florida R100RSs had the smaller header pipes and a more restrictive muffler (through until number 6183254). The R100S, R100/7, R75/7 and R60/7 continued with 38x1.5mm exhaust headers. The

carburetion on the R100/7, R75/7 and R60/7 was essentially carried over from the previous models, the R75/7 and R100/7 retaining 36x25mm intake manifolds. The clutch on the R100RS, R100S and R100/7 was a similar 180mm single disc unit to the R90S, also using a 2.8mm diaphragm spring, but with a heavier duty anti-warp clutch disc. There was a new flywheel, slightly thinner than before, and the number of teeth on the flywheel increased to 94. The transmission case received lengthwise external ribbing, and the five-speed gearbox featured 6.5mm (up from 5.7mm) gear wheels. The selector fork guide thickness was reduced by 1mm and there was a different neutral light switch. To prevent jumping out of gear, the square shift dogs on 3rd, 4th and 5th gears incorporated window sections. There were no longer sealing rings on the cam plate bearing bolts and an alternative close-ratio sporting, or competition, transmission was also available. The kick start remained an option, and the standard final drive ratio for the European R100RS was 1:3.00 (33:11), with a higher 1:2.91 (32:11) for the US. Some early US R100RSs came with the European final drive. All /7s featured the revised clutch and flywheel with different starter ratio but the R75/7 and R60/7 both had a 2.6mm clutch spring. A different final drive ratio for each version also distinguished the /7, with the US R100/7 having a higher 1:3.0 ratio than European versions.

The R100RS and R100S retained the 250 watt Bosch G1 14V 18A 22/240W alternator of the R90S and, while the 0.6-horsepower Bosch starter motor was also identical, the starter transmission ratio was increased to aid starting in colder temperatures. The other /7s featured the Bosch G1 14V 20A 21/280W alternator of the R90/6, R75/6 and R60/6. Along with a new Bosch relay, the Varta battery was uprated to 28Ah. The ignition system featured the same Bosch coils and contact breaker (with 31-degrees of advance) but there were new sparkplug leads and caps, and different Bosch W225 T30, Beru 230/14/3A or Champion N6Y sparkplugs. Very early in the model year, the ignition timing mark on the flywheel was reduced to 6 degrees before TDC instead of 9 degrees. This was to accommodate lower octane fuel and was changed after: R100RS 6080369 and US 6180040; R100S 6060396 and US 6160217; R100/7 6040680 and US 6140074; R75/7 6020327 and US 6120088; R60/7 6000207 and US 6100055.

Chassis (Type 247/77)

Although the /7 frame and swingarm was essentially unchanged from the final 1976 version, a second transverse tube was added between the front double downtubes, and the frame tubing was a thicker section. There was also additional gusseting around the steering head and the chassis type designated 247/77. The fork legs were black to fit the R100RS's accentuated black image and, because of the fairing, the steering angle of the front fork was reduced to 35 degrees (from 42 degrees). US versions still had the rectangular reflectors but these were absent on European models. The fork springs were also shorter on the R100RS than other /7s, at 543mm, while modified front fork damping provided the same 200mm of fork travel as the 1976 R90S. There was one less bleed hole in each fork damper assembly and the fork oil capacity was also reduced slightly (to 250cc). This resulted in a softer ride in the middle range of fork movement with increased stiffness at either end. While the rake was still 28 degrees, the trail was increased to 95mm. The rear Boge shock absorbers were as before, with three-way adjustable black springs, but now without top polished alloy spring covers.

The leading axle front fork on the /7 was little changed from that of the /6; nor were the spoked front wheel and single front disc brake.

All /7s, and the R100S, featured plain aluminium fork legs, 567mm fork springs and 42 degrees of steering lock on each side. The R100S forks retained the more sporting, rubber fork cups, with gaiters still featuring on other /7s. There was a new, polished steel upper triple clamp, and black anodized handlebar clamps.

All /7s, and most 1977 R100RSs, had spoked wheels with usual aluminium rims, cast hubs and 40 straight pull stainless steel spokes. These wheels were the same size as the previous /6 (1.85Bx19in on the front and 2.15Bx18in on the rear) and two blue pinstripes on each wheel rim distinguished the R100RS. Cast alloy 'snowflake'

Most 1977 R100RSs had wire-spoked wheels. The shock absorbers no longer had top spring covers.

pattern wheels were listed as an option ($400) for the R100RS only – the rear a 2.50x18in. Whilst these featured on R100RSs in brochures and many early road tests, they weren't generally available during 1977 due to supply problems, and were possibly fitted to only three 1976 European prototypes and four US prototypes – if the chassis numbers for early bikes are any guide. Muth always envisaged the R100RS with alloy wheels, initially built by BBS near Stuttgart. Nearly 3kg heavier than the spoked type, they were also prone to cracking, and all wheels manufactured prior to the end of 1982 were recalled during 1984. The replacement wheels

A few 1977 R100RSs had cast alloy wheels, these also with a rear drum brake. (Courtesy Two Wheels)

looked similar, but included additional suppor around the spokes. Tyres on the R100RS wer Continental Twins (matched front and rear) o Metzeler Block C66 Touring, in 3.25-H19 an 4.00-H18.

All /7s (including the R60/7) had a fron disc brake this year with the R100S and R100R receiving dual discs. The perforated dual fron discs were now quoted at 264mm, with 40mn ATE single piston floating calipers. The brak calipers were black on the R100S and /7, an anodized blue on the R100RS. Muth original wanted red anodized calipers, as on a Ferrar but couldn't find any company able to do that i 1976. The ATE (17.46mm on dual disc versions master cylinder still resided underneath the fue tank and the brake lines were a similar rubber/stee combination, but spaced to clear the fairing. Th rod-operated 200mm rear drum brake was a before on spoked wheel models. The few cas wheel R100RSs incorporated air scoops fo cooling the rear drum brake, with protective plasti screens over the scoops.

A much narrower, almost clip-on style, handlebar distinguished the R100RS from other sporting BMWs. Short enough to fit completely inside the fairing, the 548x22mm flat handlebar provided an aggressive riding position, contributing to the R100RS's improved stability over the R90S. The handlebar levers were black Magura dogleg-type with the same Magura handgrips as before, and the new rectangular rear-view mirrors were also black.

Standard on the /7 was a 600mm chrome-plated tubular-steel handlebar, while US /7s had a broader 680mm handlebar. Because the frame modifications improved stability there was no longer a standard steering damper on the R100S and /7s, although the R100RS retained the three-position two-stage steering damper as standard equipment this year. As on the /6, the round mirrors were black on the R100S and chrome-plated on other /7s. As there was now an additional frame brace where the horn had been located, the Bosch horn on the /7 and R100S was replaced with a new Italian single Fiamm 410 Hertz horn on the left. The R100RS had twin Fiamm horns, the left as on the /7 and a 410 Hertz on the right. Although the layout of the Hella handlebar switches was the same as before, the right indicator switch now included a thumb extension wing for ease of operation, as did the left high/low beam and flasher switch.

While instruments and instrument layout on the R100S and /7 were identical to the final /6, with the ignition switch remaining on the left head light bracket, the instrument layout of the R100RS with warning lights was more integrated into the fairing. The speedometer and tachometer were still black with white numerals, mounted on the top triple clamp, and an automotive-style plastic cover concealed the handlebar. On the R100RS the ignition key was more conveniently located, between the voltmeter and electric clock. The 180mm Bosch H4 head light, Hella tail light in polished black surround and Hella turn signal indicators in black housings were unchanged.

All /7s, including the R100RS, featured the 24-litre steel fuel tank of the R90S, with the black flush-mounted lockable filler cap that appeared on some final R90Ss – the key to the ignition was separate. The design of the tank cap wasn't perfect on early examples as it could sometimes rotate without unlocking. Constructed in two halves as before, the tank incorporated an internal expansion chamber and was retained at the rear by two plastic threaded knobs. An update on the R60/7, from 6005190

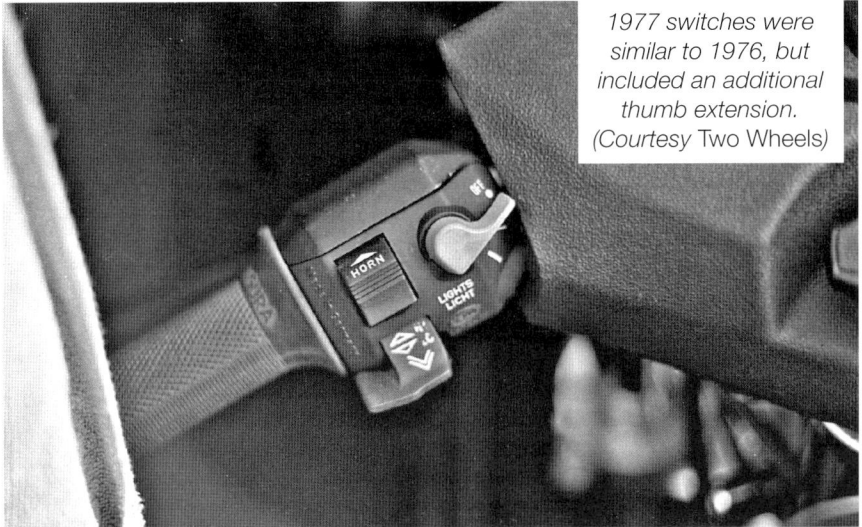

1977 switches were similar to 1976, but included an additional thumb extension. (Courtesy Two Wheels)

The right switch also included the thumb extension. (Courtesy Two Wheels)

The R100RS had the ignition key between the voltmeter and clock. (Courtesy Two Wheels)

and US 6100407, saw the petrol tank cap fitted with a 1mm breather hole. All the fuel taps were Karcoma Germa with rubber seals and enlarged internal passages.

the fork legs. Three colours were specified for the other /7s: Black Metallic with Gold stripes (532); Metallic Blue with White stripes (533); Orange Metallic with Gold stripes (034/534).

The R100S continued the style of the R90S, and had wire-spoked wheels for 1977.

The /7s also featured the R90S-style fibreglass front mudguard but without a lower brace, although the fork leg casting still retained the mount (even on the RS). The rear mudguard was painted to match the fuel tank on /7s, but black on the R100RS and R100S. /7 pinstripes encircled the side of the tank while the R100RS and R100S pinstripes were more abbreviated, as on the R90S. The handlebar-mounted fairing of the R100S was identical to that of the R90S, as was the dual seat (but with a black grab handle). The left-side handle was also black on the R100S, although chrome on other /7s. The R100S had black side covers, with gold '1000cc' decals, and for 1977, the only colour available was Metallic Red with Gold pinstripes (566). The 1977 R100RS was only available in one colour as well: flat Metallic Silver with clear lacquer and Blue pinstripes (530). The inspiration for this colour came from the pre-war BMW 328 car, and the finish was developed in conjunction with Herbol-BSF. With the support of Bob Lutz, Muth managed to persuade the accountants to agree to produce the R100RS in metallic paint with a clear lacquer by only offering one colour. The side panels were flat black with blue '1000cc' decals, while the front mudguard was painted silver with blue pinstripes and incorporated a steel brace between

Many 1977 R100RSs had a solo seat. (Courtesy Two Wheels)

There was a choice of two seats for the R100RS, a solo (almost one and a half) sport seat and the R90S-type dual seat. Both seats included a round BMW emblem on their tail and were lockable, with the dual seat featuring a black grab rail. As well as two helmet locks there was the usual lift out plastic tool tray under the seat, with a useful rear storage compartment that was quite large on the solo seat version. Locks for 1977 included separate keys for the ignition and fuel filler cap. There were new rectangular Denfeld foot peg rubbers for all /7s this year, although on the solo seat R100RS there were no passenger foot pegs.

The /7 dual seat was similar to that of the 1975 and 1976 /6, with cross pleating and a chrome grab rail. The lower metal fixtures were now black rather than chrome, and there were round BMW and specific decal model emblems on the tail. As in the past, the 26-piece toolkit was extremely comprehensive and included a spanner for adjusting the steering head bearings and swingarm. Along with the usual tyre repair kit there was a tyre pump under the seat. European models also included a first aid kit that fitted under the seat padding, US versions didn't because this compromised seat comfort.

R100RS fairing

By far the most innovative feature of the R100RS was the injection-moulded fibreglass fairing. Despite the R90S's sales success, von der Marwitz was not enamoured with the high speed instability created by the handlebar-mounted fairing – and although BMW offered aftermarket Avon or Gläser fairings, these were sensitive to side winds. Von der Marwitz asked Muth to design a fairing that offered improved weather protection and stability, while continuing BMW's design philosophy. The fairing also had to be easy to produce and, considering other fully faired designs

had failed, (such as the Vincent Black Prince and Ariel Leader) it was a big ask. The R100RS fairing was the first motorcycle component to benefit from CAD (Computer-Aided Design) technology, shared with the automotive department, and was tested in a wind tunnel. Design commenced as early as 1974, while testing began during 1975 – initially at the Technical University of Stuttgart and subsequently at Pininfarina in Italy. Although BMW paid handsomely to use the Pininfarina facilities (£2500), by attaching fabric and electrodes to the bodywork, Muth was able to design a fairing that reduced wind resistance by 5.4 per cent, side wind yawing by 60 per cent and front wheel lift by 17.4 per cent.

Under-seat storage space was impressive. (Courtesy Two Wheels)

(Lower, left) All /7s came with this comprehensive toolkit. (Courtesy Two Wheels)

The Pininfarina wind tunnel was used to develop the R100RS fairing.

The R100RS set new standards in sport touring, and the fairing would become a benchmark design.

Beautifully constructed, the 9.5kg fairing was in seven sections with a low windshield. The front upper section included a rubber head light shell and a Sekurit safety glass cover that incorporated five orange lines. These lines were purely a styling addition to the design of the windshield with no functional value. The front indicators were now flush mounted in the fairing and there was also a horizontal rectangular parking light above the head light. The front fairing section was a grill that allowed air to reach the front of the engine, while the lower sections could be removed for riding in hot weather. These were one-piece on 1977 models, requiring the exhaust pipes to be dropped for removal. Two black-painted tubular-steel brackets, incorporated into the bracket welded to the headstock, rigidly located the top of the fairing and served as mounts for the mirrors. Two additional tubes bolted to the sides, with a third set of pressed-steel brackets below the cylinders. Sealing the fairing from underneath were two rubber cups encircling the fork tubes, while open-cell foam filled the space between the fairing and the front frame down tubes.

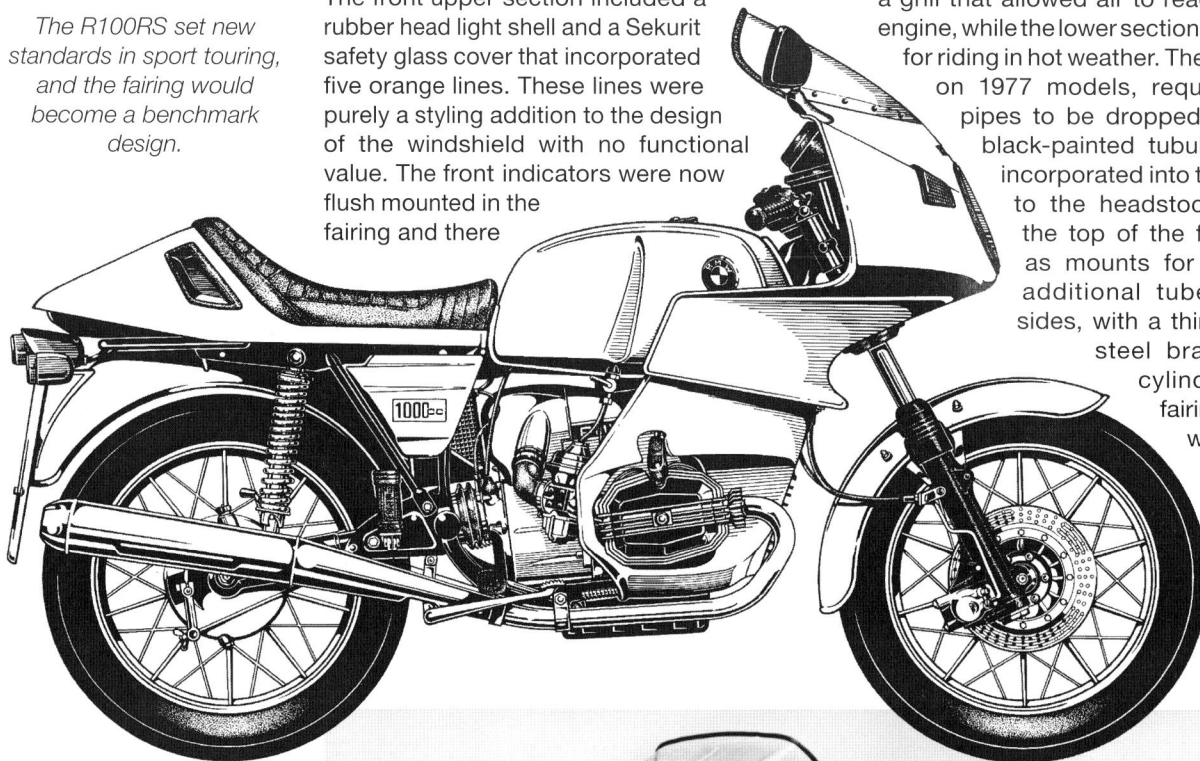

Although the R100RS appeared with cast alloy wheels in publicity pictures, these wheels were rare on production models.

/7 distinguishing features 1977 model year

Cylinders with thicker and shorter cooling fins
Improved crankcase ventilation system
1000cc models with 44mm inlet valves
Longer camshaft drive housing studs
Gasket for the oil pump pick-up and new oil filter outer cover plate
New angular rocker covers black anodized on the R100RS and R100S
R100RS and R100S with Bing 40mm Type 94 constant vacuum carburettors
R100RS, R100S and R100/7 with a heavier duty anti-warp clutch disc
Thinner flywheel with 94 teeth
Transmission case with lengthwise external ribbing
6.5mm gear wheels and no sealing rings on the cam plate bearing bolts
Selector fork guide thickness reduced by 1mm
Shift dogs on 3rd, 4th and 5th gears incorporated window sections
Starter transmission ratio increased
New Bosch relay and 28 Ah Varta battery
New sparkplug leads and caps
Frame included a second front transverse tube and additional gusseting
All /7s, and the R100S, featured plain aluminium fork legs
No standard steering damper on the R100S and /7s
Black round mirrors on the R100S and chrome-plated on other /7s
Single Fiamm horn on the left for R100S and /7
Handlebar switches with thumb extension wings
R100S and /7 ignition switch still on the left head light bracket
All /7s featured R90S-style 24-litre steel fuel tank flush mounted filler cap
All /7s with fibreglass front mudguard without a lower brace
Left-side handle black on the R100S and chrome on other /7s
/7 lower metal seat fixtures black instead of chrome
New rectangular footpeg rubbers
R60/7 with front disc brake instead of drum

R100RS handling was improved over that of the R90S.

R100RS distinguishing features 1977 model year

40mm exhaust header pipes
Black fork legs
Shorter fork springs and modified front fork damping to other /7s
Rear Boge shock absorbers without top polished alloy spring covers
Most fitted with spoked wheels with two blue pinstripes on each wheel rim
40mm front brake calipers anodized
Narrow flat handlebar that fitted inside the fairing
Black Magura dogleg handlebar levers
Black rectangular rear view mirrors
Steering damper standard
Twin Fiamm horns
Ignition key located between the voltmeter and clock
Black rear mudguard
Flat black side panels with blue '1000cc' decals
Choice of two seats, a solo and dual

67

The R80/7 replaced the R75/5 for 1978.

R100RS, R100S, R100/7, R80/7, R60/7 1978 model year

The 1978 model year was one of transition for BMW. Replacing the short-lived R75/5 was the similar R80/7, and this was effectively the final year for the R60/7 before it was replaced by the new generation R65. This year also saw a variety of additional official, police and touring models: the R60/7 T; R80/7 T; and R80/7 N. In the US, the strong German Mark had a detrimental effect, forcing up prices and resulting in diminishing sales during 1977 and 1978. It was rumoured up to 8000 motorcycles sat in dealers' showrooms and only 1092 examples of the flagship R100RS were sold in the United States throughout 1978.

In the US, noise and emission controls, and the introduction of lower octane low lead fuel, were also hurting the engine – requiring complicated engine breather systems and a general lower state of tune. In the face of cheaper and higher performing Japanese fours, the expensive boxers struggled to find a market in the US, although they continued to maintain a loyal following in Europe. But with only 29,580 motorcycles built during 1978, the future of the BMW motorcycle remained uncertain.

1978 was the final year for the R60/7.

Number sequences for 1978 were as follows: R100RS (0325) 6086001-6082865 and US (0335) 6182501-6183592; R100S (0324) 6065001-6068753 and US (0334) 6162501-6163870; R100/7 (0323) 6045001-6047995 and US (0333) 6145001-6148196; and a small series of R100/7 T (0344), 6110001-6110088. The R75/7 (0326) for 1977 were from 6220001-6220278 (no US model this year); the R60/7 (0321) between 6007001-6009844 and US (0331) 6101001-6101158. Finally, the new R80/7 (0322) were from 6025001-6021915 and US (0332) 6122501-6124909.

similar to the R75/5, but for 2.8mm larger pistons and cylinders, and the engine type was known as the M85*. There was also a lower compression version (8:1, 50 horsepower). The valve sizes were unchanged from the 750 and the claimed weight for the 800cc engine (with starter, carburettor, and oil) was 63.5kg. Also new for the R80/7, a flat-topped Bing carburettor without a spring seating the throttle valve.

There were only detail updates to the rest of the range for 1978. A new camshaft, with the same duration and valve lift but advanced 6-degrees,

For 1978 the R100/7 retained the wire-spoked wheels, and US versions a single front disc brake.

Engine

For 1978 a new model, the R80/7, replaced the R75/7, although a few R75/7s were produced as 1978 models for Europe. The R80/7 was very

was installed together with a new camshaft drive sprocket (without a tachometer drive spiral gear) and new timing chain case. Other engine updates during the year included: Seeger-pattern circlips to

retain the piston wrist-pins; a redesigned piston crown for improved combustion; and 'L' and 'R' cast into the external top surfaces of the angular rocker covers to make identification easier. The circlips and piston updates featured on all R80/7s: R100S from 6065101, and R100/7 from 6045408. The R60/7 also featured a lower compression ratio this year, down to 8.6:1 from 9.2:1. This was achieved with a 0.7mm plate at the base of each cylinder. The gearbox housing was now pressure-cast instead of chill-cast.

US examples, from R100RS 6183255; R100S 6163465; R100/7 6147574, and R80/7 6124338, now included a double-sided breather venting into both carburettor intakes, and new crankcase top cover. This replaced the previous single-sided type, and the new cover featured 'BMW' lettering cast in each side, as well as an integral air intake and a T-junction with three breather hoses. At the same time, US R100s received 38mm header pipes; a deeper sump; new cylinder heads; new mufflers, and Bing 40mm carburettors with slightly leaner jetting (160 main jets). This year, warmer Bosch W175 T30, Beru 175/14/3A or Champion N10Y sparkplugs were specified.

The R60/7 received a new final drive ratio for 1978, and all US R80/7s until number 6124337 were fitted with the 1:3.36 ratio. Those after number 6124338 had the 1:3.20 ratio. There was also a change to the R100/7 US final drive ratio from number 6147575, now sharing the 1:3.09 of European models. The R100RS was also available with an optional thermostatically controlled oil cooler.

Chassis

The /7 frame was unchanged for 1978, but the cost of manufacturing reduced considerably because the welding process now involved inert gas instead of tungsten-hydrogen. Detail updates to the front fork included: a black cover on the filler cap instead of chrome; a larger 10x13.5mm oil fill washer (from 8x11.5mm); and new upper fork spring retainer. Inside the front fork of the R100RS, R100S and R100/7 were new damper rods.

While the R60/7, R80/7, R100/7 and first R100S and R100RS retained the traditional wire-spoked wheels, during the 1978 model year

The R100S and R100RS gained a Brembo rear disc brake during 1978. (Courtesy Nolan Woodbury)

The ATE brake calipers were anodised silver from 1978. (Courtesy Nolan Woodbury)

the R100S and R100RS received 'snowflake' cast alloy wheels. All front wheels featured two larger (40x22x7mm) sealing rings, the wire wheel received an updated front hub, and the cast alloy wheels were lacquered to simplify cleaning. The rear 18-inch wheel was now quite different to the previous optional cast type, featuring a wider, 2.75-inch rim and incorporating a drilled 260mm disc brake instead of the Simplex drum brake. The brake disc was supplied by Brembo and featured the holes drilled in a pattern of alternating two holes (80 holes in double rows), instead of twos and threes. Later in the 1978 model year these Brembo discs were also occasionally fitted to the front wheel. The rear brake caliper was a twin, opposed-piston Brembo with 38mm pistons, mounted on a large alloy plate and attached to a pressed-steel brake torque rod. The Brembo rear master cylinder diameter was 15.8mm.

1978 US R100/7s, R80/7s and R60/7s featured a single front disc brake, but European R100/7s and R80/7s included a second front disc. On European /7s the cast alloy wheels and rear disc brake (of the R100RS and R100S) were also an option this year.

The dual front brakes were unchanged for the R100S and R100RS with most silver R100RSs retaining the blue anodized front brake calipers. Other R100RSs, the R100S and all /7s included silver anodized brake calipers instead of black this year. There was also a special R100/7 for the US with alloy wheels and a rear drum brake – these were the same wheels originally offered for the 1977 R100RS, a precursor to those fitted to the R100T in 1979.

There were several detail changes to the equipment for 1978. The fuel tank now included a hose attached to the overflow cavity drain, directing fuel overflow to the ground in front of the rear wheel instead of on the engine as before. The screw-type fuel filler cap had a matt finish. While the R100RS fairing was much the same, there was a new fairing head light cover and head light rubber. The lower side panels that encircled the cylinders were split so they could be removed without disturbing the exhaust system, and there was an additional metal support bracket. The R100RS also received new handlebar clamps and instrument support, along with a revised instrument light support and cover. The R100S and all /7s now featured a vinyl covered foam pad over the new upper triple clamp, a matt black tail light housing and, from May 1978, a new rear mudguard constructed of foam plastic and painted matt black. The R100S now had twin Fiamm horns like the R100RS.

The most noticeable changes to all /7s this year were to the instruments. All the MotoMeter instruments now had black faces with green numerals, white needles and non-reflective glass. There was an electronic tachometer (instead of mechanical), and an electric quartz clock for the R100S and RS. A single key operated the ignition, fuel tank cap, seat and fork lock. On US models, the head light and tail light operated whenever the engine was running and there was no head light 'on/off' switch. US models also had a loud turn signal beeper, wired to the electric start interlock. Accompanying this beeper was a change in the indicator light position to the top of the warning light panel, with the brake failure light now at the bottom. Completing the

ergonomic upgrades were softer Magura handgrips. In an effort to further improve the gearshift, the gear lever now pivoted on the rider's foot peg attachment and connected to the small shifting lever with a U rod that was covered with a rubber bellows. The pivot included a grease nipple.

Other new features included a folding cable lock stored in the frame backbone tube, and a toolkit without tyre levers because they weren't suitable for the softer alloy wheels. All dual seats included the pocket for a first aid kit, even if the kit wasn't included in the specification (as in the US). The R100RS was available in Metallic Gold (546) alongside the existing flat Metallic Silver for 1978. The Metallic Gold RS had black pinstripes, red 'R100RS' engine emblems and '1000cc' side cover decals. New colours for the R100S included Metallic Dark Red with Gold pinstripes (553) and red '1000cc' side cover decals, while the /7 was available in Metallic Black (532), Blue (533), or Orange (534), with tank pinstripes as before. Also available for 1978 was a Metallic Red /7 (531), with R100S-style gold pinstripes and black side covers and rear mudguard. The optional engine protection bars and luggage racks were also now black instead of chrome.

A new gearshift arrangement provided a more positive gear selection. (Courtesy Nolan Woodbury)

The Motometer instruments had green markings from 1978. (Courtesy Nolan Woodbury)

The R100RS Motorsport was the first of several limited editions.

The R100RS was also available in Gold for 1978.

This year also marked the first of several series of limited editions with two hundred Motorsport, painted white with orange and blue pinstripes and a red head light surround. It was available with matching white Krauser saddlebags, and many came with dark blue seat upholstery. There was also a special US model R100S without the handlebar fairing, but with higher R100/7 handlebars, clock and voltmeter housed in accessory pods and an optional touring package that included a Luftmeister fairing and Krauser luggage. Another special edition was the R100S Motorsport, or R100SRS, featuring a 70 horsepower R100RS engine, but with a smaller S handlebar fairing. The colours were identical to the similar R100RS Motorsport, and equipment extended to single and dual seats (in blue trim), engine protection bars and a km/h speedometer (with a mph speedometer in a separate box). No official data exists for the number of Motorsport models produced, but they were available in both US and non-US series. US R100S Motorsports were around numbers 6163000-6163870 and non-US 6067500-6067700. The R100RS Motorsport numbers were from around 6183000-6183592 for US and 6088000-6092865 for non-US specification.

The colour range for 1978. Only the R100RS was available in the Metallic Gold and Silver, and a Dark Metallic Red was exclusive to the R100S.

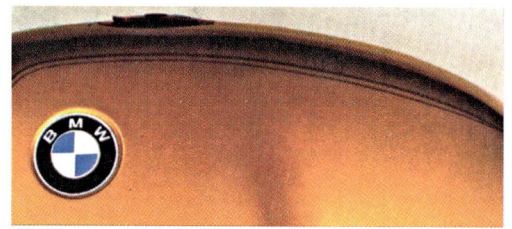

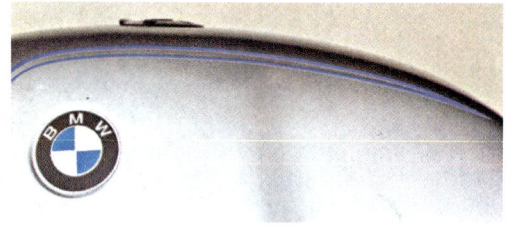

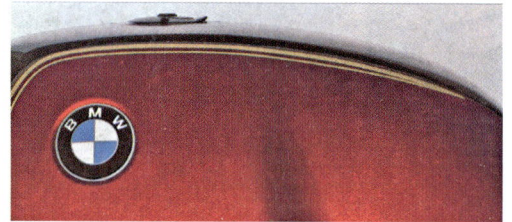

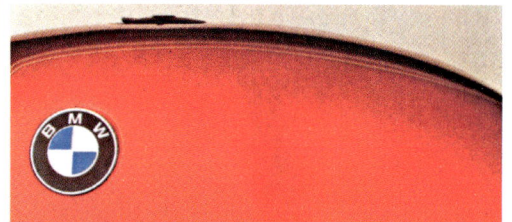

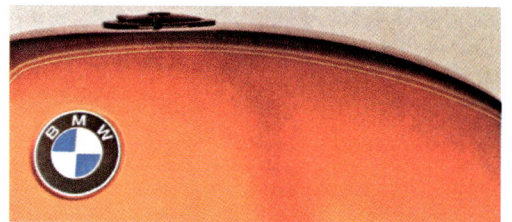

/7 distinguishing features
1978 model year

New camshaft, camshaft drive sprocket and timing chain case

Seeger-pattern piston circlips

Redesigned piston crown

'L' and 'R' cast into the top of rocker covers

US examples included a double-sided breather

US R100s with deeper sump, new cylinder heads, mufflers and leaner jetting

Warmer sparkplugs

R60/7 with lower compression ratio

Front fork with black cover on the filler cap, larger oil fill washer, new upper fork spring retainer and new damper rods

R60/7, R80/7, R100/7 and first R100S and R100RS with wire-spoked wheels

Most R100S and R100RS with cast alloy wheels

All front wheels featured two larger sealing rings

Rear 18-inch cast wheel with 2.75-inch rim and 260mm disc brake

Rear brake disc with new drilled hole pattern

New pattern discs fitted to the front wheel later in the model year

Rear brake caliper twin opposed-piston Brembo with 15.8mm master cylinder

US R100/7, R80/7 and R60/7s with single front disc brake

Rest of World R100/7 and R80/7s with dual front discs

Silver R100RSs retained blue anodized front brake calipers

All other ATE calipers silver anodized

Fuel tank with hose attached to the overflow cavity drain

Screw-type fuel filler cap with a matt finish

Vinyl covered foam pad over the new upper triple clamp

Matt black tail light housing

Black plastic rear mudguard

R100S with twin Fiamm horns

Instruments with black faces, green numerals and white needles

Instrument warning light panel with indicator at the top and brake failure at the bottom

Electronic tachometer

Single key operation for the ignition, fuel tank cap, seat and fork lock

Softer Magura handgrips

Gear lever pivoted on the rider's foot peg

R100RS included a new fairing head light cover, and head light rubber

R100RS with new handlebar clamps and instrument support

R100RT, R100RS, R100S, R100T, R100/7, R80/7, R60/7 1979 model year

In the wake of the serious sales slump, virtually the entire BMW Motorrad management team was replaced at the end of 1978. Only those in the chassis department retained their positions: Rüdiger Gutsche and Ekkehard Rapelius. Dr Eberhard Sarfert took over as general manager from Rudolf Graf von der Schulenburg and Richard Heydenreich replaced Hans-Günter von der Marwitz as Head of the Development Department. Klaus Volker Gevert repaced Hans Muth, while marketing and distribution was now under the control of Karl Gerlinger. Completing the new line up was Martin Probst, who moved from automotive engine development to head engine development. Under this new regime the boxer line-up was considerably expanded and revised for 1979.

With the release of the new generation R65 the R60/7 disappeared from the US line-up for 1979 – though it was produced in small quantities for other markets through until 1980. There were now five 1000cc models, with the R100T filling a void between the sporting R100S and basic R100/7 as a touring machine. Supplanting the R100RS, with the highest price and most equipment, was the full touring R100RT. Although its life began precariously, aimed at the fickle US market, the R100RT ultimately established a formula that was more successful than the R100RS. The R100RT lasted through until 1996.

There were also other transitory variations on the /7 theme, some specifically for the US market – such as the R100S Touring and similar R100T – because the R100/7 was especially popular there. The R100T specification also varied between markets and in the US included standard chrome saddlebag brackets and engine protection bars; voltmeter; quartz clock; an electrical accessory outlet; and rear mud flap. But

despite the high specification and keen pricing ($1415 less than the R100RT), the R100T only sold in very limited numbers.

With only 24,415 motorcycles manufactured during 1979, production was the lowest since 1974. In an effort to stem this downward spiral a R100RS was prepared for an attempt on a series of long distance records. In October 1979, at Nardo in Italy, a team of four riders (Dähne; Cosutti; Milan; and Zanini) set five new world records, including an average speed of 220.711km/h (137.14mph) over 100 kilometres (62.14m) – the lowered R100RS was only slightly modified.

Frame numbers for the new 1979 model year R100RT (code 0386) were 6155001-6157982, with two different series for the US: 6190001-6190004 and 6195001-6196039 (codes 0339 and 0399). The R100RS (0377) numbers were 6095001-6097007 and US (0395) 6185001-6185421; R100S (0376) 6070001-6070651 and US (0394) 6165001-6165152, including 1980 (0436); two series for the R100T (0344 and 0385) began at 6115001-6115002, but the general series was 6150001-6150173. There were also new number sequences for: the R100/7 (0375) 6050001-6051293 and US (0393) 6170001-6170414; and R80/7 (code 0374) 6030001-6030973, US (0392) 6126001-6126349. A small number of 37Kw R75/7s (code 0372) were produced in 1979 with numbers 6222001-6222005. The R60/7 also continued as 29Kw (0371) with Police TIC (0381) versions until 1980, numbers 6015001-6015382 and 6117001-6117273 (TIC).

Engine

For the 1979 model year the M65* engine received its most significant revision yet. Although the general specifications were unchanged, there were several subtle developments to the camshaft drive, ignition and driveshaft. There was also some engine rationalisation for 1979, the R100RT and R100S both sharing the 70-horsepower engine of the R100RS, including the same Bing 94/40/105 and 106 carburettors and 40mm exhaust header pipes. The R100T and R100/7 engine was the 65-horsepower version of the 1978 R100S (with 40mm intake manifolds and Bing 40mm carburettors) and also included the 40mm exhaust header pipes. All the 980cc engines had 44mm inlet and 40mm exhaust valves. Like the R100RS, the R100T and R100/7 now used the smaller alternator and Bosch W225 T30 or W6D, Beru 200/14/3A or Champion N7Y sparkplugs.

Developments began with the crankcases which now had black and silver highlighted 'BMW' emblems on each side, instead of an emblem indicating a particular model and capacity. The R100RS had specific crankcases as it included an oil cooler, but all /7s crankcases included cast main bearing shells, instead of forged with a circumferential 4.5mm groove

The R100RT replaced the R100RS at the head of the BMW motorcycle range for 1979.

as an additional oil supply. They also all shared a new crankshaft which incorporated riveted counterweights to the inner surfaces of the crank webs, instead of tungsten plugs. The crankshaft and balance factor for the 1000cc engine was the same as that for the 800cc. The new Viton rear crankshaft oil seal wasn't as deep as the earlier type and, to eliminate the persistent oil weep from the cylinder base, from May 1979 each cylinder base included a 93x2mm O-ring seal and modified head gaskets. During 1979 the oil filter cartridge was also revised. While the previous type utilized a paper gasket and steel washer, the end of the newer version was crimped to the outer tube, with the square section sealing rings glued to the inside of the filter. For the R100RS (and R100RT) there was now a specific oil filter with a hinge that provided easier removal and installation with the full fairing on.

All /7s also received a new camshaft drive with 50-link, single row 3/8x7/ 32in chain – now with a master link to aid servicing. This included

a spring-loaded, hydraulically damped tensioner, and there was a new front chain case and crankshaft bearing cover that assisted oil flow to the rear main bearing. The oil pump featured a new inner rotor, and there was a new oil pump pick-up strainer which could no longer split at the spot weld, thereby obscuring the pick-up hole and blocking the dipstick. The chain case now had ornamental ribbed fining, and there was a new outer cover, without any ribbing but incorporating additional side vents. European models included the new aluminium top engine cover, with integral air intake and double-sided crankcase breather that was fitted on US examples during 1978.

Some engineers at BMW always believed that the oil temperature of the 980cc was too high, so most R100RS this year (but not all) included a standard six-row oil cooler with the outlet connection at the oil filter head. Although the R100RT and R100S shared the 70-horsepower engine (with black rocker covers), they didn't receive an oil cooler.

The R100RS received an oil cooler for 1979, and a new fairing centre section.

US 1000cc models featured different cylinder heads with valve seats more suitable for low lead fuel and 38mm exhaust header pipes. US models also included a different engine top cover with slotted grill intake for the engine breather. These developments didn't initially feature on the US R80/7s until number 6126147 – which included new cylinder heads; the revised intake and breather setup; and new carburettors (64/32/321 and 322). From August 1979, all the R80/7 carburettors reverted to the domed top type.

Chassis

Chassis changes were minimal for 1979, generally confined to the equipment. The rear subframe received longer shock absorber mounts that facilitated the fitting of pannier mounts. The front fork incorporated a new upper triple clamp and

fork retainer nut, while a revised clamp secured the instrument panel more rigidly to the top triple clamp. All front forks were without rubber gaiters but included the fork sleeves with felt seals previously reserved for the R100RS and R100S. Setting the R100RT, R100RS and R100S apart were black fork legs and the inclusion of side reflectors on European models – previously fitted only to US versions. From R100RT number 6232420 and US 6175169, the front fork included additional compression spring dampers.

Standard on all /7s this year were twin front discs and cast alloy wheels. The R100RT, R100RS and R100S retained a rear disc brake and 2.75in rim, whereas the R100T, R100/7 and R80/7 included the Simplex drum brake with 2.50in rear rim. The R100S now shared its rear axle with the R100RS, along with the smaller diameter (14mm) rear master cylinder.

This year the standard seat for the R100T, R100/7 and R80/7 was the same type as on the R100S, with a fibreglass base and tail section. This included a larger black grab rail and new seat cushion, but the older style seat was still available. In addition to the /7's existing Red, Black, Blue and Orange colour options, the R100T was available in a special Red Metallic/Silver Metallic (556) with silver side covers. Other /7s were now with black side covers. A specific colour for the US was Havana Gold Metallic (511). The side cover decals indicated the model type in addition to the capacity. Twin Fiamm horns were included on all 1000cc models and US R100/7 and R80/7s also featured the broader 682mm handlebar of the R100RT. Completing the 1979 upgrades were new handlebar switches, with a more conventional left-side turn signal indicator switch, and the unconventional location of a horn button just above. The Magura handgrips were larger and reshaped, and setting off the rear was a new double chamber twin bulb tail light and black housing.

Expanding on the RS integral cockpit concept, the R100RT fairing was also developed in a wind tunnel. Even with the high and wide 690mm handlebar, the frame-mounted, pressure-moulded fibreglass fairing was able to provide hand protection. The high windshield was manually adjustable for three rake (over 10 degrees) and height positions. Air intakes under the turn indicators channelled air into the fairing through automotive style adjustable air vents with a butterfly valve.

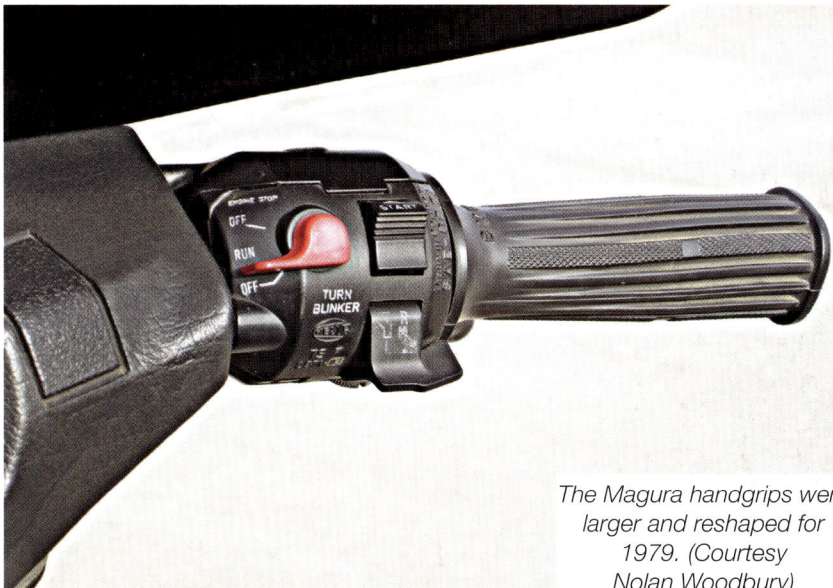

The Magura handgrips were larger and reshaped for 1979. (Courtesy Nolan Woodbury)

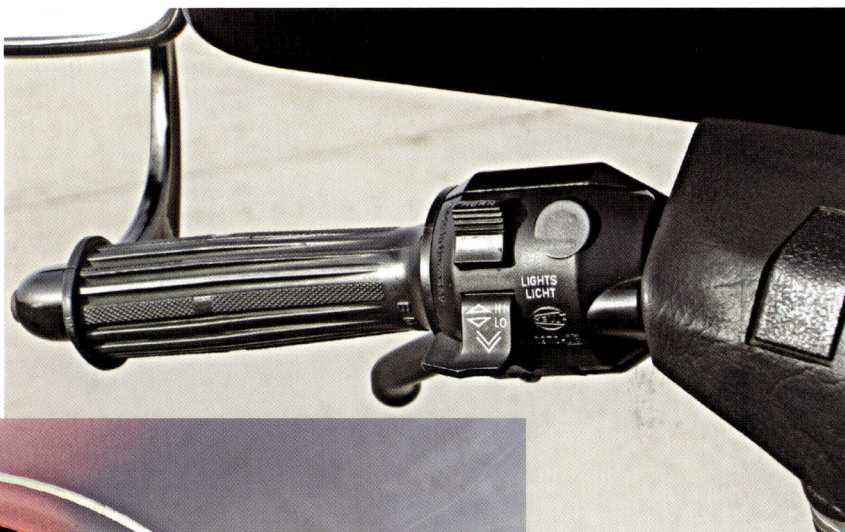

The left turn signal switch was on the left handlebar for 1979. (Courtesy Nolan Woodbury)

All 1979 twins received this larger tail light unit. (Courtesy Nolan Woodbury)

The R100RT fairing was much larger than that on the R100RS, and incorporated an adjustable windshield.

The head light cover with the same strange five orange lines was carried over from the R100RS. The instrument panel was similar to that of the R100RS with an electronic tachometer; voltmeter; quartz clock; and speedometer. There was room for additional switches and control lamps necessary for any of the wide range of optional extras. These initially included long-distance headlamps and fog lamps, and later, flip out driving lights in place of the air vents. Like the R100RS, the R100RT had a restricted 70-degrees of steering lock due to the panel fitting around the fork tubes. The fork tubes were also sealed in the fairing with rubber boots, and the front of the fairing included the open grill of the pre-1979 R100RS.

The fairing also included two large (6-litre) lockable storage compartments beneath the air vents, but there were some problems with the early model lids so these were replaced during 1979. The rear view mirrors mounted onto the fairing and there were new, stronger mounts from number 6165365 and US 6196836. The R100RT came with luggage racks for the standard lockable Krauser saddlebags and it shared the steering damper and twin Fiamm horns of the R100RS. Standard equipment also included: a 12 volt socket behind the left-hand battery panel; a cable lock (with yet another key); and a heel-and-toe rocker gearshift pedal. Setting the R100RT apart from the R100RS were cast wheels, painted a hue of Light Phoenix Gold, and colours of two-tone Brown Metallic (552) and Phoenix Gold Metallic. The other colour was Smoke Red, with Silver wheels (555). There was a different seat with strengthened upholstery and, although the upholstery was beige in the publicity brochures, production examples were black.

While the R100RS bodywork was as before, the inclusion of an oil cooler resulted in a new solid centre lower fairing panel. A dual seat was now standard, with a larger black passenger grab rail that included a rack. The solo seat remained an option and, in addition to metallic gold, there was a two-tone Blue/Silver Metallic with Red pinstriping (554).

Some 1979 R100RTs were painted metallic brown with light gold wheels.

The solo seat was still an option on the 1979 R100RS.

During 1979 a limited edition silver and triple tone blue R100S 'Exclusive Sport' was released, with paint designed by Walter Maurer from Dachau near Munich. This model also included chrome shock absorber springs; polished aluminium fork legs; rocker covers, and final drive housing. The rear mudguard and side covers were silver, and the 'R100S' decals blue. The cast wheels were also matching light silver. Unfortunately, the blue stripes were stickers, and this R100S was greeted by BMW traditionalists with disapproval so the model was very short-lived.

The limited edition Maurer-styled R100S wasn't a great success.

The R100RT soon established itself as a tourer par excellence. Here is an R100RT with a rare R100S Motorsport in 1979. (Courtesy Two Wheels)

/7 distinguishing features 1979 model year

Crankcases with black and silver 'BMW' emblems on each side

New crankshaft with riveted counterweights

New rear crankshaft seal

Cylinder base with 93x2mm O-ring seal

New oil filter cartridge

R100RS and R100RT with hinged oil filter

New camshaft drive with single row chain

Hydraulically damped chain tensioner

New front crankshaft bearing cover

New inner oil pump rotor and pick-up strainer

Chain case with ribbed fining and new outer cover with side vents

All models with double-sided crankcase breather

Most R100RS with an oil cooler

Rear subframe with longer shock absorber mounts that facilitated the fitting of pannier mounts

New upper triple clamp and fork retainer nut

No rubber gaiters on front fork for R100T, R100/7 and R80/7

R100RT, R100RS and R100S with black fork legs

Front fork with side reflectors

All with twin front disc brakes and cast alloy wheels

R100RT, R100RS and R100S with rear disc brake and 2.75in rim

R100T, R100/7 and R80/7 with rear drum brake and 2.50in rim

Brown R100RT wheels painted light Phoenix Gold

Standard seat R100S-type with a fibreglass base and tail section

Side cover decals indicated the model type and not only the capacity

Twin Fiamm horns on all 1000cc models

New handlebar switches

New twin bulb tail light assembly

Larger and reshaped Magura handgrips

R100RS fairing with solid centre lower panel

R100RT, R100RS, R100S, R100T, R100/7, R80/7 1980 model year

As most developmental resources were now directed towards the new K-series and dual purpose G/S, the 1980 larger boxer twins were ostensibly identical to those of 1979. BMW still faced many problems in the US. Not only were there further price increases, the venerable M65* engine was struggling to meet noise and emission requirements whilst still maintaining a respectable power output. As the price continued to climb in America while the performance diminished, sales stagnated to such an extent that only 3866 1000cc models were sold in the US during 1979 and 1980.

The production codes were unchanged for 1980 but the engine received some evolutionary developments. This was an interim solution until the more efficient A10 engine appeared for 1981. Offered in the US this year was a sport version of the R100T that included a low handlebar and fairing. Frame numbers for 1980 were: R100RT 6157983-6169354 and US 6196040-6196851; R100RS 6097008-6100000, 6223001-6223330 and US 6185422-6185519; R100S 6070652-6071951; R100T 6150174-6150396; R100/7 6051294-6053635 and US 6170415-6171344; and R80/7 6030974-6032475.

The R100RT was little changed for 1980, but US examples like this had a lower compression ratio.

Engine

Several modifications were made to US models for 1980, primarily to allow them to run on low lead or unleaded regular fuel, but also to enable the engine to pass more stringent EPA requirements. The combination of a high compression ratio and lower octane fuel caused detonation on 1979 US models, and from August 1979 all US 1000cc and 800cc models had a lower 8.2:1 compression ratio and smaller diameter (38mm) exhaust header pipes. The claimed power for the 1000cc models was now 67 horsepower at 7000rpm. US models also featured a redesigned sand-cast aluminium air filter box with a flat air filter and twin snorkel air intakes, identical in design to the plastic airbox that would appear for 1981. The metal top engine cover, also with 'BMW' cast into each side, incorporated ten grill vents instead of an intake bell. There were still three crankcase ventilation hoses, but the air filter and filter box were redesigned with a flat (instead of round) pleated paper filter. The housing itself was sand-cast aluminium and included a top with two snorkel air intakes. Access to the filter was much easier than before, as four spring clips located it. The new intake system was intended to lower intake noise while increasing volume – it was so successful that it featured on all 1981 engines (albeit in slightly modified form). Completing the intake modifications (on US bikes) were two 10.5mm diameter tubes connecting the air filter box to a threaded connection from each exhaust

port in the cylinder head. This Pulse-Air suction emission system was similar to one already used by Kawasaki, and included a one-way reed valve in the airbox. It was an endeavour to reduce the level of un-burnt hydrocarbons by mixing the exhaust gases with clean air. There were also hotter sparkplugs specified for US models: Champion N7Y or Bosch W6D. The larger boxers for the rest of the world included the crankcase ventilation and air intake of the 1979 US bikes for 1980. The R100T and R100/7 now featured black rocker covers in line with the RT, RS and S.

The other evolutionary development was in the lubrication system. As a direct result of experience gained through racing, from January 1980, the front oil passage in the camshaft was altered to send the oil three ways. Oil now went to the new front main bearing bushings and caps first, followed by the camshaft and the rear main bearing. Previously, oil was fed initially to the camshaft, then to the front main bearing with the rear main bearing last in the line. The new crankcases were identified by 'ALCAN' cast next to the clutch flange. There was also a small update to the lubrication bores on the rocker arm needle roller bearings, now diagonal instead of straight. These updates were incorporated from frame numbers: R100RT 6158745 and US 6196045; R100RS 6097660 and US 6185422; R100S 6070786 and US 6165103; R100T 6150266; R100/7 6051658; R80/7 6031545 and US 6126171.

Many US R100Ts were fitted out with optional touring equipment to stimulate stagnating sales.

US models from August 1979 (R100/7 6170415; R100S 6165103; R100RS 6185422; R100RT 6196045) included another set of Bing carburettors, with revised jetting (165 main jets and 2.66 needle jets) and a new choke housing. All the Bing carburettors included a new slide top spring, and for the R80/7 new carburettor piston slides.

Chassis

While there was little to visually distinguish the 1980 European boxers from the 1979 versions, US models included a few further updates: The choke lever was moved to the clutch lever handlebar bracket because there was no longer room for it on the new air filter box. The throttle cable setup included a single cable connecting to a junction with separate cables for each carburettor. There were new convex mirrors, the under seat tool tray now had a cover and audible turn signal beepers were eliminated. Completing the developments this year, was a federally mandated 85mph speedometer. The colours for the R100RT and R100S were unchanged for 1980, but the R100RS was now available in the previous Dark Blue and Silver (554) and Silver Beige Metallic (547). Three colours were provided for the R80/7; Bronco Brown (588); Dark Blue Metallic (550); and Metallic Red (531). By 1980, it was obvious that the 1000cc and 800cc boxers had a limited life in their current form. Although BMW management was committed to the water-cooled K-series, BMW's engineers were also planning the next generation boxer twin. This would be released for the 1981 model year.

/7 distinguishing features 1980 model year

US versions with 8.2:1 compression ratio and 38mm exhaust header pipes
US models with aluminium air filter box, flat filter and twin snorkel air intakes
R100T and R100/7 with black rocker covers
From January 1980 the front oil passage in the camshaft altered
Updated lubrication bores on the rocker arm needle roller bearings
US models with new Bing carburettors
US models with choke lever on the clutch lever bracket

/7 frame numbers

Type	Numbers	Model year	Production dates
R60/7	6000001–6005517	1977	05/76-06/77
	6007001–6009844	1978	07/77-12/77
	6010035–6011412	1978	12/77-01/78
	6015001-6015382	1979-80 (29kW)	09/78-04/80
	6117001–6117273	1979-80 (TIC)	09/78-06/80
	6100001–6100407	1977 (US)	06/76-05/77
	6101001–6101158	1978 (US)	08/77-11/77
R75/7	6020001–6024507	1977	05/76-06/77
	6220001-6220278	1978	09/77-04/78
	6222001-6222005	1979	01/79
	6120001–6121474	1977 (US)	07/76-06/77
R80/7	6025001-6021915	1978	04/77-07/78
	6030001-6030973	1979	06/78-08/79
	6030974-6032475	1980	09/79-06/80
	6105001–6105003	1978 R80 (TIC TN)	06/78-07/78
	6108001–6108276	1978 R80 (TIC T)	06/78-08/78
	6205001–6206315	1979-80 (37kW)	06/78-07/80
	6130001–6130118	1979-80 R80T (37kW)	09/78-07/80
	6132001–6133186	1979-80 R80T (41kW)	09/78-07/80
	6122501–6124909	1978 (US)	04/77-07/78
	6126001–6126349	1979-80 (US)	08/78-07/80
R100/7	6040001–6043414	1977	05/76-06/77
	6045001–6047995	1978	04/77-08/78
	6110001–6110088	1978 R100/7 (T)	03/78-04/78
	6050001–6051293	1979	06/78-08/79
	6051294–6053635	1980	09/79-07/80
	6140001–6142451	1977 (US)	05/76-06/77
	6145001–6148196	1978 (US)	07/77-07/79
	6170001–6170414	1979 (US)	09/78-08/79
	6170415–6171344	1980 (US)	09/79-07/80
R100T	6115001–6115002	1979	07/78
	6150001–6150173	1979	11/78-07/79

Type	Numbers	Model year	Production dates
	6150174–6150396	1980	09/79-07/80
R100S	6060001–6063149	1977	05/76-06/77
	6065001–6068753	1978	04/77-07/78
	6070001–6070651	1979	06/78-07/79
	6070652-6071951	1980	09/79-07/80
	6160001–6161385	1977 (US)	05/76-06/77
	6162501–6163870	1978 (US)	07/77-07/78
	6165001–6165152	1979-80 (US)	08/78-09/79
R100RS	6080001-6085159	1977	03/76-06/77
	6086001-6092865	1978	04/77-07/78
	6095001-6097007	1979	06/78-08/79
	6097008-6100000	1980	09/79-06/80
	6223001-6223330	1980	06/80-07/80
	6180001-6181263	1977 (US)	05/76-06/77
	6182501-6183592	1978 (US)	04/77-07/78
	6185001-6185421	1979 (US)	08/78-07/79
	6185422-6185519	1980 (US)	11/79-06/80
R100RT	6155001-6157982	1979	06/78-08/79
	6157983-6169354	1980	09/79-07/80
	6190001-6190004	1979 (US)	04/78
	6195001-6196039	1979 (US)	08/78-07/79
	6196040-6196851	1980 (US)	09/79-07/80

CHAPTER V

R100 & R80 1981-85 (TYPE 247)

Continual refinement of the 1000cc boxer engine resulted in its quintessential development for 1981. With significant improvements to the engine and chassis, from 1981 until 1984 the R100 boxer represented the culmination of a classic design. Although the later monoshock twins were functionally superior, the twin shock BMW was more aesthetically balanced, maintaining a traditional classic profile.

R100RT, R100RS, R100CS, R100 1981 model year

A rationalisation of the line-up coincided with the introduction of the improved A10 engine for 1981. The R100RT and R100RS continued with a similar style, and the R100S evolved into the R100CS. There was now only one basic model in the range, the R100. Although still offered for police applications as the R80TIC, the only regular 800cc model this year was the R80 G/S. Its outstanding success led to a proliferation of 800cc versions during 1982 and 1983.

Frame numbers for 1981 were: R100RT (code 0446) 6230001-6232899 and US (code 0449) 6240001-6241232; R100RS (0427) 6075001-6080001 and US (0437) 6225001-6225628; R100CS (0426) 6135001-6136503 and US (0436) 6188001-6188163; R100 (0425) 6035001-6037528 and US (0435) 6175001-6175593; there was also a police R100 TIC (0445) 6193001-6193433.

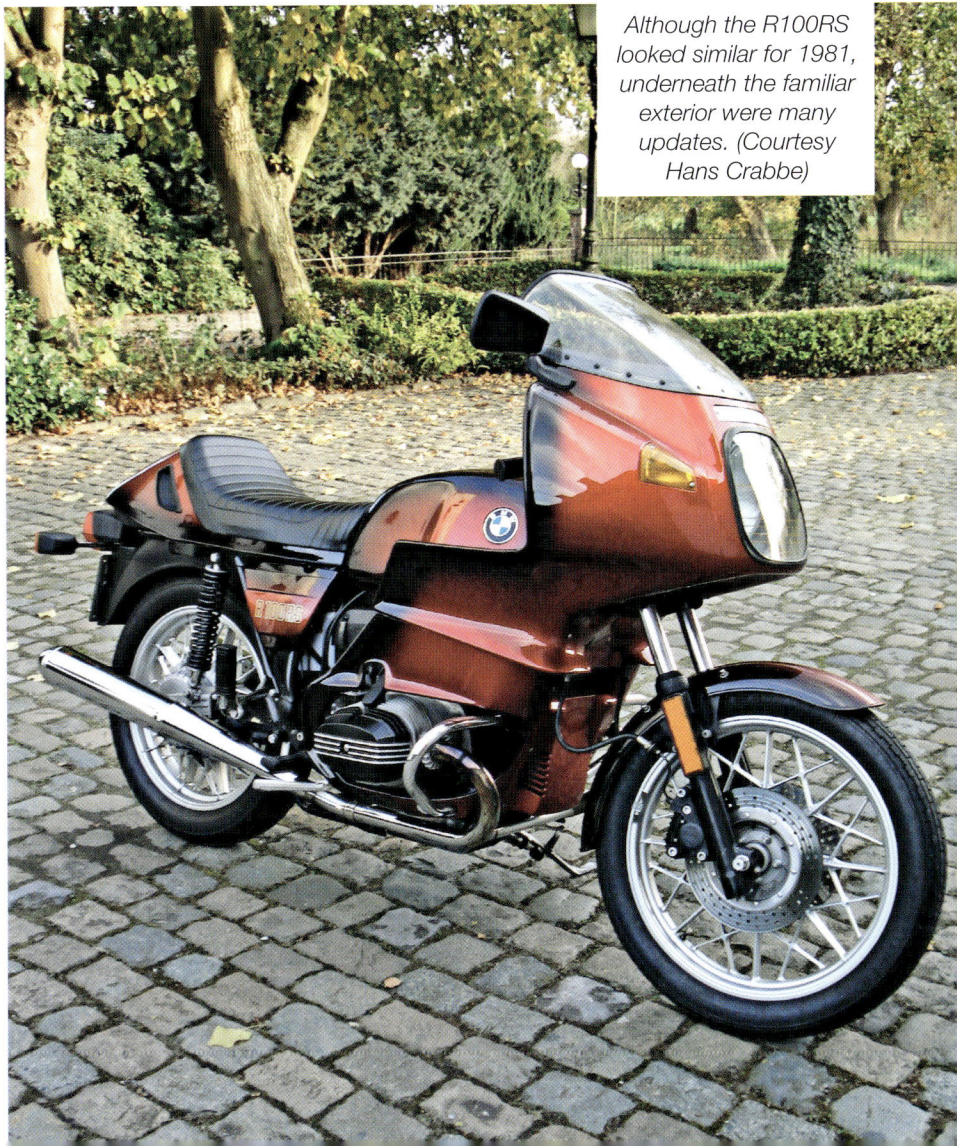

Although the R100RS looked similar for 1981, underneath the familiar exterior were many updates. (Courtesy Hans Crabbe)

Engine (Type A10)

There were many more engine updates this year, beginning with crankcase strengthening underneath the starter motor. The R100RS had specific crankcases as it was still the only model with an oil cooler, the R100RT sharing the engine housing with the R100CS and R100. All crankcases included modified oil passages; a deeper sump cover with transverse oil baffle plates; new drain plugs, and dipstick. This increased the oil capacity to 2.75-litres on the R100RS (with the standard oil cooler) and 2.50-litres on the other R100s, resulting in lower oil temperature. The R100CS shared the engine of the R100RT, along with black rocker covers.

One of the main updates was new cylinders – Nicasil (by Mahle of Stuttgart) or Galnikal (by Kolben-Schmidt of Neckarsulm). Later supplies were also obtained from the Italian manufacturer, Gilardoni. All the coatings were identical but for the brand name. Instead of lining aluminium cylinders with cast-iron, silicon-carbide was applied directly to the aluminium cylinders. The weight-saving was 3.4kg with wear qualities significantly improved. The cylinders could no longer be rebored, and were matched to the piston; however, with improved heat dissipation, wear was virtually nonexistent. No liquid sealant was used at the base of the cylinder, and the O-ring was increased from 2mm to 2.2mm. The rear cylinder studs were now the same as the front (305mm), and the piston pin offset from the centreline was reduced to 1.0mm (from 1.5mm). While European examples retained the 9.5:1 compression ratio, producing the same 70 horsepower but at a slightly lower 7000rpm,

US models still had the lower 8.2:1 compression ratio. There was no claimed power figure for US examples.

The crankshaft was unchanged, except for a new lock ring and thrust washer for the substantially lighter pressed-steel (rather than billet-cast) flywheel. This was akin to a three-spoked cross with riveted ring starter gear, the flywheel O-ring inside the flywheel cap. Accompanying the new cylinders were new cylinder heads and new exhaust valve seats. The exhaust valve seat width was reduced from 2.0mm to 1.5mm, although valve recession from lead free fuel was still a problem in the US. The crankcase ventilation on all 1981 models was now the same revised diaphragm controlled double-sided breather that first appeared on US 1979 examples. This included the new vented top engine cover and a revised chain case cover (to accommodate the new ignition) – now with black highlighting between the ornamental fining, previously reserved for the smaller R65.

Experience with the smaller R65 proved the benefits of a lighter clutch and flywheel, especially in combination with the driveshaft shock absorber, and this was passed on to the A10 engine. The thinner (5.5mm) 165mm clutch also had a stronger diaphragm spring and spring plate. The weight of the flywheel and clutch assembly was reduced from 6kg to around 2kg, with a vast improvement in throttle response. This new clutch was accompanied by a new operating mechanism – running in ball-and-needle bearings – that included a new pushrod, clutch piston, and gearbox end clutch lever, resulting in a 30 per cent reduction (100Nm to 70Nm) in draw effort.

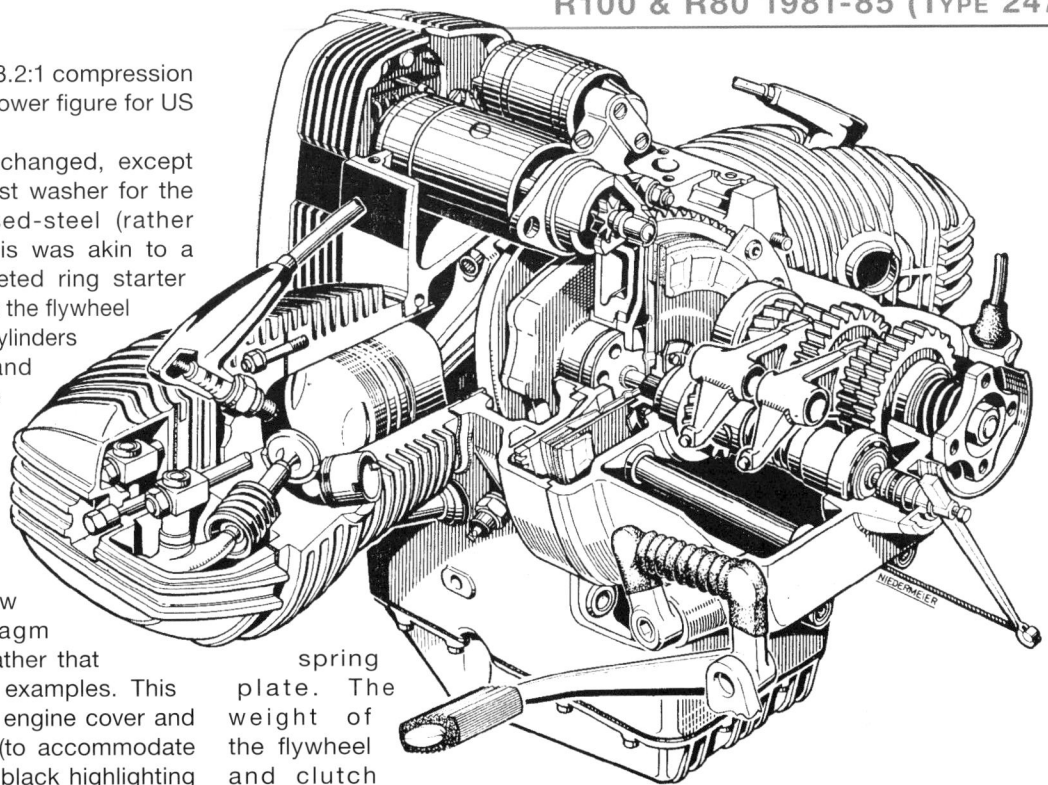

The boxer engine featured a much lighter clutch assembly from 1981.

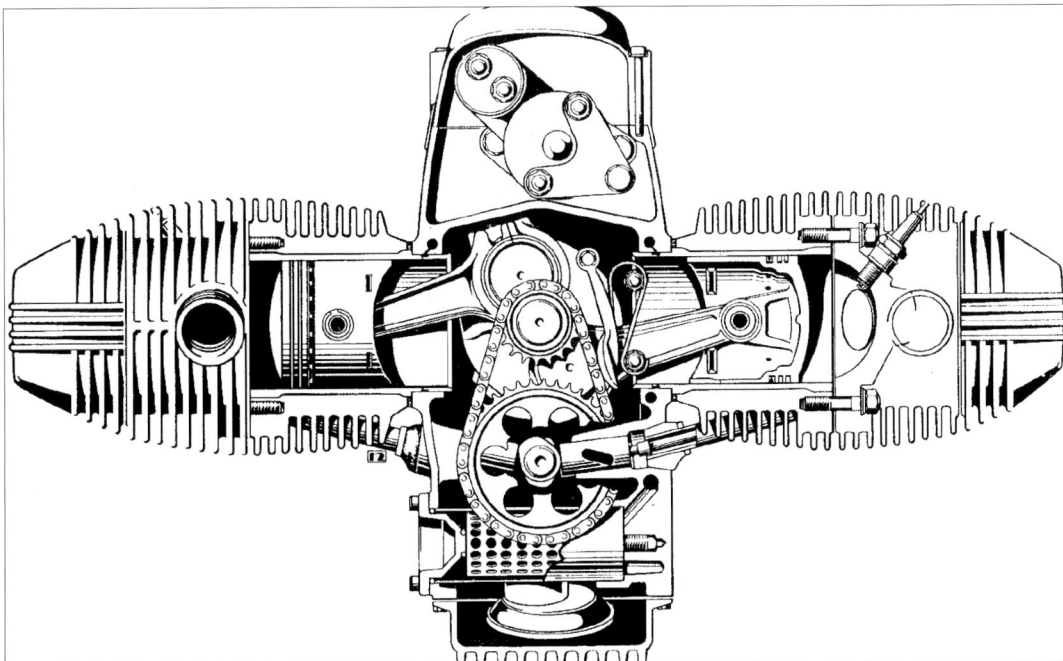

Engine updates included lighter and harder-wearing Nikasil or Galnikal cylinders.

The five-speed transmission ratios were unchanged, but there was a new main shaft drive pinion and seal, and input shaft. Other updates included a new rear transmission cover; new kick start ratio and spline for the optional kick start, and Heim joints for the gearshift mechanism. During 1981, the black 'FW2' gearbox oil seal was updated to a 'KACO' seal to eliminate oil leaks

New for 1981 was a lighter pressure die-cast final drive housing. (Courtesy Hans Crabbe)

between the gearbox and swingarm. While the shaft drive tunnel in the swingarm was now a single component, and only flattened on the inside, the driveshaft ramped coupler shock absorber was new. The final drive pinion needle output bearing was now 15x30x18mm (instead of 15x32x17mm), and the driveshaft gaiter received a new hose clip. Completing the new rear end was a lighter and stronger pressure die-cast final drive housing, similar to that of the monoshock R80 G/S, and it also included fins for improved cooling. US R100s retained the 1:2.91 final drive, with the European R100 featuring the 1:3.0 ratio.

The new 40mm Bing carburettors included a more positive location for the throttle slides, with a supplementary piston guideway. There was also the new flat pleated paper rectangular air filter and airbox design that featured on 1980 US models. Although the airbox was the same design, the body and top were now black plastic rather than cast-aluminium, with two removable, forward facing plastic snorkels. The smoother plastic finish was claimed to reduce turbulence and restriction, permitting leaner jetting, and the new setup also allowed easier access to the air filter. US versions retained the twin air intake pipes but now incorporated a vacuum shut-off, connected to the reed valve inside the airbox. This also improved cold weather performance, and throttle response throughout the rev range, as the carburation wasn't as lean as before.

The airbox was plastic on post-1981 boxer twins. (Courtesy Hans Crabbe)

The R100RS retained 40mm Bing carburettors. (Courtesy Two Wheels)

There were some changes to the exhaust system, all models now receiving the 38x1.5mm diameter exhaust pipes previously reserved for the R80 and US versions. An additional rear crossover balance pipe behind the sump helped broaden the power band. Completing the exhaust updates were new exhaust spider nuts and more efficient mufflers, with specific mufflers for the US.

All R100s received an updated electrical system including a more powerful Bosch G1 14V 20A 280W alternator; new micro element electronic Wehrle E1951B/14V voltage regulator; improved battery charging; and a 0.7kW Bosch starter motor to ensure the engine turned over reliably every time. One of the more practical updates was the Bosch TSZH electronic ignition. This transistorised breakerless system used a Hall effect trigger with integral centrifugal advance and two lighter 6V coils, the timing (advance from 1550-3000rpm with 32-degrees maximum) was unchanged. The sparkplugs (on all 1000cc models) were Bosch W5D, Beru 14-5D or Champion N6Y for Europe, US sparkplugs were Bosch W6D, Beru 14-6D or Champion N7Y. Also new, the BMW Mareg28 Ah battery and Hella TBB 53 turn signal indicator units.

Chassis

The frame and swingarm received some subtle updates for 1981. The rake was still 28.5 degrees with 95mm of trail, but a new rear subframe improved access to the battery. BMW's engineers learned from their development of the monoshock R80 G/S, designing a stiffer swingarm with an additional cylindrical tube. The swingarm included new pivot pins, seal rings and tapered roller bearings – these bearings were changed again in January 1981. New chassis identification plates were fitted from April 1981, and all 1981 R100s included a warning plate regarding the transistorised ignition.

Warning stickers abounded on BMW motorcycles of this era. (Courtesy Nico Georgeoglou)

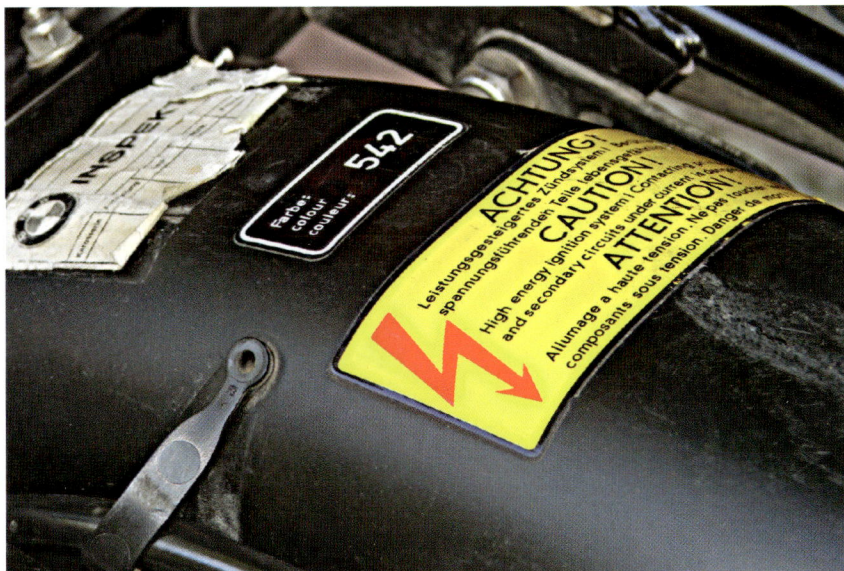

Although the cast-aluminium 'snowflake' wheels looked similar to before, the front wheel on all R100s was now a wider 2.15Bx19in. The tyre size (3.25Hx19) was unchanged. The rear wheel on the R100RT and R100RS remained 2.75Bx18in with a 4.00Hx18 tyre. Unlike the R100S with its rear disc brake, the R100CS had the narrower 2.50Bx18in rear wheel with a rear drum brake. This rear wheel, together with new brake lever, brake shoes, and rear brake cam, was also shared by the R100. All wheels were silver, with the special R100RT Phoenix gold discontinued.

The R100 and R100CS had a rear drum brake and a new casting. (Courtesy Hans Crabbe)

Some R100CSs had wire-spoked wheels and the older-style drum brake.

While some brochures and catalogues showed the R100CS with wire-spoked wheels and plain alloy fork legs, most examples had black fork legs and cast wheels. The R100CSs featuring wire-spoked wheels were sold primarily in Australia, with different hubs to the earlier types and new distance bushings. The alloy rim sizes were the same as the R100S of 1977, a 1.85Bx19in on the front and a 2.15Bx18in on the rear, with an earlier style 200mm Simplex rear brake.

action saw oil transferred from the top to the lower chamber, with the shock eventually settling at a point determined by the controlling orifice in the central pumping rod. Although the spring travel was reduced to 85.5mm, the shocks were extremely effective and the Nivomat was the most advanced suspension available for a touring motorcycle in 1981. Unfortunately, troublesome seals tarnished the Nivomat's reputation.

The front brake calipers were Brembo for 1981. (Courtesy Two Wheels)

The front wire-spoked wheel for the R100CS was similar to the pre-1978 front wheel.

While retaining the relatively narrow 36mm fork tubes, the Sachs-built front fork was new, and each leg required less fluid (220ml), although the spring travel was unchanged. Although most R100RTs, R100RSs and R100CSs had black fork legs this year, on some R100s they were plain alloy. The forks included shorter (539mm), but thicker (4.25mm), springs and new dampers. The fork legs were cast to accept the rectangular reflector. The fork design was changed during 1981 (from R100RT 6232420 and US 6175169; R100RS 6077830; and R100 6193063) to include an additional compression coil spring at the base of the damping rod. Although the rear Boge shock absorbers were unchanged, the R100RT featured self-levelling Nivomat units that were optional on other R100s. The Nivomat incorporated a high-pressure oil/gas chamber in the lower part of the body, with a low-pressure chamber in the top. Repeated shock absorber

The perforated front brake disc diameter was now quoted at 260mm and had new twin 38mm piston Brembo calipers with aluminium pistons. These calipers with Textar asbestos-free pads, combined with the relocation of the Magura front brake master cylinder to the handlebar, vastly improved braking performance from the earlier ATE floating piston calipers. Wet weather braking was claimed to be improved by 40 per cent. The master cylinder piston diameter was 15mm (down from 16mm), and the front brake lines included a T-junction with pressure switch

located on the top frame tube, underneath the fuel tank. The same Brembo disc as before was at the rear, but with the smaller 14mm master cylinder of the 1979 R100S to provide an improved leverage ratio.

Although the speedometer, head light and tail light were unchanged, the electronic tachometer was new, with the RPM indication on the lower face. The new instrument light display included a 'High Beam' warning light at the bottom, replacing the 'Brake Failure' item. US versions still had the 85mph speedometer and hard-wired head light this year. The R100RT and R100RS retained the two-stage hydraulic steering damper, and the side and centre stands were redesigned with rubber plugs on the base of the centre stand. The side stand was no longer self-retracting and the centre stand was 10mm longer. Along with a new rear turn signal indicator bracket, there was a new set of footpeg mounts to reduce vibration – in a slightly higher and more rearward location. This provided more space between the rider's feet and the carburettors, the thread holes no longer painted to minimise thread wear. The passenger footpegs were adjustable. There was a recall early in 1981 to replace the right side footpeg, as its location could prevent ease-of-operation of the rear brake. While the remote gearshift linkage was similar to the previous version, there was no longer a grease nipple at the pivot.

The front brake master cylinder was now on the handlebar, instead of underneath the fuel tank. (Courtesy Nico Georgeoglou)

The instrument panel was very similar to that of the previous model. (Courtesy Nico Georgeoglou)

The choke lever was now on the left handlebar. (Courtesy Nico Georgeoglou)

All R100s now had the choke lever on the left handlebar clutch assembly. The Magura throttle assembly retained the excellent cam and chain system, but was of the type fitted to 1980 US models, with a single cable connecting to a junction block and two cables running to each carburettor. This was claimed to reduce friction, although one feature missing from the new throttle assembly was a throttle stop. New black round mirrors were fitted to the R100CS and R100. The frame tube cable lock still featured on the R100RT, R100RS and R100CS (optional on the R100). The ignition key location remained on the left head light mount and, while the R100CS retained twin Fiamm horns, the R100 still had only a single horn on the left.

A cable lock was provided on most R100s, as was a tyre pump. (Courtesy Nico Georgeoglou)

93

The bodywork for all models was much as before. The front mudguard received a new metal brace with shorter mounting bolts but the longer front mudguard was still an option. On the R100RT, the centre section of the fairing was closed off with fewer slots and there was a new windshield. This was trimmer than before, without any of the creases that distorted the vision on the earlier version. The windshield attachment was also improved to allow easier refitting. The R100RT was available in Metallic Amazon Green (520) with gold pinstripes and decals, and Lava Red Metallic (509).

A limited edition R100RS for 1981, the black and gold JPS.

The R100CS continued the style established by the R90S back in 1974.

New colours were also available for the R100RS: Polaris Graphite Metallic (507) or Lava Red Metallic (508) – both without pinstripes and white side cover decals; Stratos Silver Metallic with red pinstripes; and a John Player Special Edition, released to coincide with the racing 6-series JPS cars, black with gold wheels and decals. Most R100CSs were Classic Metallic Black (506) with gold pinstripes but they were also available in Dunkel Red Metallic (553). Although the most popular colour for the R100 was Metallic Silver with Blue pinstripes (505), it was also available in Black (519) or Metallic Atlantic Blue (504). The R100CS had specific 'R100CS' side cover decals this year. A wide range of optional equipment was available for the R100, extending to engine protection bars; Nivomat shock absorbers; electrically-heated handlebar grips; white or black panniers; magnetic tank bag; additional instruments, and super toolkit. The optional touring windshield for the R100 was redesigned, with simplified mounts.

R100 distinguishing features 1981 model year

- Strengthened crankcases with modified oil passages
- Deeper sump with new drain plugs and dipstick
- Nicasil or Galnikal cylinders
- Cylinder base O-ring thickness increased to 2.2mm
- 305mm rear cylinder studs
- Piston pin centre line offset reduced to 1.0mm
- Lighter pressed-steel flywheel
- Thinner and lighter clutch with stronger spring and plate
- New clutch operating mechanism with ball and needle bearings
- Exhaust valve seat width reduced to 1.5mm
- Double-sided engine breather
- New vented top engine cover
- New chain case cover
- New gearbox main shaft; drive pinion and seal; and input shaft
- New rear transmission cover
- New kick start ratio and spline for the optional kick start
- Heim joints for the gearshift mechanism
- New driveshaft ramped coupler shock absorber
- Stronger final drive pinion needle output bearing
- Lighter and stronger pressure die-casting final drive housing
- New 40mm Bing carburettors
- Flat paper rectangular air filter and plastic airbox
- All models with 38mm exhaust pipes and additional rear crossover balance pipe
- More powerful Bosch 280W alternator
- Bosch TSZH electronic ignition with 6V coils
- New rear subframe provided improved battery access
- Stiffer swingarm with an additional cylindrical tube and new bearings
- Wider 2.15Bx19in front wheel
- R100CS with 2.50Bx18in rear wheel and drum brake
- New 36mm front fork
- R100RT with self-levelling Nivomat rear shock absorbers
- 260mm front disc brakes with twin piston Brembo calipers
- Magura front brake master cylinder located on the handlebar
- 14mm master cylinder for rear disc brake
- New electronic tachometer
- New instrument warning light display
- Redesigned side and centre stands with the side stand manually retracting
- Centre stand 10mm longer
- New footpeg mounts to reduce vibration
- Footpeg thread holes no longer painted
- Choke lever on the left handlebar clutch assembly
- Throttle assembly with a single cable splitting into separate cables to each carburettor
- Front mudguard with a new metal brace and shorter mounting bolts
- R100RT with closed centre fairing section and new windshield

R100RT, R100RS, R100CS, and R100 1982 model year

With most developmental resources going into the forthcoming K-series, there were few changes to the 1000cc boxer twins for 1982. R100 production codes were unchanged for 1982 and frame numbers were: R100RT 6232900-6236060 and US 6241233-6242332; R100RS 6390001-6392801 and US 6225629-6226208; R100CS 6136504-6138122 and US 6188164-6188166; R100 6037529-6040000 and US 6175594-6176319. An R80 was also produced for official use and used as the TIC police model.

Engine and transmission

As most engine and transmission updates were introduced for the 1982 model year, engine developments were minor this year. The protective tube pushrod rings were now braised onto the cylinders to increase the pre-load on the rubber seals and prevent oil weeping. Early in 1982, the crankcase finishing hole plugs were updated and the oil filter seal was a 4mm O-ring instead of a washer and paper gasket. The oil dipstick was also changed from silver-grey to black.

The transmission also received some developments early in 1982. From R100RT 6234533 and US 6242150; R100RS 6390466 and US 6226148; R100CS 6137305; R100 6039007 and US 6175989; R80 6012938, and R80 TIC 6211170, the gearbox series number was placed on the side of the gearbox housing instead of the top, enabling the number to be read without removal of the

air filter housing. The gear selecting mechanism was updated after gearbox number 56 476 to improve gear selection. A green paint mark was placed above the gearbox number, indicating an improved hairpin selector spring and selector disc, and a mechanical device installed to prevent mis-shifting. Further gearbox improvements occurred from gearbox number 58 225 on models: R100RT 6235211; R100RS 6391446; R100CS 6137659; R100 6039576 and US 6176014. The transmission received new helical input primary gears and a new fifth gear. To reduce noise and wear the mesh angle was now 17.5 degrees, and the new gears were marked with a cross. Improved clutch plates and a fully enclosed clutch housing were standard from June 30th, 1982, model numbers: R100RT 6235850; R100RS 6392366 and US 6226174; R100CS 6137944; R100 6040199 and US 6176211; R100 TIC 6193369; R80 6012984; R80 TIC 6211523; R80RT 6420016.

The R100 was essentially unchanged for 1982. (Courtesy Hans Crabbe)

Chassis

Frame updates for 1982 included strengthening of the side stand frame mount, and a new side stand. The side stand now featured a corrugated step and rubber stop, and was spring loaded. This modification occurred after R100RT 6234677; R100RS 6390944; R100CS 6137484; R100 6039221, and R80 6012949. Shortly afterwards, the frame number was stamped on the right downtube, above the side stand instead of the steering head, from frame numbers R100RT 6235895 and US 6242301; R100RS 6392466 and US 6226176; R100CS 6137994; R100 6040238 and US 6176222; R100 TIC 6193423; R80 6013030; R80 TIC 6211546; R80RT 6420171 and US 6172020. Early in the model year (week 49, 1981), the frame radius was altered to provide easier access to the oil filter cover.

Other minor developments this year included a one key lock and the R100RT Nivomat shock receiving an extra spring to ensure it could handle a full load. These shocks were marked with an 'L' on the lower mounting hole. Many Karcoma (but not Germa) fuel petcocks now had the feed angling backwards instead of down to clear the throttle and choke cables.

The optional 40-litre pannier bags were a new rectangular style, with an improved latch to the frame mount. New rear turn signal indicator brackets featured on US models from R100RT 6242152, R100RSs 6226150, R100CS 6188165, and R100 6175996.

Some R100RSs were offered in white with red pinstripes for 1982. (Courtesy Jeff Whitlock/ Mac Kirkpatrick)

The RSR was another limited edition R100RS.

The range of colours was also expanded slightly for the 1982 model year. The R100RS was available in an optional Mother-of-Pearl Metallic White (571) with red pinstripes. There was a numbered limited edition R100RSR in Black with white and red pinstripes, primarily for the Japanese market. The R100CS (colours unchanged from 1981) was still available in Europe for 1982, with black fork legs and cast alloy wheels, but was dropped from the official US line-up even though a very small number were manufactured. Instead of the R100CS, two versions of the R100 were offered in the US; the Touring and the Sport. The Sport came with the CS sport fairing and narrow handlebar as standard, while the Touring was fitted with standard saddlebags. Both these US model R100s included non-painted fork legs and black rocker covers; 'R100' side cover decals; and cast alloy wheels with a rear drum brake. R100 colours were the same as for 1981.

The R100RS still had an oil cooler and closed central fairing section. Blue was one of the less common colours. (Courtesy Nico Georgeoglou)

R100 distinguishing features 1982 model year

Protective tube pushrod rings now braised onto the cylinders

Oil filter seal now a 4mm O-ring

Black oil dipstick

Gearbox number on the side of the gearbox housing

New gear selecting mechanism

New helical input primary gears and a new fifth gear

New clutch plates and a fully enclosed clutch housing

Strengthened side stand frame mount and new side stand

Frame radius changed to improve access to oil filter

One key locking

Nivomat shock with an extra spring

New rectangular style optional panniers

R100RT, R100RS, R100CS, R100, R80RT 1983 model year

In an effort to overcome stagnating R100RT sales, the R80RT joined the R100RT for the 1983 model year. The R80RT was almost identical to the larger version but with the R80 engine, a rear drum brake, and without standard luggage or Nivomat rear suspension. Although the performance was extremely leisurely, it was popular and, when the revised boxers were offered in 1984, the R80RT survived. It wasn't until 1987 that the R100RT would make a return. The R100 models continued much as before, the R100CS still not available in the US. For Europe the R100CS had black fork legs and cast alloy wheels.

The frame numbers for the 1983 model year were: R100RT 6236061-6237429 and US 6242333-6243216; R100RS 6392802-6395887 and US 6226209-6226731; R100CS 6138123-6138797 and US 6188167-6188174; R100 6400001-6401588 and US 6176320-6176735; R80RT (code 0444) 6420001-6424026 and US (code 0448) 6172001-6173121.

Engine

Although the 1000cc boxer was nearing the end of its envisaged production, a few small updates were introduced for 1983. From January 1983, the cylinder base O-rings returned to the 2mm thickness of pre-1981 – to overcome the barrel deformation caused through incorrect assembly (the worst case scenario). From week 9, 1983, an improved oil retaining ring was fitted to the clutch end of the crankshaft, and, from week 20, the oil seal for the alternator was grooved.

With the four-cylinder K-series destined to replace the 1000cc boxer, the boxer's future now lay with the smaller capacity 800cc engine. This was already powering the R80/GS and, unlike the 1000cc models, there was only one specification R80RT engine. US and European examples using ostensibly the same engine as the earlier R80/7, but with the lower 8.2:1 compression ratio, Nikasil cylinders, lighter clutch and flywheel, and electronic ignition. There were new valve seats for the 42mm and 38mm valves and shorter (44mm) valve guides. Distinguishing the R80RT were plain alloy, rather than black, rocker covers. To compensate for the moderate horsepower, the R80RT came with a 1:3.36 (37:11) final drive ratio. The R80RT also had new 32mm Bing carburettors with different throttle return springs. From R80RT 6421094 a 148 main jet was fitted to improve low speed running and, from May 1983 (R80RT 6243167 and US 6173082), all R80 carburettors

had new needles, throttle valves and 135 main jets. US versions now had a 40 idling jet and 2.68 atomizer. The Bosch electronic ignition system for the R80RT was the same as for the R100 but with different sparkplugs: Bosch W7D, Beru 14-7D, or Champion N10Y.

Reinforced clutch housing and harder wearing clutch plates were fitted early in the model year (R100RT 6236140; R100RS 6392820 and US 6226222; R100CS 6138170 and US 6188167; R100 6400621 and US 6176912; R80RT 6420740 and US 6172253. This was to alleviate clutch slipping problems on full load caused by undersized ground housing. From these frame numbers, a 0.2mm washer was installed to spring load the dished spring. The size of this pre-load washer was increased to 0.4mm after frame number R100RT 6236173; R100RS 6392868 and US 6226235; R100CS 6138204; R100 6400644; R80RT 6420811 and US 6172267. Soon afterwards (after frame number R100RT 6236312 and US 6242478; R100RS 6393187; R100CS 6138269; R100 6400792 and US 6176497; R80RT 6421255 and US 6172379) the washers were discontinued. Marked by a brown paint mark, the clutch housing was now stiffer and more accurately machined.

Further gearbox modifications occurred after gearbox number 79 720, with an improved gear selector camplate, including deepened detent valleys to eliminate false neutrals. First featured on the R80G/S and ST, this update provided an additional 0.6mm clearance for the hairpin spring. From gearbox number 88 401 (with kick start) and 88 478 (without kick start), all the components of the gear selector mechanism were more precisely finished to reduce friction and improve gear selection.

Chassis

The R80RT was ostensibly identical to the R100RT, sharing the touring fairing that still included an adjustable windshield. The R80RT had no voltmeter, clock, or luggage as standard equipment, but these were available as an option. The front fork was also the same, but with plain aluminium fork legs, and the brakes and wheels were shared with the R100. The front brakes were twin Brembo, while the rear wheel and brake was a 2.50Bx18in with rod-operated 200mm Simplex. The rear suspension was also the standard R100 Boge twin shock absorbers, with Nivomat an option. Standard equipment on the R80RT included a steering damper, twin Fiamm horns, and external power socket. R80RT colours were Pacific Blue Metallic (544) and Red Metallic (566). Other models also received new colours: the R100RT now in Spheric Sliver Metallic (573) and Magenta Red Metallic (572), and the R100RS in Alaska Blue Metallic (542), alongside the existing Polaris Graphite and White.

The R80RT was the final twin shock absorber boxer.

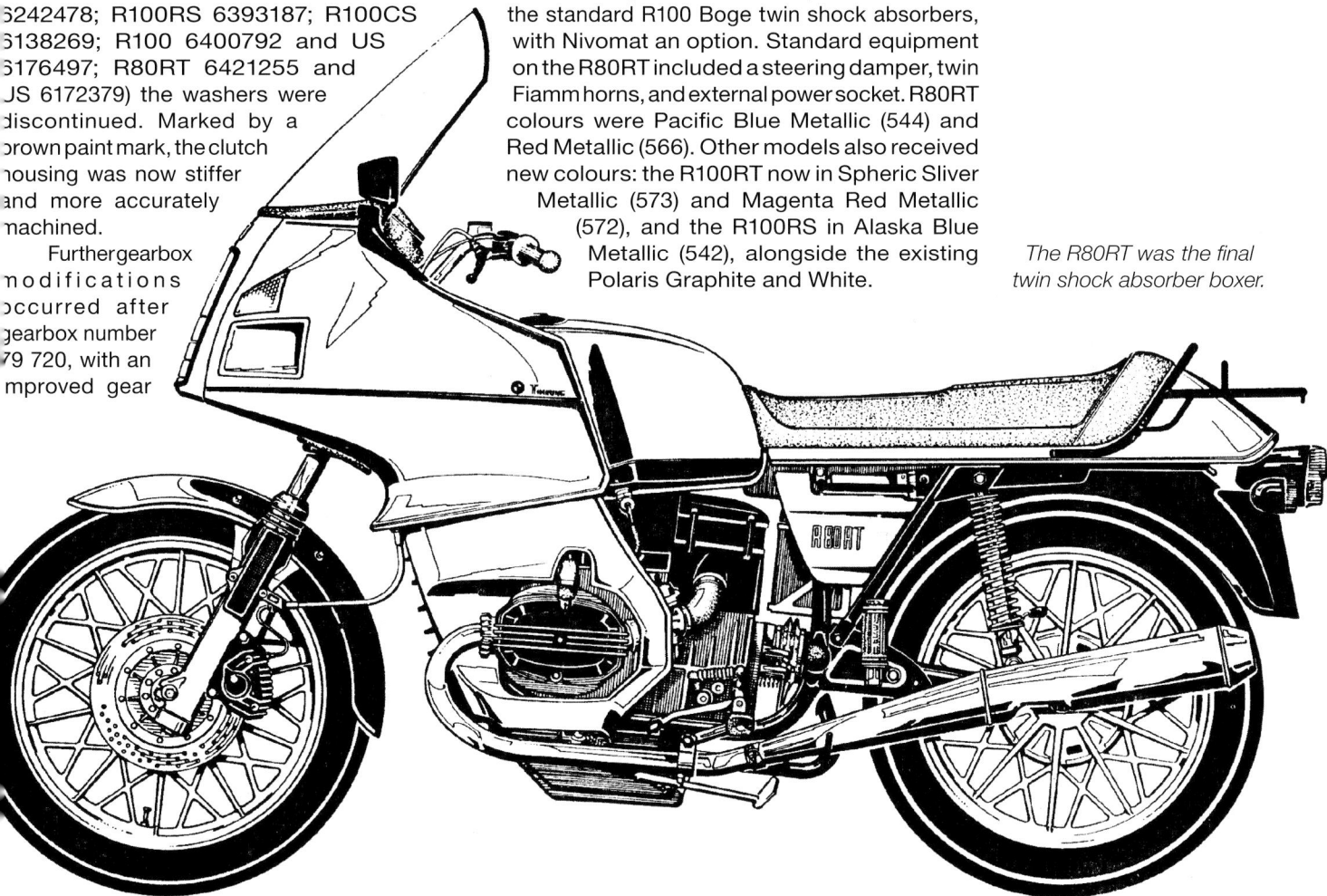

As BMW gradually phased out production of the twin shock absorber, R-series chassis updates for the 1983 model year were minor. A four-position front brake lever was standardised after R100RT US 6242440; R100CS 6138235 and US 6188168; R100 6400685 and US 6176446; and R80RT US 6172280. From January 1983 there was a revised side stand with a new stop, positioned closer to the frame. This was fitted after R100RT 6236401 and US 6242527; R100RS 6393505; R100CS 6138298; R100 6400921 and US 6176510; R80RT 6421404 and US 6172572. The centre stand was also redesigned, with a sheet metal lever instead of tubular-steel. The stand pivots were redesigned and the bushes at the frame were countersunk to prevent loosening through use. From week 33, the gear shift pedal received grease-filled needle roller bearings at the pivots instead of bushes.

The front fork was also updated in January 1983 from R100RT 6236572; R100RS 6393753 and US 6226333; R100CS 6138324; R100 6401020; R80RT 6421668 and US 6172638. The damper valve was revised to provide a quieter action, with more accurately machined valve discs and a coil spring to eliminate axial play. Other developments during 1983 included a new air filter top (from May) and an additional locating dowel for the final drive (from March). There was a new wiring harness and modifications to the pannier latches and keys. From January 1983, the speedometer and tachometer glass face covers were replaced by plastic items, and this year also saw the return of the 140mph speedometer on US examples.

Only a few R100CSs were built after 1982.

R100 and R80 distinguishing features 1983 model year

2mm thick cylinder base O-rings
New oil retaining ring at clutch end of the crankshaft
Grooved alternator oil seal
Reinforced clutch housing and new clutch plates
Improved gear selector camplate with deeper detents
Gear selector components were more accurately machined
Four-position front brake lever
New side and centre stands
Front fork damper valve revised
New air filter top
New wiring harness
Additional locating dowel for the final drive
Plastic speedometer and tachometer face covers
Needle roller bearings for gearshift lever pivot

R100RT, R100RS, R100CS, R100, R80RT 1984-85 model year

Although K100 production had commenced as a replacement for the 247-series, the R100 continued for one more year in its traditional twin-shock form. The R100CS continued for 1984 with plain fork legs and 'R100' side cover decals, and a R100CS Motorsport – in dark blue with orange and light blue pinstripes – was also available in small numbers. As BMW intended to retain the boxer in smaller capacities only, in order to celebrate the end of the 247 line several final editions were produced towards the end of 1984. Ironically, just as the 1000cc twins were about to be superseded, the R100RT finally became accepted in the US. But the success of the R80RT eclipsed even that of the rejuvenated R100RT, and it was the 800cc version that survived in the wake of the new K-series. The R80RT then reappeared in 1985 followed by a new R100RT in 1988.

Frame numbers for the 1984 and 1985 model years were R100RT 6237430-6237516 and US 6243217-6244165; R100RS 6395888-6396033, US 6226732-6227337 and 6308001-6308050; R100CS 6138798-6138864; R100 6401589-6401795, US 6176736-6177382 and 6186001-6186040; R80RT 6424027-6425163, US 6173122-6174022 and 6186101-6186300. There was no further engine or chassis development but, from R100RS 6398757 and US 6226353; R100CS 6138324; R100 6401022; R80RT 6421671 and US 6172638, the gear shift mechanism included the ball joint setup of the R80 G/S. During 1984, the cast wheels included additional support material around the spokes to eliminate cracking.

R100RS final editions were produced in separate series for Europe and the US. A numbered R100RS Series 500 in blue and silver with matching silver panniers was available outside the US. The fairing came with a small numbered plaque on the side, and the seat was thicker with different upholstery. The fairing screen was also tinted. The US R100 final editions, of which 250 were made, were white with thin red, orange and blue pinstripes and panniers, as standard with single and dual seats and a BMW System II helmet. They had a 'Last Edition' plaque on the side covers. For the US there was also a small run of limited edition R100CSs and R100RTs, but it is not known how many were produced. Additionally, California received a specific version with slightly different pinstripes.

These final series were intended to be the end of the line for the 247-type, but pressure from enthusiasts saw the R100 resurrected just two years later in Monolever form. The new four-cylinder K100 was technologically and functionally superior but, as it lacked the charisma of the boxer, it wasn't greeted as enthusiastically as expected. The K100 chassis was more rigid and the handling superior, but the four-cylinder engine vibrated disconcertingly and lacked character. With the new technology came increased bulk and weight, and the K100 weighed in at a considerable 249kg with a full tank of fuel. As soon as the 247-series finished, it was replaced by the Monolever R80 and R80RT, with a 1000cc version appearing for 1988. Although, for many enthusiasts, the new R100s were a pale imitation of the original, the large capacity boxer twin was far from dead and would last another decade.

One final series R100RS was the European specification 'Series 500'.

Frame numbers 1981-84

Type	Numbers	Model	Production dates
R80 (TIC)	6210001-6212790	1981-84 (37kW)	09/80-11/84
R80RT	6420001-6424026	1983	07/82-08/83
R80RT	6424027-6425163	1984	09/83-11/84
R80RT (US)	6172001-6173121	1983	08/82-06/83
R80RT (US)	6173122-6174022	1984	08/83-10/84
R80RT (US)	6186101-6186300	1985	11/84-12/84
R100	6035001-6037528	1981	06/80-08/81

Type	Numbers	Model	Production dates
R100	6037529-6040000	1982	09/81-06/82
R100	6400001-6401588	1983	06/82-08/83
R100	6401589-6401795	1984	09/83-10/84
R100 (US)	6175001-6175593	1981	09/80-08/81
R100 (US)	6175594-6176319	1982	09/81-08/82
R100 (US)	6176320-6176735	1983	09/82-08/83
R100 (US)	6176736-6177382	1984	06/83-09/84
R100 (US)	6186001-6186040	1984	12/83
R100 (TIC)	6193001-6193894	1981-84	11/80-09/84
R100CS	6135001-6136503	1981	06/80-08/81
R100CS	6136504-6138122	1982	09/81-08/82
R100CS	6138123-6138797	1983	09/82-08/83
R100CS	6138798-6138864	1984	09/83-10/84
R100CS (US)	6188001-6188163	1981	09/80-08/81
R100CS (US)	6188164-6188166	1982	10/81-08/82
R100CS (US)	6188167-6188174	1983-84	09/82-09/84
R100RS	6075001-6080001	1981	06/80-12/81
R100RS	6390001-6392801	1982	12/81-08/82
R100RS	6392802-6395887	1983	09/82-10/83
R100RS	6395888-6396033	1984	11/83-11/84
R100RS (US)	6225001-6225628	1981	09/80-08/81
R100RS (US)	6225629-6226208	1982	09/81-08/82
R100RS (US)	6226209-6226731	1983	09/82-08/83
R100RS (US)	6226732-6227337	1984	09/83-09/84
R100RS (US)	6308001-6308050	1984	12/84
R100RT	6230001-6232899	1981	08/80-08/81
R100RT	6232900-6236060	1982	09/81-08/82
R100RT	6236061-6237429	1983	09/82-08/83
R100RT	6237430-6237516	1984	09/83-10/84
R100RT (US)	6240001-6241232	1981	06/80-08/81
R100RT (US)	6241233-6242332	1982	09/81-08/82
R100RT (US)	6242333-6243216	1983	08/82-08/83
R100RT (US)	6243217-6244165	1984	09/83-09/84

CHAPTER VI

POST-1984 AIR-COOLED TWINS

With the new generation water-cooled K-series set to replace the 1000cc twins from 1985, the flat twin remained in the line-up to satisfy the traditional enthusiast and maintain a classic tradition within the company. The 800cc R80/GS and R80ST continued much as before, and initially the smaller R45 and R65 were also available for 1985, but soon discontinued. In the wake of the dual-purpose R80 G/S success, two new street R80 G/S-based twins, the R80 and R80RT, also became available for 1985. The renaissance of the boxer twin was underway, even before the final death knell.

Conceived in the style of the first /5, these revamped twins were the antithesis of most mid-1980s motorcycles. Resisting the trend of emphasising engine performance through increased complexity without consideration of weight saving, the new boxer twins reiterated the traditional BMW boxer formula – simplicity, agility and lightness were placed ahead of ultimate horsepower. Looking remarkably similar to the pre-1984 twins, the new R80 offered improved brakes and handling but, unfortunately, it could not match the earlier R100 for performance.

By 1987, with the K-series no longer seen as BMW's road to the future, the R80-series was further expanded. Calls by traditionalists for a resurrection of the 1000cc boxer twin resulted in a new R80-based R100RS and R100RT. By 1988, a complete line up of R80-based twins joined the K100 and K75, lasting into the next decade.

R80 and R80RT 1985 model year

Even when it was conceived back in 1976, the air-cooled 247-series boxer twin was limited as a high performance design and always envisaged as a short-term solution. By the early 1980s, increasing noise and emission requirements painted a bleak future for the 247 engine, already struggling to reliably produce 70-horsepower in production form. While the decision was made to replace the larger capacity twins with the four-cylinder K-series, the boxer twin had a

The two new street boxers for 1985 were the R80 and R80T, with monoshock rear suspension.

surprising reprieve with the R80 G/S. As a result, BMW decided to continue development of the boxer twin for applications up to 60 horsepower – the figure deemed to provide a balance between power and reliability. For 1985, the 800cc twin range was made up of five models (R80; R80RT; R80ST; R80 G/S, and R80 G/S Paris Dakar). As the evolution of the final 247-series was continued, only the two pure street models (R80 and R80RT) are discussed here (G/S motorcycles and their derivatives are outside the scope of this book).

Assembled alongside the K-series in the Spandau factory in Berlin, the new R80 was derived from the R80 G/S and R80ST but incorporated many K-series features. The 50-horsepower engine was shared with the G/S and ST but, instead of a two-into-one exhaust system, the R80 and R80RT received an upswept conical two-into-two exhaust system that reduced noise levels by 3dBA and improved midrange power.

No longer with matching engine and frame numbers, R80 (production code 0453) frame numbers for the 1985 model year were 6440001-6443233 and US (0463) 6480001-6480542, with the R80RT (0457) frame numbers 6470001-6472957 and US (0464) 6490001-6490812.

Although producing only 50 horsepower, the R80 was still a very pleasant and capable all-round motorcycle.

Engine

The 800cc engine was basically that of the R80ST with a few updates aimed at reducing noise. From November 1984, all 800cc engines received new cylinder heads with revised bases and supports for the rocker shafts. To eliminate noise emanating from the valve operating mechanism, from January 1985, new rockers with axial bearings and plastic washers were installed. Instead of zero axial end float, there was now 0.03-0.07mm. Further noise reduction came through the installation of twelve rubber buttons between the cylinder head fins. The valve seat material was also changed to overcome the valve seat recession problem with unleaded fuel. From February 1985 there was a new crankcase oil pressure relief valve, with a 16mm (instead of 11mm) compression spring, and a 14mm blind plug. These modifications also appeared on the R80 G/S and R80 ST, although the general 800cc engine specifications were unchanged for the R80 and R80RT. The valve sizes remained at 42mm and 38mm, with a Bosch TSZH electronic ignition and the Bosch double-ended ignition coil of the R80 G/S. Carburetion was by Bing V64/32/353-354mm carburettors, the 32mm Bing carburettors now sharing the float bowls of the larger 40mm type. US models retained the SAS secondary air injection emission system and the R80 had black rocker covers. A Bosch 280W alternator powered the electrical system, and the battery was increased from 16Ah to 20Ah for more reliable starting in colder weather. The new twins also included an attractive, but restrictive, new exhaust system, with a large welded pre-muffler interconnecting the left and right exhaust pipes before the twin mufflers. This effectively retained the horsepower of the previous engine and was a claimed three decibels quieter. The R80 included only a single exhaust gasket up until October 1985, and the claimed power was also modest, with 50 horsepower produced at 6500rpm.

Further updates to the 800cc twins occurred in March 1985, with another new gearbox input shaft; kick start spline; input helical driving gear, and thrust mount. The input helical driving layshaft now had a 17.5-degree gear cut, instead of the previous 15-degree. The final drive assembly, with a more substantial casting for 1985, was also new. This included a new crown wheel set and a 25x47x15mm inner tapered roller bearing (from the K-series), instead of the previous 35x50x20mm needle roller type. The R80 final drive ratio was 1:3.20 (10/32), with the R80RT and R65 receiving a 1:3.36 (11/37).

Chassis

A combination of R80ST and K-series components formed the chassis of the revamped boxer. The frame was inherited from the R80ST, a twin loop main frame similar to that of the first /5, but with a Monolever swingarm. The steering head angle was 28.85-degrees, providing 116mm of trail. While the frame and swingarm were similar to the R80 G/S and R80ST, the wheels, brakes and suspension had more in common with the K-series. The K-style centre-axle included beefier 38.5mm fork tubes and provided considerably less travel than before (175mm). To improve front end rigidity the fork also incorporated an integral fork brace with the front mudguard, and a larger diameter hollow axle (25mm). Unlike the previous Type 247 series, the forks included a forward mount for the Brembo 08-series brake calipers. The fork legs were plain alloy for the 1985 R80, US versions incorporating reflectors in each fork leg.

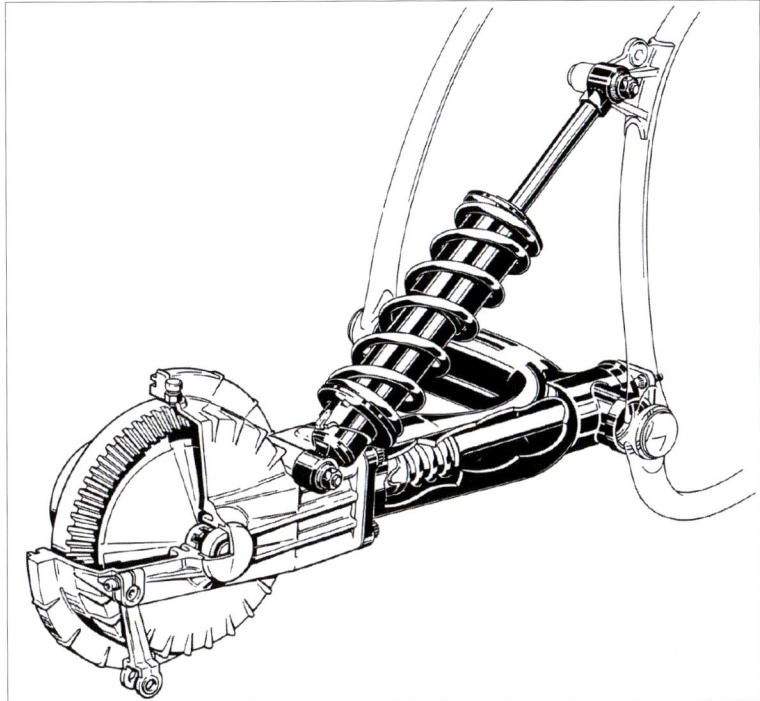

The monoshock suspension unit attached directly to the final drive housing.

The 1985 European R80RT had a single front disc brake. The fork legs were plain alloy this year.

The single gas-charged Boge rear shock absorber provided 121mm of travel, and attached to the trailing loop of the main frame, via a forged steel mount. It also mounted on the rear axle housing (like the K-series) instead of the swingarm, the laid-down position resulting in a higher leverage ratio than on the R80 G/S and R80ST. Both the front fork and rear shock absorber were non-adjustable, although the rear shock absorber did include four spring pre-load settings.

Although BMW boxer twins had featured a 19-inch front wheel since the first /5, the R80 received an 18-inch front wheel. The same MT H 2.50x18in front and rear, these cast alloy wheels were K-series derived and now accommodated tubeless tyres. The Y-fork and H-cross section was designed to provide spoke elasticity with rim rigidity. The rear wheel incorporated a 200mm drum brake and the rear hub featured a four bolt retaining system (unlike the R80 G/S and R80ST). A narrow 90/90H18 front tyre (usually a Metzeler Perfect ME11) contributed to agile steering without compromising braking performance, the rear tyre was a reasonably large 120/90H18 (often a Metzeler ME99). The front brake was also upgraded, with a larger slotted 285x5mm disc, a dual 36mm piston Brembo caliper and 14mm master cylinder. The R80 and R80RT had a single front disc for Europe, while twin front discs brakes were fitted on US examples for 1985.

While the steel fuel tank retained the same classic shape as the previous 247-series, it now held only 22-litres. This was due to the relocation of some electrical components from the head light shell to the frame backbone. The fuel filler tank cap was an EPA-mandated spring-loaded type. While the narrower seat also continued the previous theme, the abbreviated plastic front mudguard was more angular. 5.5-litres of storage space was provided underneath the seat and new side covers facilitated visual checking of the battery acid level. Continuing the classic theme were the smaller diameter MotoMeter instruments and single, or sometimes twin, round Bosch horns. The ignition key was moved to the handlebar protective cover and the new handlebar switches were specific to the R80. More logical than the K-series, the left switch block on US versions didn't incorporate a light switch as the head light was hard-wired. A 21-piece toolkit was standard, as was a 12V power socket. The side stand was improved, and the centre stand pipe diameter increased to 38.5mm for improved strength and stability. The R80RT fairing now incorporated a clock and voltmeter, and factory accessories for both R80s were plentiful, extending from panniers and tank bag to four-way flashers and a 30Ah battery.

For the US, the R80RT received standard luggage and a dual disc front brake.

The R80 dashboard included smaller diameter instruments.

Both the R80 and R80RT were modest performers, the 50-horsepower boxer engine working quite hard to propel the 210kg R80 to a top speed of 176km/h (109mph), and the 227kg R80RT to170km/h (105.6mph). The range of colours was limited: Polaris Silver Metallic, Colorado Red or Black Metallic for the R80, and Colorado Red Metallic or Yukon Blue Metallic for the R80RT.

The R80 and R80RT both had a rear drum brake.

The success of the monoshock R80 soon saw a proliferation of models based on the 800cc boxer motor.

R80 distinguishing features 1985 model year

Rockers with axial bearings and plastic washers to reduce noise

Twelve rubber buttons inserted between the cylinder head fins

New seat material to overcome the valve seat recession with unleaded fuel

New crankcase oil pressure relief valve with a 16mm compression spring

20Ah battery

Exhaust system with a large pre-muffler

New gearbox input shaft, kick start spline, input helical driving gear and thrust mount

New final drive assembly with inner tapered roller bearing

Centre-axle fork with 38.5mm fork tubes, plain alloy legs, 175mm travel and integral brace

25mm axle

Single Boge rear shock absorber mounted on the rear axle housing

2.50x18in Y-fork and H-cross section wheels

200mm rear drum brake

Rear hub with four bolt retaining

285mm front disc brake with twin piston Brembo caliper

22-litre fuel tank

Narrower seat with 5.5-litres of under seat storage space

Angular front mudguard

New side covers

Smaller diameter instruments

Ignition key on the handlebar protective cover

New handlebar switches

Centre stand pipe diameter increased to 38.5mm

R80RT fairing now with clock and voltmeter

R80, R80RT and R65 1986 model year

New for the 1986 model year was the R65; very similar to the R80.

The R80 and R80RT continued for the 1986 model year largely unchanged and, with the demise of the smaller 248-series, were joined by the R65. The R65 was also produced in RT form; as a police model and as a specific 27-horsepower version for the German market, as well as being available in the US with a

covers plain aluminium to set the engine apart from the 800 with its black covers. The final drive ratio for the 205kg R65 was 1:3.36 (11/37). The R65 chassis was identical to the R80 and for the 1986 model year the fork legs were black on all twins. All twins this year had a single front disc brake as standard.

R80 and R65 distinguishing features 1986 model year

650cc R65 introduced
R65 with plain aluminium rocker covers
Black fork legs
All twins with a standard single front disc brake

R100RS, R80RT, R80 and R65 1987 model year

Although BMW intended the K-series to replace the larger boxers, repeated calls for the reintroduction of the 1000cc twin saw the release of a new R100RS towards the end of 1986 for the 1987 model year. Based on the R80 Mono and not the earlier Type 247, the resurrected R100RS was initially intended as a limited edition of 1000 units but stayed in production until 1993. The R80RT, R80 and R65 continued as before for 1987. Frame numbers for the 1987 model year were: R100RS (0455) 0160001-0161672; R80RT 6475888-6478620 and US 6491268-6491452; R80 6445827-6447156 and US 6480907-6481120, and R65 6074775-6118807. Only a few R65s were built for the US this year; the concept of a small capacity engine in a larger dimensioned motorcycle was anathema in the US.

slightly de-tuned (from Europe) 45 horsepower. Production codes were unchanged from the previous year and frame numbers for the 1986 model year were: R80 6443234-6445826 and US 6480543-6480906; R80RT 6472958-6475887 and US 6490813-6491267; and R65 (48 HP) 6073001-6074774 and US 6128001-6128516.

Although ostensibly identical to the previous R65 type 248 engine, the new R65 engine was updated to provide a wider power band and run more easily on unleaded fuel. Engine dimensions stayed at 82x61.5mm and, with a 8.7:1 compression ratio, the power was reduced from 50 to 48 horsepower at 7250rpm. The maximum torque of 47.8Nm (35.2 ft/lb) was developed at a lower 3500rpm. Valve sizes on the R65 were 40mm and 36mm, the carburettors 32mm Bing V64/32/359-360, and the rocker

The resurrected R100RS of 1987 was initially intended as a limited production run of 1000 units.

Engine

With increasing noise and emissions controls to be instigated in Europe from 1988 (ECE R 40), the resurrected R100RS was inevitably compromised as a performance motorcycle. While the R100RS started life as a 70-horsepower high performance motorcycle it was now derived from the R80, and the 1000cc engine was designed to provide more relaxed power over a wider rev range and run on regular unleaded fuel.

The R100RS engine dimensions of 94x70.6mm were shared with the earlier version but the cylinder heads included the smaller 42mm inlet valves of the R80, along with the larger 40mm exhaust valves of the 1984 R100RS. From June 1987 (on all boxer twins), the valve seat angles were changed to 43 degrees for the inlet and 30 degrees for the exhaust (from 45 degrees for both) to improve their life on unleaded fuel. The R100RS compression ratio was slightly up on the R80 at 8.45:1, carburetion was by 32mm Bing V64/32/363-4 carburettors, and the pre-muffler exhaust system was the same as the R80. While the power was reduced to 60 horsepower at 6500rpm, the maximum torque of 74Nm (55ft/lb) was now produced at a low 3500rpm (compared to 6000rpm on the earlier engine). Although on-the-road performance was similar at legal speeds, the new R100RS was noticeably down on top speed (185km/h or 115mph). It featured a standard oil cooler and 30Ah Mareg battery, but in all other respects the engine was as for the R80. Included was the same 280 watt alternator, and, also shared with the R80, the 1:3.00 (11/33) final drive.

Chassis

Underneath the RS bodywork was a similar Monolever chassis to the R80 and R65. The front fork was the same K-series type with 38.5mm fork tubes, and the single rear shock absorber a Boge. Twin front disc brakes were standard on the R100RS, but the rear brake was a 200mm drum instead of the disc on the earlier R100RS. Also shared with the R80 were the 18-inch wheels, although the R100RS wheels were black with plain alloy accents.

Although the style of the monoshock R100RS replicated the earlier version, it was based on the R80, and down on power compared to the original.

The fairing was carried over from the 1984 R100RS, but now featured larger black mirrors; the front section of the pre-1979 R100RS, including vented grill, with the oil cooler at the top. No hydraulic steering damper was included, but the protective pad on the RS was the same as before and looked strange without the damper knob – a round BMW badge sat in its place. Unlike the R80, the R100RS was fitted with dual Fiamm horns, and two types of saddlebags were available as an option; the R-type or squarer K-type. The colours for the R100RS were Mother-of-Pearl White Metallic with blue stripes, or Henna Red with black stripes and black fairing base. With its shorter (1447mm) wheelbase, lighter weight (229kg), and more rigid frame, the resurrected R100RS provided more agile and surefooted handling than the earlier version. However, the reduction in horsepower did little to endear it to a new breed of enthusiasts.

New for 1988 was the R100RT, ostensibly an amalgam of the R80RT and R100RS.

R100, R80 and R65 distinguishing features 1987 model year

R100RS with 42mm inlet valves and 40mm exhaust valves
New valve seat angles from June 1987
R100RS with 32mm Bing carburettors
R100RS with a standard oil cooler
R100RS with 30Ah battery
R100RS with twin front disc brakes as standard
R100RS with 200mm rear drum brake
R100RS 18-inch wheels black with plain alloy accents
R100RS fairing with larger black mirrors and vented front grill
No hydraulic steering damper on R100RS
R100RS with dual Fiamm horns

R100RT, R100RS, R80RT, R80 and R65 1988 model year

With most boxer development centred on the Paralever GS there were few updates to the existing line-up. This year the R100RT was added, ostensibly a combination of the R100RS engine and R80RT chassis. The R80RT and R80 were now no longer available in the US, and 1988 was the final year for the R65 (except in 27-horsepower for the German market). With response to the resurrected R100RS being overwhelmingly positive it now went into regular production. Frame numbers for the 1988 model year were: R100RT (0459) 6016001-6017067 and US (0469) 6292601-6293172; R100RS 0161673-0162358 and US 6247001-6247548; R80RT 6478620-6483775; R80 6447157-6448032, and R65 6118808-6131123.

Updates to the street boxer range were minor for 1988. The steering head angle was reduced slightly to 27.8 degrees and 120mm of trail to lighten the steering, and after June 1988 the clutch pushrod and release bearing were revised. The single disc R80RT, R80 and R65 received R100GS solid discs and a 38mm Brembo caliper from July 1988, but the twin disc R100s retained the previous slotted type disc.

Despite its modest power output, the R100RT was still an effective touring motorcycle.

As an amalgam of the existing R80RT and R100RS, the R100RT wasn't exactly groundbreaking. The R100RT bodywork was identical to that of the R80RT, and the chassis equipment to the R100RS. As on the R100RS the engine included a standard oil cooler, front brakes were twin discs and there was no hydraulic steering damper. Standard equipment included a quartz clock; voltmeter and panniers, and a single key operated the ignition, steering lock, fuel tank cap, seat and panniers. The weight of the R100RT was 234kg and colours for 1988 were Bermuda Blue with Dual Silver pinstripes and a black seat.

R100, R80 and R65 distinguishing features 1988 model year

Reduced steering head angle of 27.8-degrees and 120mm of trail
New clutch pushrod and release bearing
Single disc models with a solid disc and 38mm Brembo caliper from July 1988
R100RT introduced with R80RT bodywork and R100RS engine and chassis

R100RT, R100RS, R80RT and R80 1989 model year

By 1989, motorcycle production at the Berlin Spandau plant was around 24,000 units with the R-series boxer accounting for about half of that. Motorcycle sales worldwide gradually declined during the 1980s and BMW relied strongly on their domestic German market. By 1989 Germany accounted for a third of motorcycle sales, BMW achieving about a 10 per cent share of the German market. Within this static climate development was curtailed, with resources focused on the four-cylinder K1. Apart from the introduction of the Paris-Dakar R100 GS, there was no change to the R-series this year. Frame numbers for the street R models for the 1989 model year were: R100RT 6017068-6018000 and US 6293173-6293399; R100RS 0162359-0163754 and US 6247549-6247599; R80RT 6483776-6486351, and R80 6448033-6448814.

R100RT, R100RS, R80RT and R80 1990 model year

Like the 1989 model year the R-series evolved into 1990 with very little development. Production of the R100RS was gradually scaled down (and it wasn't available in the US this year) with only 337 being produced. Frame numbers for the 1990 model year were: R100RT 6167001-6168000 and US 6293400-6293579; R100RS 0163755-0164009; R80 RT 6486352-6488024, and R80 6448815-6450000. The minimal updates for 1990 included an improved rear drum brake, the brake

pad width increased to 27.5mm (from 25mm), along with new mounts for the brake shoes. The R80RT gained dual disc front brakes as standard.

R100RT, R100RS, R100, R80RT and R80 1991 model year

With most R-series development centred on the successful G/S models this year, the street R-series was again largely unchanged. Although the R100RS was no longer available in the US, the regular R100 made a return for the US market in 1991. This was essentially an R80 with the R100RS/RT engine, only lasting for one year before it was replaced by the R100R for 1992. With only 157 produced, it was one of the rarest more modern BMW boxer twins. In Germany, all R80s were now available with a 27-horsepower engine. Frame numbers for the 1991 model year were: R100RT 6337001-6337902 and US 6293580-6293729; R100RS 0164010-0164292; R80RT 6488025-6490000, and R80 0121001-0122608.

Optional on all R-series was the US-style Secondary Air System (SAS). Designed to reduce HC emissions by 30 per cent and CO emissions by 40 per cent, the SAS used exhaust pressure pulses to move two diaphragm valves in the air filter housing, drawing in fresh air. Two tubes directed this fresh air into the cylinder head and exhaust system, behind the exhaust valve. The combination of additional air with the high exhaust temperature ensured more complete combustion of HC and CO. Exhaust misfiring was controlled

The R80 continued virtually unchanged for many years; the 1992 version was very similar to that of 1985.

by interrupting the secondary air supply when the engine wasn't under load, the left SAS valve had no effect on engine performance or fuel consumption.

Although the twin disc R100RT, R100RS and German market R80 retained the earlier slotted front disc rotors, the single disc R80 received a new disc rotor for 1991. To eliminate squeaking the brake disc was attached to the carrier by rollers, allowing the brake disc to float with the brake pads and utilise the full amount of pad surface. The colours were rationalised for 1991, all R100 and R80 street models available in Red Metallic, Topaz Red Metallic, and Bermuda Blue Metallic.

R100 and R80 distinguishing features 1990 and 1991 model years

Wider rear brake linings (1990)
SAS system optional
Floating front disc rotors for single disc models

R100R, R100RT, R100RS, R80RT and R80 1992 model year

As the release of the new generation R259 boxer twin was still more than a year away, for the 1992 model year BMW released the interim – the R100R Roadster. Based on the R100GS, and designed to reflect BMW's classic twin tradition, the R100R was sold alongside the existing twins and was surprisingly successful. During 1992 the R100R was BMW's best-selling motorcycle, accounting for 23 per cent of production, with 8041 sales. Although it was arguably a parts-bin special, the R100R had a certain appeal. The styling and execution was questionable, but the chassis was functionally superior to the earlier street boxers and the engine made adequate power. The existing range of 1000cc and 800cc boxers continued much as before, although the R100RS was now in its final year. As a final effort, before the advent of the R1100RS, nearly 1000 were produced. Also built during 1992, a special series of 30 Rennsport in traditional blue and silver with a numbered plaque. The wheels were no longer black highlighted on this limited edition.

The final limited edition R100RS was the Rennsport of 1992.

The layshaft starter used a smaller electric motor but provided the same torque, with an intermediate transmission. The overall reduction in weight was 2kg. With the R100GS compression ratio of 8.5:1, the power of the R100R was 60-horsepower, with maximum torque of 76Nm (56 ft/lb) produced at only 3750rpm. The R100R exhaust system featured a large pre-muffler, 38mm chrome-plated header pipes and a low mounted round stainless steel K100 muffler. Instead of mounting the oil cooler on the engine protection bar as on the GS, this was now positioned in front of the engine. The classic look extended to the older style sparkplug caps and the rounder rocker covers first seen on the R68, lasting on the sporting twins until the 1976 /6. As on all boxers for 1992, the SAS emission control system was an option on the R100R.

Each Rennsport carried a numbered plaque.

Frame numbers for 1992 were: R100R 0240001-0247618 and US 0280001-0280546; R100RT 6337903-6338475 and US 6293730-6293881; R100RS 0164293-0165331 and US 6247600-6247750; R80RT 0270001-0271732; R80 0122609-0123285.

R100R

Engine

As with the earlier R80ST, the R100R was based on its dual-purpose stable mate, in this case the R100GS. Except for the different exhaust system and the older-style rocker covers, the R100R and R100GS engines were identical. Included on the R100R was the larger sump of the 1991 GS, lighter layshaft starter and 40mm Bing carburettors (although US models retained 32mm carburettors).

Chassis

The silver painted R100R frame and Paralever swingarm came from the successful dual purpose R100GS. Featured for the first time on a street boxer twin, the Paralever contributed to excellent handling. The steering head angle and 101mm of trail was unchanged from the R100GS, as was the long wheelbase of 1513mm. Another first for a BMW motorcycle was the use of Japanese Showa suspension. The non-adjustable 41mm front fork provided 135mm of travel and the rear single gas pressurised Showa shock absorber included adjustable rebound damping. There

were six spring pre-load settings and 140mm of travel and, as with the R80, the shock absorber bolted directly to the final drive housing.

Although only intended as an interim model, the R100R was BMW's best-selling motorcycle during 1992. The frame was painted silver this year.

The Paralever swingarm was designed to minimise the effects of driveshaft movement under acceleration. As the ideal swingarm length for the shaft drive twin was an impractical 1,700mm, BMW's engineers, René Hinsberg and Horst Brenner, created the Paralever double-joint swingarm. Inside the single sided swingarm was a second universal joint, freeing the rear gear case and hub assembly and allowing it to float on the

rear axle. An alloy strut connected the gear case to the frame, just below the swingarm pivot. Thus, the swingarm, stay arm, gear case and frame formed a parallelogram, with pinion torque feeding into the lower strut instead of the swingarm. The slight fore and aft movement of the gear case was absorbed by the laid down single shock absorber. As the parallelogram arrangement increased the radius of the wheel elevation curve, it provided the same effect as a 1400mm long swingarm. Although the Paralever increased the weight by 1.6kg, it allowed the full travel of the Showa to be used more effectively.

Further emphasising the classic image were cross-spoked wheels, with Akront aluminium rims, a 2.50x18in on the front, and 2.50x17in on the rear. The front brake was a single perforated floating 285x5mm disc with a four-piston Brembo caliper from the K-series. The cable-operated 200mm rear drum brake was the same as the GS. Also from the GS was the tall 24-litre fuel tank. The round 180mm head light came from the K75, but with a chrome shell, while the plastic nacelle contained R100GS instruments. The 720mm chrome-plated handlebar was similar to the R80ST, with K-series handlebar switches and end weights to minimise vibration, but without the K-series self-cancelling indicator function. Specific R100R features included the handlebar cover, side covers, passenger grab handle and rear mudguard.

The foot controls were also similar to the GS, with the same reversed gearshift linkage. Styling considerations extended to the two-tone seat with a silver rear rack. The seat core and foam were new but seat height was still relatively high at 800mm. From March 1992, an optional chrome kit was available which comprised a chrome-plated fork stabiliser; valve covers; carburettor tops; instrument panel; direction indicator housings; fuel tank cap; mirrors, and exhaust nuts. R100R colours for 1992 were Classic Black with Silver pinstripes (656), Amethyst Metallic (685), and from January 1992, Turquoise Green (525). BMW hit the nail on the head with the R100R, it was the right machine at the right time. Naked machines were

The instrument layout and controls of the R100R were new.

beginning to reassert themselves and, although not powerful, the R100R was light enough (218kg) with the Paralever swingarm and shorter travel suspension contributing to arguably the finest handling boxer yet.

The R100RT, R100RS, R80RT and R80 continued as before, but now all featured a Marzocchi front fork. The colours were Classic Black Metallic 656 (all models), Red Metallic 654 (R80, R80RT and R100RT), and Pine Green Metallic 684 (R100RS and R100RT).

R100 and R80 distinguishing features 1992 model year

Final R100RS Rennsport series in traditional blue and silver

R100R based on the R100GS released

R100R featured a layshaft starter, 40mm Bing carburettors, and old-style rocker covers

R100R frame painted silver and included a Paralever swingarm

R100R with 41mm Showa front fork and single Showa rear shock absorber

R100R with cross-spoked wheels and aluminium rims

R100R with single front disc brake and four piston Brembo caliper

R100R with cable-operated rear drum brake

R100R with K75 round head light

R100RT, R100RS, R80RT and R80 with Marzocchi front fork

R100R, R100RT, R80R, R80RT and R80 1993 model year

The creation of the new generation R259 boxer for the 1993 model year engulfed most of BMW's developmental resources and, as a result, the existing R-series continued much as before. Surprisingly, in the wake of updated K-series and the R259, the R100R sales success continued. In some markets the new R80R replaced the R80, and in Germany the R80R was available in 50- and 27-horsepower form. Frame numbers for the 1993 model year were: R100R 0247619-0250000 and 0165501-0166916 with US 0280547-0280788; R100RT 6338476-6339226 and US 6293882-6294013; R80RT 0271733-0272533, and R80 0123286-0123509.

With the formula of the moderately powered, light and simple twin firmly established, there were only cosmetic changes to the R100R for 1993. The R80R was very similar to the R100R, but without an oil cooler. Setting the 1993 R100R (and R80R) apart, on turquoise green metallic (525) examples, were large 'BOXER' emblems on the sides of the fuel tank. These retained the silver frame and rear rack, while on black R100Rs, these features were also black. Colours for the 1993 model year were: Classic Black Metallic 656 (all street R models); Mystic Red Metallic 527 (R100RT, R80RT and R80); Turquoise Green Metallic 528 (R100RT, R100R and R80R); and Amethyst Metallic 685 (R100R and R80R).

The R100RS R259 boxer replaced the R100RS from 1993.

The R100R was little changed for 1993, although the frame and rear rack were now black.

New garish decals appeared on the 1993 R80R.

R100R, R100R Mystic, R100RT, R80R, R80RT and R80 1994 model year

By 1994 it was inevitable that production of the traditional air-cooled boxer twin would end; it was only a matter of how long it could survive. The R100R received dual disc front brakes, the SAS emission system was standard, and it was joined by a special Mystic version. Designed to appeal to the connoisseur of classic motorcycles, the Mystic was a particularly attractive rendition of the R100R. All R80s were available in either 50- or 34-horsepower this year, with kits available to transform a 50-horsepower engine into 34-horsepower, and vice versa. For 1994 the US RT100RT included heated grips, a custom touring seat, and rear top case. In Australia it was called the R100LT.

Frame numbers for the 1994 model year were: R100R 0166917-0167941 and US 0280789-0280858; R100R Mystic 0169001-6435634 and US 0400001-0400145; R100RT 6339227-6339787 and US 6294014-6294248; R80RT 0272534-0273337, and R80 0123510-0123695. Colours for the 1994 model year were: Classic Black Metallic 656 (all street R models), Mystic Red Metallic 527 (R100RT and R80RT) and Turquoise Green Metallic 528 (R100RT, R100R, R80RT and R80R).

R100R Mystic

Although incorporating only cosmetic alterations to the R100R, the Mystic managed to impart a quality image that was lacking with the standard R100R. Along with the special Red Metallic paint, the frame was painted black, the side covers were new and there was a shorter licence plate bracket. The handlebar was lower, and the seat and tailpiece restyled. Additional chrome-plated components included the head light support, instrument surround with new warning light setup, and indicator supports. The muffler was also turned 3cm to the inside, along the longitudinal axis.

Some versions of the R100RT were sold with standard luggage.

117

The R100R Mystic was essentially an R100R with some styling touches.

One of the Mystic's styling features was chrome-plated instrument surrounds.

R100 distinguishing features 1994 model year

R100R with dual disc front brakes

R100R with SAS emission system standard

Mystic with red metallic paint and black frame

Mystic with new side covers and restyled seat and tailpiece

Mystic with lower handlebar and shorter licence plate bracket

Mystic with chrome head light, indicator supports and instrument surround

Mystic muffler turned 3cm to the inside, along the longitudinal axis

The Mystic featured the traditional wire-spoked wheels of the R100R. All R100Rs had dual front disc brakes for 1994.

R100R, R100R Mystic, R100RT, R80R, R80RT and R80 1995 model year

For the 1995 model year BMW released four 'farewell model' R100 boxers. Alongside the R100GS Paris Dakar Classic were three street models: the R100R Classic, R100R Mystic and R100RT Classic. The standard R80 was discontinued but the R80RT remained in production. Frame numbers for the 1995 model year were: R100RT 6339788-6340000 and US 6294249-6294455; R100RT Classic 0470001-0470400; R100R 0167942-0169000 and US 0280859-0280929; R100R Classic 6469000-6470000; R100R Mystic 6435635-6437226 and US 0400146-0400255; R80RT 0273338-0273599.

Four 'Farewell Model' boxers were offered for the 1995 model year.

Distinguishing the R100R Classic was its black finish, with many components highlighted in black. This included a black seat with new upholstery, head light support, instrument console and grab handle. The handlebar levers were silver epoxy and the avus black fuel tank was embellished with white double lines and a 'R100R Classic' model designation. Along with double front disc brakes and the SAS system, standard features included cylinder protection bars, hazard warning flashers and a luggage rack.

A wide range of optional equipment was available for the R100R Classic.

The R100R Mystic was finished in Mystic red metallic. It differed from the R100R Classic by featuring a chrome-plated instrument console, a more sporting seat and different tail section. The R100RT Classic was finished in two-tone metallic paint (Arctic Grey and Graphite), the upper half of the fairing and fuel tank accentuated by a double silver line. The tank carried the designation 'R100RT Classic' and completing the specification, a rear 22-litre top case and side panniers, special comfort seat, cylinder protection bars and heated handgrips.

Black highlighting distinguished the R100R Classic.

The R100RT Classic was the final version of the R100RT, one of BMW's longest model runs.

1996 model year

Production of the Classic boxers finished at the end of 1995, they were available in limited numbers for the 1996 model year.

At the end of 1994 BMW announced that production on the range of traditional air-cooled boxers would cease at the end of 1995. As production lasted only a few months into the 1996 model year there was no difference to any of the four 'Farewell Models.' R100R Classic frame numbers for the 1996 model year were 0125001-0125874. Although the street R models finished in December 1995, production of the GS Basic continued for a little longer. An R80GS Basic was the final air-cooled boxer, the last leaving the Spandau production line on December 19, 1996. The end finally came for one of BMW's most classic engine designs. It remained in production for 27 years and was remarkably similar at the end as it was when it began. Considering the Type 246 was originally perceived as an interim engine design, it was astonishing it lasted so long. The air-cooled boxer twin endured because it was reliable and charismatic. Ultimately, noise and emission regulations killed it, but for the many thousands who bought and rode air-cooled boxers they remained indestructible.

The final traditional boxer was the R80 GS Basic of 1996.

R100 Classic distinguishing features 1995 and 1996 model years

R100R Classic with black seat, head light support, instrument console and grab handle

The R100RT Classic with two-tone metallic paint, standard top case and panniers

Frame numbers (1985-96)

Type	Numbers	Model	Production dates
R65 (48HP)	6073001-6074774	1986	06/85-08/86
R65	6074775-6118807	1987	09/86-08/87
R65	6118808-6131123	1988	09/87-10/88
R65 (45 HP US)	6128001-6128516	1986-87	07/85-05/87
R65 (RT TIC)	6460001-6461092	1986-88	07/85-11/88
R65 (27HP)	6430001-6433529	1986-93	04/85-06/93
R80 Mono	6440001-6443233	1985	03/84-07/85
R80 Mono	6443234-6445826	1986	09/85-08/86
R80 Mono	6445827-6447156	1987	09/86-08/87
R80 Mono	6447157-6448032	1988	09/87-08/88
R80 Mono	6448033-6448814	1989	09/88-08/89

Type	Numbers	Model	Production dates
R80 Mono	6448815-6450000	1990	09/89-06/90
R80 Mono	0121001-0122608	1991	06/90-08/91
R80 Mono	0122609-0123285	1992	09/91-08/92
R80 Mono	0123286-0123509	1993	09/92-08/93
R80 Mono	0123510-0123695	1994	09/93-01/95
R80 Mono (US)	6480001-6480542	1985	07/84-08/85
R80 Mono (US)	6480543-6480906	1986	09/85-08/86
R80 Mono (US)	6480907-6481120	1987	09/86-07/87
R80RT Mono	6470001- 6472957	1985	07/84-08/85
R80RT Mono	6472958-6475887	1986	09/85-08/86
R80RT Mono	6475888-6478620	1987	09/86-08/87
R80RT Mono	6478620-6483775	1988	09/87-08/88
R80RT Mono	6483776-6486351	1989	09/88-08/89
R80RT Mono	6486352-6488024	1990	09/89-08/90
R80RT Mono	6488025-6490000	1991	09/90-04/91
R80RT Mono	0270001-0271732	1992	04/91-08/92
R80RT Mono	0271733-0272533	1993	09/92-08/93
R80RT Mono	0272534-0273337	1994	09/93-08/94
R80RT Mono	0273338-0273599	1995	09/94-11/95
R80RT Mono (US)	6490001-6490812	1985	07/84-07/85
R80RT Mono (US)	6490813-6491267	1986	09/85-08/86
R80RT Mono (US)	6491268-6491452	1987	09/86-04/87
R100RS Mono	0160001-0161672	1987	07/86-08/87
R100RS Mono	0161673-0162358	1988	09/87-08/88
R100RS Mono	0162359-0163754	1989	09/88-08/89
R100RS Mono	0163755-0164009	1990	09/89-08/90
R100RS Mono	0164010-0164292	1991	09/90-08/91
R100RS Mono	0164293-0165331	1992	09/91-10/92
R100RS Mono (US)	6247001-6247548	1988	08/87-03/88
R100RS Mono (US)	6247549-6247599	1989	09/88-09/89
R100RS Mono (US)	6247600-6247750	1992	02/92-08/92
R100RT Mono	6016001-6017067	1988	07/87-08/88
R100RT Mono	6017068-6018000	1989	09/88-09/89

Type	Numbers	Model	Production dates
R100RT Mono	6167001-6168000	1990	09/89-06/90
R100RT Mono	6337001-6337902	1991	06/90-08/91
R100RT Mono	6337903-6338475	1992	09/91-08/92
R100RT Mono	6338476-6339226	1993	09/92-08/93
R100RT Mono	6339227-6339787	1994	09/93-08/94
R100RT Mono	6339788-6340000	1995	09/94-11/94
R100RT Classic	0470001-0470400	1995	11/94-02/95
R100RT Mono (US)	6292601-6293172	1988	08/87-08/88
R100RT Mono (US)	6293173-6293399	1989	09/88-09/89
R100RT Mono (US)	6293400-6293579	1990	02/90-08/90
R100RT Mono (US)	6293580-6293729	1991	11/90-08/91
R100RT Mono (US)	6293730-6293881	1992	09/91-08/92
R100RT Mono (US)	6293882-6294013	1993	09/92-08/93
R100RT Mono (US)	6294014-6294248	1994	09/93-08/94
R100RT Mono (US)	6294249-6294455	1995	09/94-02/95
R80R	0260001-0263503	1992-94	03/91-06/94
R100R	0240001-0247618	1992	03/91-08/92
R100R	0247619-0250000	1993	09/92-02/93
R100R	0165501-0166916	1993	02/93-08/93
R100R	0166917-0167941	1994	09/93-07/94
R100R	0167942-0169000	1995	09/94-03/95
R100R Classic	6469000-6470000	1995	03/95-07/95
R100R Classic	0125001-0125874	1996	07/95-12/95
R100R US	0280001-0280546	1992	09/91-08/92
R100R US	0280547-0280788	1993	09/92-08/93
R100R US	0280789-0280858	1994	09/93-01/94
R100R US	0280859-0280929	1995	12/94-12/95
R80R Mystic	0390001-0390090	1995-96	03/94-03/95
R100R Mystic	0169001-6435634	1994	12/93-08/94
R100R Mystic	6435635-6437226	1995-96	09/94-12/95
R100R Mystic US	0400001-0400145	1994	03/94-08/94
R100R Mystic US	0400146-0400255	1995	09/94-09/95

CHAPTER VII

RACING /5S, /6S AND /7S

Even before the /5 was conceived, BMW had a long and illustrious racing history. It began with Franz Bieber's victory in the 1924 German Road Championship on an R37, and continued into the late 1920s with the R63 of Paul Köppen and Ernst Henne in the Targa Florio. By the time the Second World War broke out in 1939, BMW's 500cc Kompressor was one of the leading racing motorcycles in Europe. After the war, the Kompressor was resurrected, forming the basis of BMW's racing program and spawning the fabulous RS54.

The 500cc RS54 engine shared the Kompressor's bevel-gear driven double overhead camshaft setup, with short rockers and two straight cut gears in the cylinder head, but it was updated with a pair of more modern Fischer-Amal 30mm carburettors. The RS54 was also fitted with a single-plate dry clutch, matched to an all-indirect four-speed gearbox, and an Earles leading link front fork. Walter Zeller won the 1954 German Championship and, following the return of von Falkenhausen to head the competition department in 1955, the factory racer was further developed. For the 1956 Grand Prix season, former 350cc World Champion Fergus Anderson was signed alongside Zeller and Ernst Hiller, although Anderson was killed at Floreffe in Belgium early in the season. Zeller claimed second overall in the 500cc World Championship, behind John Surtees on the MV Agusta.

Although 1956 was the high point of post-war BMW solo racing, it also coincided with a severe downturn in motorcycle sales and a reduction in racing development. Results during 1957 were less impressive, and at the end of the year BMW officially withdrew their support for solo racing. They continued to provide machines to selected riders for 1958, including legendary champion Geoff Duke, now without a factory ride following Gilera's retirement from racing. Dickie Dale raced the RS during 1959, and Japanese rider Fumio Ito joined Hiller on the RS during 1960. By now it was obvious the BMW twin was never going to succeed in the solo arena, although it continued to have a long and successful career powering Grand Prix sidecars.

During this time the production R50 and R69S had limited success in endurance events. London BMW dealer MLG entered an R50 in the 1958 Thruxton 500-mile race for production bikes, fourth place encouraging them to enter again in 1959. This time John Lewis and Peter Darvill won, and later that year, Darvill, partnered with Bruce Daniels, won the Barcelona 24-hour race. They narrowly failed to win at Montjuich in 1960, but with factory assistance, the MLG R69S won again in 1961. Even by 1964 the BMW twin was competitive, with Darvill and Norman

Walter Zeller was BMW's leading solo racer during the 1950s, on the Earles Fork RS54 and its factory derivatives. (Courtesy Ivar de Gier)

Price managing a second place in the Barcelona endurance event.

Although the R69S had isolated success in long distance racing during the 1960s, von der Marwitz always envisaged the /5 as a more suitable basis for competition. The R69S was difficult to set up for racing and required a specific riding approach to attain its best. Von der Marwitz may not have succeeded totally in creating a motorcycle that handled as well as a Manx Norton but, by the standards of the day, it was surprisingly close. Not only did the /5 handle better than the /2, the engine design was considerably stronger. Von der Marwitz gave BMW a motorcycle that had real sporting potential, and could acquit itself in production and production-based racing.

R75/5 Racers; Dähne and Butenuth

The chief racing exponents of the R75/5 in Europe were Hans-Otto Butenuth and Helmut Dähne. A heavy plant engineer with an oil company, Butenuth was a veteran BMW racer, beginning his career on an RS54 Rennsport in 1957, culminating in victory in the 1971 German Championship on a factory-prepared RS. Born in November 1944, after joining BMW in 1959 as an apprentice mechanic, Dähne rose to become a development engineer and test rider. In 1967, Alex von Falkenhausen lent him an R69S engine to race. "He allowed me to reduce it from 600cc to 500cc, in the factory and after work. I won the race. He was so satisfied he gave the engine to me as a present. So I had to race. This is how my racing career started." He began racing seriously in 1968, and as an amateur won the 1970 German B-grade championship. During 1971, Dähne began racing an R75/5 in German production racing events.

As soon as the R75/5 was released, Hans-Otto Butenuth rode a near standard machine in the 1970 Isle of Man Production 750cc TT. Although one of the slowest machines in the field, Butenuth achieved a very creditable 6th, covering the five laps at an average speed of 93.54mph (150.5km/h). With only British machines ahead of him, Butenuth finished comfortably ahead of all the Honda 750 Fours. This promising result prompted BMW to provide Butenuth with a special racing R75/5 for the 1971 Isle of Man Production 750cc TT. This year

the race was shortened to three laps, Butenuth finishing fourth at 93.75mph (150.8km/h). The private machines of Tom Dickie and Tony Anderson managed seventh and ninth, a promising result in a field dominated by Triumphs and Nortons. Dickie also managed eighth in the Formula 1 750cc TT. Helmut Dähne also applied to ride his R75/5 in the 1971 Isle of Man Production TT, but was rejected by the British ACU because it didn't consider him experienced enough.

With the advent of Formula 750 in 1972, Butenuth and Dähne entered the inaugural Imola 200 in April, on special R75/5s. Developed with unofficial factory assistance, Dähne and Butenuth put up a good showing but were out-paced by the hoard of factory teams. Dähne's machine had a narrower GP-style frame, shortened forks, and the engine was fed by Dell'Orto carburettors. His 13th overall at Imola earned him his first ride in the TT.

Helmut Dähne on his way to fourth place in the 1972 Isle of Man 750cc Production TT. (Courtesy Two Wheels)

Butenuth wasn't entered this year but Dähne, armed with his Imola F750 machine as well as the production R75/5, had a very successful week at the TT. He managed fourth in the 1972 Production TT at an average speed of 92.3mph (148.5km/h), and 11th in the F750 race at 92.65mph (149km/h). Dähne continued to develop his R75/5 during 1973. Retaining the short wheelbase frame of the 1970 model, this year he came 14th at the Imola 200. Dähne also managed fourth place in the 750cc Production TT, but conditions reduced his average speed to a slower 90.32mph (145.3km/h). Butenuth, riding a prototype R75/5 with sand-cast crankcases, managed seventh in the 750 Production TT. Dahne also finished ninth in the F750 TT, at 96.79mph (155.7km/h). The 1973 season was a moderately successful one for Dähne, who also won five production races in Germany on the R75/5. The year 1973 was the final year for a 750cc limit in the production TT, but BMW already had the R90S waiting for 1974.

Dähne rode in both the 1973 750cc Production and Classic TTs, finishing ninth here in the Classic. (Courtesy Helmut Dähne)

racing program. In April 1970, a Canadian entered R75/5 finished second in the 24-hour Harewood marathon race, covering 1635 miles (2630.7km), and encouraging Butler & Smith to seek a repeat of its earlier Danville result. New Vice President, Peter Adams, decided to sponsor the entry which was coordinated by Volker Beer and AMOL Precision. Helmut Kern spent 92-hours blue printing the 750cc engine in time for the race in September 1970. Liebmann, partnered by Charles Dearborn, won convincingly, three laps ahead of the second place Honda 750.

At the end of 1970, Beer organized for the factory to supply many racing components already tested by Dähne in Germany. Four racing frames and a variety of engine parts, ranging from magnesium castings to titanium conrods, were provided to Udo Gietl so he could build two 750RS racing bikes for the 1971 season. German-born, but US educated, Gietl was an electrical engineer with experience at NASA and on the Polaris submarine navigation systems. In 1959 at the age of 19, he helped a friend rebuild an R68, and when the people at Butler & Smith saw it they offered him a job. Gietl's racing experience began with motocross in 1961 and, after spending time in the army repairing communications gear in Korea, and at Cape Canaveral, by the end of the 1960s he was back at Butler & Smith.

Butler & Smith R75/5 Racers

On the other side of the Atlantic, a parallel racing program also operated. BMW motorcycles were distributed in the US by Butler & Smith, based in New York and owned by the Bondy family prior to 1970. During 1969, Butler & Smith service manager, Helmut Kern, persuaded Michael Bondy to enter two telescopic fork R69US models in the Danville (Virginia) 5-hour endurance club race. The teams were Kurt Liebmann/John Potter and Fred Simone/Bill VanHauton, from the AMOL Precision dealer/machine shop in Dumont, New Jersey. With minimal preparation by Edward Mitchell, Udo Gietl and Helmut Kern, the BMWs surprised everyone with a comfortable 1, 2 victory. During 1970, Butler & Smith moved to a new facility in Norwood, New Jersey and Volker Beer (their full-time BMW factory representative) recommended an expansion of the

Butler & Smith's first race was an entry in the 1970 VIR five-hour endurance race, won by Kurt Liebmann and Charles Dearborn. (Courtesy Udo Gietl)

The first Butler & Smith GP racer of 1971 had a 250mm Fontana brake. (Courtesy Udo Gietl)

By 1971 Gietl was working full-time on the F750 project and, in conjunction with AMOL Precision Gietl, produced one racer for Liebmann with another later in the year, for Justus Taylor. The resulting 750RS racer was commendably narrow, but didn't handle as well as expected as the frame wasn't sufficiently strong around the steering head. Only two of the four frames were used and, while Gietl and Kern commissioned C&J in California to build two similar frames, the handling on these was also deficient. A third F750, using a production R75/5 frame, was built for Charles Dearborn, along with a production racer for Liebmann. While the 750RS had limited success that year, Liebmann (with John Potter) again won the Danville 5-hour production race on the R75/5. Dearborn also won the production race at Bridgehampton in August.

The narrow frame on this early racer was a special BMW Motorsport type, also used by Dähne in Europe. (Courtesy Udo Gietl)

129

The fuel tank and fairing were fibreglass, and the tachometer was an electronic Krober. (Courtesy Udo Gietl)

The Butler & Smith franchise was sold to the Adams in 1971, and it expanded the operation by opening a West Coast office in Compton, California. Helmut Kern was general manager, with Edward Mitchell (parts manager), Matt Capri (sales manager) and Miles Rossteucher (shop mechanic). At the end of 1971, with R75/5 sales stagnant, Kern approached expatriate Briton, Reg Pridmore, to ride in the 1972 West Coast Production series. Pridmore tested one of Udo Gietl's special R75/5s and recalls: "When I rode the bike I was quite impressed. It had no brakes, but it ran quite well. BMW wanted to move a lot of 750s that were sitting around. People thought the BMW was a good old man's touring machine and didn't believe it was a good handling performance machine. I enjoyed a good rapport with Butler & Smith. They kept developing the bikes and things just got better and better. We had a lot of success, and they sold a lot of bikes."

An R75/5 production racer was built on the West Coast using many components from Gietl's GP bikes. A 19-inch wheel was fitted on the rear, and the cylinders shaved to increase the compression ratio. During 1972 and 1973, the engine received shorter conrods and 10.8:1 83mm Venolia pistons with lightweight wrist-pins, located closer to the piston crowns. The rockers pivoted on George Wenn needle bearings and Jerry Branch ported the cylinder heads. Valve train weight was reduced with S&W valve springs, hollow steel tappets and aluminium pushrods. From the GP bikes there was a heavily drilled flywheel to reduce weight, and tungsten plugs inserted in the crankshaft. Lubrication modifications saw an additional oil groove cut into the base of the cylinder, with a high pressure orifice feeding this groove for additional piston skirt lubrication. By the end of its development the transmission was also five-speed. Just about all these racing developments eventually found their way onto the production models, again evidence that racing improves the breed.

Kurt Liebmann raced the GP 750 during 1971, but without success. (Courtesy Udo Gietl)

Square windows were cut in the air intake hoses, and holes drilled in the air filter housing. While the chassis was stock, Kern spent considerable time and effort reworking the front suspension. With Ferodo AM4 green linings in the front drum brake, the B&S R75/5 was possibly the most effective production racing motorcycle in the United States during 1972 and 1973. Pridmore managed 15 wins and 6 second places out of 23 starts, winning the AFM production class championship. As the series was confined to the West Coast it had limited exposure, However, when *Cycle* magazine tested the R75/5 racer in its May 1974 issue, Pridmore received nationwide fame. *Cycle's* performance figures at Orange County Raceway were impressive, especially so considering the surprisingly stock looking and very quiet mufflers. Into a strong head wind, the R75/5 ran a 12.7-second standing quarter-mile at 104mph (167.3km/h). Pridmore also took the AFM 750cc Grand Prix title on the 750RS.

During 1972, the East Coast racing program continued with Udo Gietl developing the 750RS, both with the standard and racing frame. The engine now produced 86 horsepower but performance was limited by the AMA-sanctioned four-speed gearbox. The machine was commendably light and, with the special racing frame, weighed only 150kg. Raced by Liebmann, Dearborn and Pridmore, the 750RS had some success this year. Liebmann contested the 100-mile Junior race at Daytona, where he failed to finish, but went on to win the Pocono 50-mile road race in August and AAMRR open class Grand Prix title. Dearborn also managed another win on the R75/5 in the street class at Bridgehampton in April, and, teamed with Liebmann, took first place in the Two-Hour production race a week later. Dearborn's best finish on the GP bike was third at Virginia in September 1972.

Encouraged by the AMA request for manufacturer involvement in competition, Butler & Smith continued to race the F750 racers during 1973, but again they were outclassed. The racers now featured a Harley-Davidson full fairing, a Ceriani front fork with twin Honda disc brakes, and now had a five-speed gearbox. Ridden by Liebmann, Justus Taylor and Pridmore in the AMA National Road Race Championship, Pridmore summed them up with: "those early GP bikes were, what you might say, shoestring racers."

At the end of 1973 Pridmore introduced frame builder, Englishman Rob North, to Kern and Capri. North migrated to Southern California during 1973, and Pridmore, who was racing a North sidecar racer at the time, suggested North provide a

frame and fuel tank similar to those of his highly successful Triumph and BSA 750cc triples. North subsequently built two frames, both closely patterned on the Triumph version. This development coincided with an expansion in workshop facilities at Norwood, with a new dyno, flow bench and welding equipment. Gietl agreed to the North proposal for a Triumph-style racing frame, although he had Todd Schuster on the East Coast fabricate a swingarm that was longer by 2 inches. The wheelbase was quite long, at 1470mm (57.9 inches), but the double-cradle chrome-molybdenum steel frame was strong and immediately tamed the handling of the R75/5. The driveshaft ran in the right-side of the swingarm, but with an exposed U-joint to save weight. The engine was also located higher than that of the Triumph, for improved ground clearance.

Justus Taylor raced the GP bike during 1973. The fuel tank was now aluminium and the fairing was from a Harley-Davidson. (Courtesy Udo Gietl)

Justus Taylor at speed on the banking at Daytona in 1973. Braking was now via twin front discs. (Courtesy Udo Gietl)

The North frame on the 1974 Butler & Smith racers was patterned on that of the successful BSA and Triumph triples, and included a sculptured fuel tank. (Courtesy Two Wheels*)*

Two North-framed F750 machines were prepared in time for the 1974 Daytona 200-mile race, both extensively modified boxer twins. Overbored to the maximum allowed (1mm), the 763cc engine was based on Pridmore's successful R75/5 production racer, with input from many of California's leading Hot-Rod exponents. It was further developed throughout 1974 and 1975. Jerry Branch reworked the cylinder heads with 44mm intake valves and straight intake ports, as the carburettors no longer needed to clear the rider's shins, while Sig Erson developed the camshaft. Along with lightweight steel cam followers, the rocker assemblies included needle thrust

bearings. After experimenting with aluminium and titanium pushrods, Gietl settled on steel units that flexed less. The camshaft drive was initially by a single-row chain to minimise power loss; however, as revs increased and heavier valve springs were required, the chain sprockets failed and the duplex chain was reinstalled. According to Reg Pridmore "roller cam followers were tried at one stage. It revved like a banshee but didn't show the reliability the boss was looking for." Due to their stronger bearing supports the crankcases were /6, with all excess metal machined. There were also modifications to the lubrication and crankcase ventilation system, with a smaller diameter oil pump, enlarged oil passages and high volume crankcase ventilation. At peak revs it was found the stock oil pump drew five horsepower, and the smaller oil pump reduced cavitation. A tiny oil reservoir was incorporated in the crankshaft journals. All the machine work was done by Kurt Liebmann's father, Oscar, at his company, AMOL Precision.

Carburetion was by Mikuni, initially 38mm but later reduced to 36mm. The 83mm 12:1 pistons were Venolia and the gudgeon pin, located 12mm closer to the crown, allowed each machined Alfin cylinder to be 22mm shorter, improving ground clearance. Ignition was electronic Krober, with twin sparkplugs per cylinder, two triggers and four coils. The crankshaft rod journals incorporated a second oil supply hole and weight saving extended to lighter counterweights (by 80 grams), re-balanced with metal inserts and removal of the generator. The 10mm shorter conrods were titanium and, to improve throttle response, the standard flywheel was drilled to weigh only 1.6kg (from 3.6kg). The larger sump carried another 1.1-litres of oil, and a Triumph oil cooler kept everything cool at 9500rpm. Initially producing between 82- and 85-horsepower, by 1975, the 750cc engine was rumoured to produce 100 horsepower at the crank. During 1973, the AMA sanctioned five-speed gearboxes and, as the R75/5 only featured a four-speed gearbox, a five-speed Kaiser-converted unit was used. By 1975 the gearbox was a BMW unit, but with a drum shifting mechanism instead of cam-plates. There was a choice of eight final drive ratios, ranging from Daytona's 1:2.62, to a 1:4.25 for the twisting Sears Point circuit.

Knowing that his BMW racers suffered a horsepower deficiency compared to the competition, over its two and half year developmental period, Udo Gietl concentrated on improving the suspension. The racing Ceriani forks, similar to those of the racing MV Agustas, had Betor triple clamps, while the twin Girling shock

When they appeared at Daytona in 1974, the North-framed racers looked promising, but were outclassed.

Pridmore and Kern at Daytona in 1975.

absorbers featured heavier damping with light springing. This suited the peculiar characteristics of shaft drive and steering and handling were vastly improved. The magnesium wheels were designed by Gietl, cast by Morris and machined by AMOL. Braking was by double 230mm drilled cast-iron disc brakes with dual-piston Lockheed calipers on the front, and a single disc on the rear. At 152kg ready to go, the B&S racer was lighter than the Yamaha and Suzuki two-strokes, capable of around 265km/h (164.7mph).

The North-framed machines were hopelessly outclassed at Daytona in 1974, with only Pridmore qualifying. Pridmore managed to get up to 12th before a cracked valve forced his retirement. It was rumoured that Pridmore's machine displaced 1000cc, but his retirement with a cracked valve eliminated the embarrassment of a post-race teardown. Reg says, "The two Rob North GP racers were really good, but their effort in GP racing was knocked down by all the TZ Yamahas. The BMW was competitive against the 350s, but then the 700s and 750s came along. I found that on certain shorter tracks I could beat 80 per cent of them, but it lacked horsepower at places like Daytona." While not especially suited to Daytona, the B&S GP machines were effective in regional road racing. Their high point was a magnificent 1-2 victory at Summit Point, West Virginia, in April 1974. In the Open Expert GP, Justus Taylor led home Kurt Liebmann, despite fracturing an intake valve.

Pridmore at Daytona 1975. Updates from the previous year included a two-into-two exhaust system and new shock absorbers.

The final race for the North-framed 750 BMWs was at Laguna Seca in 1975. Here, Gary Fisher diced for the lead on the monoshock version. (Courtesy Udo Gietl)

Although four-strokes appeared dead in AMA racing, Butler & Smith entered Liebmann and Pridmore on the F750 racers, in the 1975 Daytona 200. Now at the peak of their development, producing around 100 horsepower at the crank and running to 10,500rpm, they were probably the fastest pushrod twins ever. Pridmore was running 13th, a good effort in the field of 80, but problems saw him finish 30th. Gary Fisher was drafted alongside Pridmore for the remaining races of the 1975 AMA F750 season, and during 1975 Gietl experimented with monoshock rear suspension on Gary Fisher's bike. In the final race for the F750 BMWs (at Laguna Seca), Fisher put the monoshock bike on the front row, dicing with Kenny Roberts for the lead during the race until the monoshock failed. Pridmore also proved the F750 BMW's potency by out accelerating the Yamaha 700s at Road Atlanta. Often top ten finishers in AMA Nationals, and faster than the once-dominant Harley V-twins, the B&S GP racers remain testimony to the magnificent era when BMW in America was committed to racing, against all odds, and when racing development trickled onto the production bikes.

R90S and R100S Production Racers

The release of the R90S at the end of 1973 was fortuitous for BMW, as it coincided with a move away from 750cc-based Production racing to 1000cc. For the Bol d'Or 24-Hour endurance race at Le Mans, 23 September 1973, BMW prepared a factory R90S. Ridden by Dähne and Gary Green, this finished third, covering 3200km (1988.4m). Dähne, assisted by Helmut Bucher, also continued to develop his older R75/5 racer for Production events. With the Production TT capacity limit now 1000cc, they installed a new 900cc engine with five-speed gearbox and dual disc front end on the R75/5 chassis. "I always raced with the short wheelbase R75/5 chassis, even with the R90S engine. This was for weight and handling reasons. I never had any stability problems," says Dähne.

In the 1974 Isle of Man 1000cc Production TT Butenuth also raced an R90S. This was a special 1000cc version developed by Paul Blum. Butenuth came second at 97.7mph (157.2km/h) and Dähne third at 97.01mph (156.1km/h). Dähne was also entered on a R50R and R75R in the 1974 Senior and Classic TTs, although his R90S was substantially faster. Dähne went to work for the Metzeler tyre company as race manager in May 1974, but continued a close association with the BMW factory.

The 1975 Production TT was a 10-lap handicap race with two riders and Dähne teamed with Werner Dieringer. The Daytona Orange R90S (still in the short chassis) engine featured a larger sump; Krober electronic ignition; titanium conrods; high compression pistons; larger valves; hotter cam; larger Dell'Orto carburettors; megaphone racing exhaust, and a close-ratio transmission.

After two laps Dähne was in the lead by a minute, when he knocked a hole in the right-side cylinder head cover, causing severe oil loss and engine seizure. Dähne carried a spare rocker cover strapped to the side of the bike but the damage was already done. He finished ninth in the Open Classic TT on the same bike later in the week, the first four-stroke home. He averaged 99.67mph (160.36km/h) for the six-lap race, and his best lap of 101.89mph (163.94km/h) was the first 100mph lap by a BMW at the Isle of Man. BMW also returned to the Bol d'Or in 1975, Dähne teaming with René Guili to finish fourth.

Dähne before the Isle of Man 1975 Production TT. He was comfortably in the lead before retiring after oil loss, caused by wearing a hole in the rocker cover.

Dähne returned to the Isle of Man in 1976, this time determined not to suffer from the ground clearance problems of the previous year. Special 10.5:1 Mahle pistons, with raised gudgeons and shorter conrods, trimmed 22mm off each side. The crankshaft and flywheel were lightened by 2kg, and there were lighter, thinner (10mm rather than 12mm) alloy pushrods enabling the engine

Dähne's 1975 R90S racer retained the short wheelbase R75/5 chassis but still suffered ground clearance problems, as evidenced by the ground rocker cover.

to rev safely to 8000rpm. Dähne commented that: "The valve train was very fragile. So I developed a two-part alloy pushrod with a spacer in the middle, together with mushroom cam followers. It cured the valve spring breakage problems by absorbing some of the valve shock when the cam came very abruptly off bottom dead centre. I also made a major change to the valve gear by obtaining an unmachined crankcase off the production line. This was sleeved to allow the cam follower and pushrod to line up straight because in the standard engine they're six degrees out of line, with the pushrod always being moved sideways. This was done in anticipation of the larger, 94mm, cylinders for the later R100." The power of Dähne's R90S was 80-horsepower at 7000rpm, and the weight was 185kg.

A 1mm thicker top triple clamp tightened the handling for the bumpy TT course and, teamed with Butenuth, Dähne led the 10-lap 1976 Production TT from start to finish, averaging 98.82mph (159km/h). Under the handicap system, they were credited

Although not credited with victory under the handicap system, Dähne and Butenuth convincingly beat the rest of the field in the 1976 Production TT.

with fifth – the first time the fastest finishers didn't win a TT. Dähne's fastest lap of 102.52mph (164.95km/h) remains the best ever lap of the Isle of Man by a pushrod boxer twin. Martyn Sharpe and Abe Alexander on another R90S finished second across the line, averaging 95.5mph (153.7km/h), but were credited with 15th overall. Dähne returned to TT in 1977 with a boxer twin for the TTF1 race, but retired after one lap.

The release of the R90S also coincided with the expansion in production, and production-based racing in America. As Reg Pridmore and the Butler & Smith R75/5 were the most competitive combination in West Coast production racing during 1973, it was no surprise to see them on the leader board with the new R90S during 1974. Liebmann campaigned the production R90S on the East Coast. Gietl and Kern, with Todd Schuster assisting with fabrication, worked on the R90S, boosting the power output to around 90 horsepower. Although chassis specification had to remain basically stock, they used wider wheel rims with an offset to clear the driveshaft. Pridmore found the R90S to be a forgiving bike: "I used to ground the heads a lot but the handling was OK with some suspension changes. If you hit something down on another bike it would pick up the front end and usually throw you away. A lot of times the BMW gave warning signs of lifting, then it would come back. I didn't fall off them a lot."

During 1974, Pridmore rode the new R90S to some success in west coast Production racing. (Courtesy Two Wheels)

Pridmore was denied a win in at Laguna Seca when an ignition wire broke, but made amends at Ontario where he finished so far in front of the Yoshimura Kawasakis of Yvon Duhamel and Steve McLaughlin, they assumed they had won. On the podium, Duhamel said to Pridmore: "What are you doing here? Didn't you crash?" Reg rates this victory as his most memorable on the R90S, and one of the most unforgettable in his career. He continued to ride the production R90S (now Daytona Orange) during 1975, finishing fourth in the Daytona production race. But as production racing evolved into Superbike racing in the US, so did the R90S.

Butler & Smith R90S and R100S Superbikes

With the demise of competitive four-strokes in open class racing in the US, and a consequent massive drop in public interest, for 1976 the AMA created the Superbike series for racing motorcycles based on production models. The Superbike rules required the machines to look stock, even retaining a tail light, but underneath the street bodywork they were highly developed racers. Udo Gietl was on the AMA Competition Board rules committee and instrumental in the creation of this series, coining the word 'Superbike.' In that first year of Superbike, only Butler & Smith exploited the new Superbike regulations to the full. Initially, Superbike preparation was a sole East Coast (Norwood) project, but, ultimately, it became a combined effort by both racing arms of Butler & Smith. Team manager Udo Gietl, with Todd Schuster, Kenny Augustine, AMOL Precision and West Coast executives Helmut Kern and Matt Capri, worked tirelessly to create the R90S Superbikes, arguably the most spectacular BMW racing motorcycles ever built.

Gietl began preparing the R90S Superbikes for the upcoming Daytona Superbike race in October 1975. He knew that, to compete with the Kawasaki Z1, he would need as much power as possible, with better handling. Gietl then went to extraordinary lengths to achieve it. 95mm forged Venolia pistons bumped the capacity to 1000cc and provided more than 12.6:1 compression. Three different brands of piston ring were used: a special L-section top ring; Chevrolet middle ring, and a Perfect Circle oil control ring. As the engine had to rev safely to 9200rpm, the gudgeon pins were machined from K11 heat-treated steel. Inside the cylinder head were titanium 46mm inlet and 39mm exhaust valves. Augustine flowed the cylinder heads, Schuster bored and worked the 38mm Dell'Orto carburettors to 40mm, and the camshaft was by Sig Erson (with 12.8mm of intake valve lift). The shorter Smith pushrods were of 4130 steel and very thin steel valve lifters came from Germany. To increase cornering clearance the cylinder barrels were shortened and the conrods were 10mm shorter, German forged titanium (125mm instead of 135mm). The rocker covers were bevelled and fitted with steel skid plates, the crankshaft was rebalanced for higher rpm and included two holes for the conrod bearings and the counterweights were removed. As the BMW crankshaft was only supported at the ends, without a centre bearing, it was always prone to flex at high rpm.

Gietl fabricated an all-metal dry clutch and, while the close-ratio gearbox retained the stock BMW third, fourth and fifth gears, AMOL Precision made up closer first and second gears. Four coils fired the twin sparkplugs per cylinder, and all superfluous components (such as the electric start and air filter box) were discarded. Pridmore retained points ignition while Fisher and McLaughlin's was electronic, and the large front-mounted oil cooler came from an English MGB sports car. As stock mufflers were required by the regulations, these were gutted and fitted with a reverse-cone megaphone, designed by C.R. Axtel for Harley XR750s. When they lined up at the inaugural Superbike race at Daytona in March 1976, the Butler & Smith R90Ss produced 92 horsepower at the clutch. During the season it was continually developed, eventually producing 102 horsepower at 8600rpm (with roller follower camshafts).

Gietl also looked hard at the chassis regulations, stretching them to the limit. A loophole indicated that the swingarm could be modified and the rear suspension relocated, and this is exactly what he did. Gietl reworked the swingarm to incorporate a single, semi-horizontal, Koni F1 racing car shock absorber. Udo said: "Earlier, Volker Beer provided an R90S with a bent frame from a crash and Schuster and I developed the monoshock with this bike. Riding it gave me a better understanding and ultimately led to the 1976 Superbikes." All this fabrication had to be done in secrecy, so the welding was done at the Norwood shop with the assistance of AMOL Precision. A spacer behind the gearbox shifted the engine forward 25mm, and upwards 10mm, and the engine was also repositioned 5mm to the right, to allow clearance between the Michelin slick tire and driveshaft. As gusseting and added stiffness to the production fame was permitted, Gietl and Schuster added a pair of diagonal frame

The three Butler & Smith R90S Superbikes lined up at Daytona in 1976. Fisher's bike is closest to the camera. (Courtesy Two Wheels)

members, connecting the steering head to the swingarm pivot. This also enabled one of the lower frame cradles to be removed, the motor now hanging in the frame, facilitating quicker engine removal for servicing.

The stock BMW forks were reworked, strengthened with a huge alloy top triple clamp and braced. The internal fork rubber bumper was replaced by a short bottoming spring. Front fork travel was limited to six inches, and rear suspension travel, five inches (with either suspension layout). Wider WM4 and WM5 (later this was a TZ750 WM6) 18-inch alloy wire-spoked wheels allowed wider

Michelin slick tyres, with the rear laced 8mm to the left for even more clearance. Initially the brakes were still the stock ATE floating caliper type, with 260mm aluminium discs. The overall weight was at the AMA regulation 370 pounds (168kg). All the testing was done in secrecy on the flow bench, dyno and illegal test rides. "One of these test rides came at the cost of some skin in one of the crashes I had," says Udo... "The bikes didn't feel fast compared to my heavily modified street bike but the dyno said otherwise. Time moves quickly when you are having this much fun, and soon it was show time at Daytona."

Three R90S Superbikes were prepared and Gietl's plan was to run two riders, Pridmore and Fisher, with one machine as a spare. But, at the last minute, McLaughlin was drafted in. Peter Adams wanted a third rider, and Matt Capri convinced Adams and Kern to include McLaughlin. As Gietl says: "we were up to the hilt. We arrived at Daytona with three complete bikes, but very few spares, hardly even an extra piston ring. The West Coast guys also knew nothing of the monoshock until Daytona. I did this secretly, giving the welders a six pack of beer to complete it. When Helmut Kern saw it he was livid, and it caused a lot of friction in the team." As Udo left the twin shock mounts in place it was decided, as Pridmore was the number one rider, to leave his bike twin shock to allay any possible protest. Reg tells it slightly differently: "I didn't like the tension in the shorter rear spring, and I couldn't make the damping keep up with the lack of movement in the shock. So I couldn't ride

it and had Helmut Kern remount the twin shocks." Udo says: "We had a huge selection of springs, and Kern selected a heavier spring for Reg, while Steve and Gary used much softer ones."

Unexpected humidity, and the high compression, resulted in ignition problems during practice, but the speed was impressive and the bikes were reasonably fresh for the main race. Fisher was timed at 144.5mph (232.5km/h) and all three riders qualified for the final. Fisher was first, Pridmore second and McLaughlin third. In the first US Superbike National final on March 5, Fisher built-up a large lead until a fouled shift lever caused the transmission to pop out of gear. He over-revved the engine, breaking a rocker arm two laps from the finish. McLaughlin assumed the lead until Pridmore caught him. On the final lap, Pridmore led, but McLaughlin drafted past across the finishing line to win by three inches. Pridmore was initially credited with victory, but the

Throughout much of the race, Pridmore led McLaughlin by a close margin. (Courtesy Two Wheels)

139

photo finish equipment later proved McLaughlin the winner. It was one of the closest race finishes ever at Daytona, and the race average was 99.8mph (160.57km/h). So dominant were the BMWs that they made the rest of the field look second-rate.

At the next round at Laconia, New Hampshire, the experimental aluminium brake discs were problematic. McLaughlin missed a shift, over-revving and shearing the flywheel, while Fisher and Pridmore were beaten by Baldwin's Brembo-braked Moto Guzzi Le Mans. Twin-piston Lockheed front calipers with Hurst-Airheart steel discs graced on the front for Laguna Seca. While Fisher retired with a broken oil cooler leak, Pridmore and McLaughlin diced for the lead, McLaughlin crashing spectacularly on the final lap, allowing Pridmore to win.

Pridmore also went on to win the fourth and final race of the inaugural Superbike season at Riverside, a favourite track that he knew well, ensuring victory in the 1976 AMA Superbike Championship. Gietl's book-keeping showed the racing season had cost Butler & Smith $250,000,

McLaughlin celebrates with Pridmore after one of the closest finishes in Daytona history. (Courtesy Two Wheels)

but it ensured the sales success of the R90S in the US, and forever changed the perception of BMW motorcycles. According to Udo Gietl, "at least 13 racing bikes came out of the Butler & Smith Norwood shop during the 1970s," and, with the PR job done, Peter Adams decided to pull the plug on the expensive program. Udo goes on to say, "Peter Adams had to come to terms with the expenditure so termination of the project was inevitable. The sad, and disturbing, part for me was all the racing equipment went to Compton on the West Coast where it was destined to be sold." For racing machines, the R90S Superbikes were extremely reliable, with the same pistons that took first and second at Daytona still in the bikes at Laguna Seca. After Daytona, *Cycle* magazine nicknamed the B&S bikes the "Bavarian Murder Weapons," but the obsessive racing season came at a cost. The marriages of Pridmore, McLaughlin, Fisher, Gietl, Augustine and Schuster all ended. "This was the only part that wasn't a team effort!" says Udo.

Although Butler & Smith was no longer seriously involved in racing the R90S Superbike, one machine was entered for the 1977 Daytona Superbike race. Monoshock rear suspension was banned by the AMA Superbike this year, and the Butler & Smith R90S was a West Coast entry coordinated by Helmut Kern. Now painted red R100S colours (but still an R90S because this was the only homologated model), Pridmore rode it at Daytona, qualifying fastest. McLaughlin rode Udo Gietl and Todd Schuster's Bel Ray-sponsored R90S, while Pierce rode a North Chester Motorcycle Parts entry. McLaughlin qualified second, but his motor failed in the race and he didn't finish.

After finishing second at Daytona, Pridmore went on to provide BMW with its only AMA Superbike Championship.

McLaughlin and Pridmore again lined up on BMWs for the 1977 Daytona Superbike race, but this year they rode for different teams. Pridmore (on the right) finished fourth. (Courtesy Two Wheels)

Pridmore finished fourth in the 1977 Daytona Superbike race (behind Cook Neilson's Ducati and the Kawasaki Z1s of Wes Cooley and Dave Emde), but the difference in trap speeds between Pridmore's 142mph (228.5km/h) and Cooley's 153.06mph (246.27km/h) signified the end of any official Butler & Smith involvement in Superbike racing. As Pridmore said: "I wasn't too upset. The new bike had different steering geometry and I thought the handling was much worse, making it harder to go into turns." Gietl and Schuster continued their involvement, assisting Ron Pierce to provide the McLaughlin Daytona-winning bike (also now painted red), another victory at Loudon in June 1977. The San Jose bike (Fisher #21) also gave BMW another AMA Superbike victory, when Harry Klinzmann won at Laconia in 1978.

For the 1978 season Gietl and Schuster (GS Performance) continued developing their R90S Superbike. Udo managed to persuade Peter Adams to provide some assistance: "Peter Adams was extremely enthusiastic about the racing program, and also sympathetic when it ended. When asked to continue on a small scale on my own, he agreed to the use of the Norwood facility, some parts, exceptional discounts and time off. Without his support this last R90S project would never have happened."

An independent team was formed, with Gietl responsible for design and drivetrain; Schuster for chassis, machining and fabrication, and Tom Cutter for assembly, maintenance and track support. In the hands of the already successful Miami rider John Long, they almost provided BMW with their second AMA Superbike Championship. Development saw the engine modified to improve reliability. With later R100 crankcases, to reduce crankcase pressure loss, the breather fed into a foam-filled box through reed valves. The 95mm Venolia pistons were lighter by 50-60 grams,

McLaughlin and Pridmore again lined up on BMWs for the 1977 Daytona Superbike race, but this year they rode for different teams. Pridmore (on the right) finished fourth. (Courtesy Two Wheels)

enabling tighter clearances, and the 45mm inlet valves were from a Chrysler Hemi V8. Schuster fabricated 40mm smooth bore Dell'Orto carburettors and, for shorter tracks, Gietl installed a 36mm intake restrictor. For improved intake flow, the stock curved intake manifolds were cut off and fabricated straight ones welded on at a different angle. The 330-degree camshaft was by Crane, with double coil Crane springs, Smith pushrods and Wiesmann steel tappets straight out of an aftermarket automotive catalogue. Later in the season, Gietl fitted a set of Harley-Davidson XR750 lightweight roller tappets. The Carillo conrods were nickel steel, still 10mm shorter than stock and, when combined with the steel wristpins mounted 12mm higher in the pistons, this allowed for 22mm shorter cylinders. Ignition was by Bosch total loss CDI, still with four coils

and twin sparkplugs per cylinder, the top plug firing at 34 degrees BTDC and the lower plug at 32 degrees. "This was a setting I first tried on the Butler & Smith Superbikes, and it worked," said Gietl. Other modifications extended to a heavily milled flywheel, contributing to a reduction in engine weight to only 52kg. The transmission was a special reworked close-ratio set from BMW. For the Loudon race after Daytona, Gietl built a second engine with roller cam followers, and a chrome molybdenum steel camshaft ground by Crane. The camshaft ran in needle bearings, and the ignition was replaced by a Krober electronic magneto. The power was approximately 102-104-horsepower at 8700rpm, and the camshaft, compression ratio and port sizes were altered for each track, as were the gear ratios and final drive.

The GS Performance R90S that finished second in the 1978 AMA Superbike Championship. The mechanical anti-dive system was designed by Gietl and installed after Daytona. (Courtesy Udo Gietl)

Improving the handling was Schuster's priority. The engine was moved forward 15mm in the frame to improve weight distribution, and two welded struts connected the swingarm pivot to the steering head. Extra plates also strengthened the steering head, and the head angle was decreased to 28.5 degrees (from 31 degrees). The swingarm was extensively reinforced, and the twin Koni shock absorbers considerably re-worked. The wheels remained wire-spoked (a WM4 at the front and WM5 on the rear, with Michelin slicks), while the stock BMW 36mm fork included very soft springing and modified damping. After Daytona, to restrict fork travel under hard braking, Gietl incorporated a mechanical anti-dive with the twin Lockheed brake calipers mounting on a floating alloy rocker arm pivoting from the front axle. Each rocker was linked by ball joint and pushrod to the lower fork crown, transmitting rotational torque to the lower crown. This setup allowed some dive during braking, but aided cornering ground clearance. The twin front discs were light-weight plasma-coated aluminium, or cast-steel for shorter circuits. Superbike regulations allowed a 20 per cent weight reduction from stock, providing the Gietl-Schuster BMW a considerable weight advantage over the Suzuki and Kawasaki 1000s.

The GS Performance R90S handled extremely well and was perfectly balanced. At Daytona, Long finished third, out dragged to the finish line by Reg Pridmore, now on a Kawasaki. A second at Loudon, followed by fifth at Sears Point, retirement at Pocono and fourth at Laguna Seca, saw Long ending the season with a points tie for the 1978 AMA Superbike Championship with Pridmore. Due to a starting infringement at the second Loudon race, lowering their third place to eleventh, Long was credited with second overall. It was an astonishing achievement for a privately entered pushrod twin to succeed so well in a field of factory-prepared fours. Long also won the Canadian Superbike Championship, clinching it with a win at Mosport. This last victory represented the end of an era. An era where the shaft-drive pushrod BMW twin was a real racing force, and could compete with the best the rest of the world could offer. At the end of 1978, the GS Performance R90S was sold to

a Massachusetts dealer, but Long continued to campaign it during 1979, finishing fourth at Daytona, and ninth at Loudon.

Ex-AMA 250 champion Dave Emde also rode one of the ex-Butler & Smith R90Ss in BOTT. Sponsored by San Jose BMW, Emde was so fast in the wet at Loudon in 1981 that his team also entered him in the Superbike race. Starting from the back of the grid Emde ran as high as third before finishing fourth. While that was the end of the BMW twin in AMA Superbike, Long continued to race the GS R90S until 1983, in the Battle of the Twins Grand Prix Class.

Australian Castrol Six-hour Production Race

Production racing was extremely popular in Australia in the early 1970s, and the Castrol Six-hour race for production motorcycles was the premier motorcycle racing event on the calendar. Broadcast nationally on live television, the rules were strictly administered. The race was first run in 1970 and while several R75/5s were entered in the early years, they didn't figure prominently on the tight 1.9km circuit that favoured smaller and lighter motorcycles. However, in 1973 the BMW R75/5 surprised the field, Tony Hatton riding the six hours single-handedly with only two fuel stops to finish third.

John Long is congratulated by Tom Cutter and Todd Schuster after a fine finish on the GS Performance R90S. (Courtesy Udo Gietl)

Bob Pressley at speed on an R75/5 in the 1970 Australian Castrol Six-hour race for production motorcycles. (Courtesy Two Wheels)

Even before the 1974 Castrol Six-hour race was run, it was packed with drama. The organisers decided to ban motorcycles with fairings, eliminating the R90S, so the BMW distributors, Tom Byrne, entered an R90/6. Bryan Hindle and Clive Knight crossed the line first, covering 346-laps at an average speed of 112.22km/h (69.73mph), with another R90/6 (Gary Thomas and Graham Kairl) third. Unfortunately, BMW's victory was short-lived, as an examination by the scrutineers after the race resulted in both BMWs' exclusion from the results. The spacers in the front forks were from the R90S and, apparently, incorrectly positioned, pre-loading the springs for more ground clearance. As the factory manual was imprecise, this finding was contentious, but

indisputable, and the R90/6s were excluded. The bonus for BMW was that 50,000 people watching the race on TV saw the R90/6 cross the finish line first.

A rule change allowed the R90S to be eligible for the 1975 Castrol Six-hour race, and this year Kenny Blake rode solo, finishing second. No longer allowed to ride the six hours solo, Blake teamed with Hatton for the 1976 race and, again, finished second. The promise of the previous four years was finally realised in 1977. Taking maximum advantage of being able to run for more than two hours between fuel stops, the BMW R100S of Blake and Joe Eastmure set a new race record, covering 355-laps in six hours. Helmut Dähne and Tony Hatton finished fifth on a similar machine. Although not the fastest or best handling, the ultra-reliable R100Ss proved that, with a smooth riding technique, they were more than a match for the higher performance Kawasakis or better handling Ducatis. Although Blake and Dave Burgess rode the R100S to fourth place in the 1978 Castrol Six-hour race, they failed to qualify in the top fifteen and the future for the venerable boxer twin in this event looked ominous. The reality of beating the new wave of improved Japanese Superbikes hit home, and for the 1979 Castrol Six-hour no official BMWs were entered.

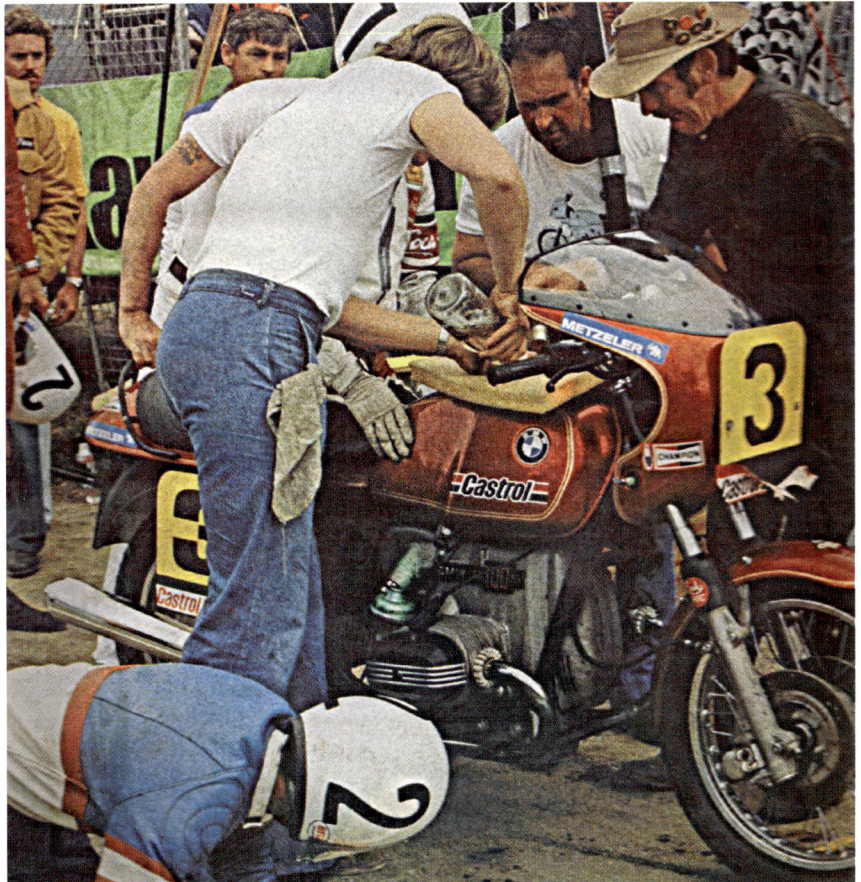

Rider changeover for the winning R100S in the 1977 Castrol Six-hour race. As the BMW had the advantage of a larger fuel tank and fewer pit stops, it was imperative that the tank was filled to the maximum. (Courtesy Two Wheels)

Helmut Dähne shared a second R100S in the 1977 Castrol Six-hour race, finishing fifth. (Courtesy Two Wheels)

APPENDIX

TECHNICAL SPECIFICATIONS

R50/5

Year	1970-73
Bore (mm)	67
Stroke (mm)	70.6
Capacity (cc)	498
Compression ratio	8.6:1
Valve timing (2mm valve clearance, ± 2.5-degrees) intake opening	TDC
Intake closing	40° ABDC
Exhaust opening	40° BBDC
Exhaust closing	BDC
Horsepower	32 at 6400rpm
Left carburetor	Bing 1/26/113
Right carburetor	Bing 1/26/114
Main jet	135
Needle jet	2.68
Jet needle no.	46-234
Needle position	3
Idle jet	35
Sparkplugs	Bosch W230 T1, Champion N7Y, Beru 230/14/3A
Ignition timing	9 deg BTDC
Points gap	0.35-0.40mm
First gear	3.896:1
Second gear	2.578:1
Third gear	1.875:1
Fourth gear	1.50:1
Fifith gear	–
Final drive	09:32
Overall width	740mm
Seat height	810mm
Overall length	2100mm (2450mm 1973)
Wheelbase	1385mm (1435mm 1973)
Weight including oil and fuel	210kg (205kg 1971)
Top speed	157km/h (98mph)

R60/5

Year	1970-73
Bore (mm)	73.5
Stroke (mm)	70.6
Capacity (cc)	599
Compression ratio	9.2:1
Valve timing (2mm valve clearance, ± 2.5-degrees) intake opening	TDC
Intake closing	40° ABDC
Exhaust opening	40° BBDC
Exhaust closing	BDC
Horsepower	40 at 6400rpm
Left carburetor	Bing 1/26/111
Right carburetor	Bing 1/26/112
Main jet	140
Needle jet	2.68
Jet needle no.	46-234
Needle position	2
Idle jet	40
Sparkplugs	Bosch W230 T1, Champion N7Y, Beru 230/14/3A
Ignition timing	9 deg BTDC
Points gap	0.35-0.40mm
First gear	3.896:1
Second gear	2.578:1
Third gear	1.875:1
Fourth gear	1.50:1
Fifth gear	–
Final drive	11:37
Overall width	740mm
Seat height	810mm
Overall length	2100mm (2450mm 1973)
Wheelbase	1385mm (1435mm 1973)
Weight including oil and fuel	210kg (205kg 1971)
Top speed	167km/h (104mph)

R75/5

Year	1970-73
Bore (mm)	82
Stroke (mm)	70.6
Capacity (cc)	745
Compression ratio	9.0:1
Valve timing (2mm valve clearance, ± 2.5-degrees) intake opening	10° BTDC
Intake closing	50° ABDC
Exhaust opening	50 BBDC
Exhaust closing	10° ATDC
Horsepower	50 at 6200rpm
Left carburetor	Bing 64/32/3 (64/32/9 from

	1971)
Right carburetor	Bing 64/32/4 (64/32/10 from 1971)
Main jet	140 (150 from 1971)
Needle jet	2.73 (2.70)
Jet needle no.	46-241
Needle position	3
Idle jet	44-950
Sparkplugs	Bosch W200 T30, Champion N7Y, Beru 200/14/3A
Ignition timing	9 deg BTDC
Points gap	0.35-0.40mm
First gear	3.896:1
Second gear	2.578:1
Third gear	1.875:1
Fourth gear	1.50:1
Fifith gear	–
Final drive	11:32 (10:32 1971)
Overall width	740mm
Seat height	810mm
Overall length	2100mm (2450mm 1973)
Wheelbase	1385mm (1435mm 1973)
Weight including oil and fuel	210kg (205kg 1971)
Top speed	175km/h (110mph)

R60/6

Year	1974-76
Bore (mm)	73.5
Stroke (mm)	70.6
Capacity (cc)	599
Compression ratio	9.2:1
Valve timing (2mm valve clearance, $\pm$ 2.5-degrees) intake opening	TDC
Intake closing	40° ABDC
Exhaust opening	40° BBDC
Exhaust closing	BDC
Horsepower	40 at 6400rpm
Left carburetor	Bing 1/26/111 (1/26/123 from 1976)
Right carburetor	Bing 1/26/112 (1/26/124 from 1976)
Main jet	140
Needle jet	2.68
Jet needle no.	4
Needle position	3

Idle jet	35
Sparkplugs	Bosch W230 T1, Champion N7Y, Beru 230/14/3A
Ignition timing	9 deg BTDC
Points gap	0.35-0.40mm
First gear	4.40:1
Second gear	2.86:1
Third gear	2.07:1
Fourth gear	1.67:1
Fifth gear	1.50:1
Final drive	11:37
Overall width	740mm
Seat height	810mm
Overall length	2180mm
Wheelbase	1435mm
Weight including oil and fuel	210kg
Top speed	167km/h (104mph)

R75/6

Year	1974-76
Bore (mm)	82
Stroke (mm)	70.6
Capacity (cc)	745
Compression ratio	9.0:1
Valve timing (2mm valve clearance, $\pm$ 2.5-degrees) intake opening	10° BTDC
Intake closing	50° ABDC
Exhaust opening	50 BBDC
Exhaust closing	10° ATDC
Horsepower	50 at 6200rpm
Left carburetor	Bing 64/32/9 (64/32/13 from 1976)
Right carburetor	Bing 64/32/10 (64/32/14 from 1976)
Main jet	135 (145 from 1976)
Needle jet	2.77 (2.66 from 1976)
Jet needle no.	46-241
Needle position	3
Idle jet	45 44-950
Sparkplugs	Bosch W200 T30, Champion N7Y, Beru 200/14/3A
Ignition timing	9 deg BTDC
Points gap	0.35-0.40mm
First gear	4.40:1
Second gear	2.86:1
Third gear	2.07:1
Fourth gear	1.67:1

Fifith gear	1.50:1
Final drive	10:32
Overall width	740mm
Seat height	810mm
Overall length	2180mm
Wheelbase	1435mm
Weight including oil and fuel	215kg
Top speed	175km/h (110mph)

R90/6

Year	1974-76
Bore (mm)	90
Stroke (mm)	70.6
Capacity (cc)	898
Compression ratio	9.0:1
Valve timing (2mm valve clearance, $\pm$ 2.5-degrees) intake opening	10° BTDC
Intake closing	50° ABDC
Exhaust opening	50 BBDC
Exhaust closing	10° ATDC
Horsepower	60 at 6500rpm
Left carburetor	Bing 64/32/11
Right carburetor	Bing 64/32/12
Main jet	150
Needle jet	2.68
Jet needle no.	46-241
Needle position	1
Idle jet	45 44-950
Sparkplugs	Bosch W200 T30, Champion N7Y, Beru 200/14/3A
Ignition timing	9 deg BTDC
Points gap	0.35-0.40mm
First gear	4.40:1
Second gear	2.86:1
Third gear	2.07:1
Fourth gear	1.67:1
Fifth gear	1.50:1
Final drive	11:34
Overall width	740mm
Seat height	810mm
Overall length	2180mm
Wheelbase	1435mm
Weight including oil and fuel	215kg
Top speed	188km/h (117mph)

R90S

Year	1974-76
Bore (mm)	90
Stroke (mm)	70.6
Capacity (cc)	898
Compression ratio	9.5:1

Valve timing (2mm valve clearance, ± 2.5-degrees)	
intake opening	10° BTDC
Intake closing	50° ABDC
Exhaust opening	50 BBDC
Exhaust closing	10° ATDC
Horsepower	67 at 7000rpm
Left carburetor	Dell'Orto PHM38AD (PHM38BD from 1976)
Right carburetor	Dell'Orto PHM38AS (PHM38BS from 1976)
Main jet	155
Needle jet	260
Jet needle no.	–
Needle position	3
Idle jet	60
Sparkplugs	Bosch W200 T30, Champion N7Y, Beru 200/14/3A
Ignition timing	9 deg BTDC
Points gap	0.35-0.40mm
First gear	4.40:1
Second gear	2.86:1
Third gear	2.07:1
Fourth gear	1.67:1
Fifth gear	1.50:1
Final drive	11:33
Overall width	740mm
Seat height	810mm
Overall length	2180mm
Wheelbase	1435mm
Weight including oil and fuel	220kg
Top speed	200km/h (124mph)

R60/7

Year	1977-80
Bore (mm)	73.5
Stroke (mm)	70.6
Capacity (cc)	599
Compression ratio	9.2:1
Valve timing (2mm valve clearance, ± 2.5-degrees)	
intake opening	TDC (6 BTDC from 1978)
Intake closing	40 ABDC (34 ABDC from 1978)
Exhaust opening	40 BBDC (34 BBDC from 1978)
Exhaust closing	TDC (6 ATDC from 1978)
Horsepower	40 at 6400rpm
Left carburetor	Bing 1/26/123
Right carburetor	Bing 1/26/124
Main jet	140
Needle jet	2.68
Jet needle no.	46-234
Needle position	2
Idle jet	40
Sparkplugs	Bosch W200 T30, Champion N7Y, Beru 200/14/3A
Ignition timing	9 deg BTDC
Points gap	0.35-0.40mm
First gear	4.40:1
Second gear	2.86:1
Third gear	2.07:1
Fourth gear	1.67:1
Fifth gear	1.50:1
Final drive	11:37
Overall width	746mm
Seat height	810mm
Overall length	2180mm
Wheelbase	1465mm
Weight including oil and fuel	215kg
Top speed	167km/h (104mph)

R75/7

Year	1977-79
Bore (mm)	82
Stroke (mm)	70.6
Capacity (cc)	745
Compression ratio	9.0:1
Valve timing (2mm valve clearance, ± 2.5-degrees)	
intake opening	10° BTDC
Intake closing	50° ABDC
Exhaust opening	50 BBDC
Exhaust closing	10° ATDC
Horsepower	50 at 6200rpm
Left carburetor	Bing 64/32/11 (64/32/313 from 1978)
Right carburetor	Bing 64/32/12 (64/32/314 from 1978)
Main jet	150 (145 from 1978)
Needle jet	2.66
Jet needle no.	46-241
Needle position	3
Idle jet	50
Sparkplugs	Bosch W200 T30, Champion N7Y, Beru 200/14/3A
Ignition timing	9 deg BTDC
Points gap	0.35-0.40mm
First gear	4.40:1
Second gear	2.86:1
Third gear	2.07:1
Fourth gear	1.67:1
Fifth gear	1.50:1
Final drive	10:32
Overall width	746mm
Seat height	810mm
Overall length	2180mm
Wheelbase	1465mm
Weight including oil and fuel	215kg
Top speed	177km/h (110mph)

R100/7

Year	1977-78
Bore (mm)	94
Stroke (mm)	70.6
Capacity (cc)	980
Compression ratio	9.1:1
Valve timing (2mm valve clearance, ± 2.5-degrees)	
intake opening	10 BTDC (16 BTDC from 1978)
Intake closing	50 ABDC (44 ABDC from 1978)
Exhaust opening	50 BBDC (56 BBDC from 1978)
Exhaust closing	10 ATDC (4 ATDC from 1978)
Horsepower	60 at 6500rpm
Left carburetor	Bing 64/32/19
Right carburetor	Bing 64/32/20
Main jet	150
Needle jet	2.68
Jet needle no.	46-241
Needle position	3
Idle jet	50
Sparkplugs	Bosch W200 T30, Champion N7Y, Beru 200/14/3A
Ignition timing	9 deg BTDC
Points gap	0.35-0.40mm
First gear	4.40:1
Second gear	2.86:1
Third gear	2.07:1
Fourth gear	1.67:1
Fifth gear	1.50:1
Final drive	11:34
Overall width	746mm
Seat height	810mm
Overall length	2180mm

Wheelbase	1465mm
Weight including oil and fuel	215kg
Top speed	188km/h (117mph)

R80/7

Year	1978-80
Bore (mm)	84.8
Stroke (mm)	70.6
Capacity (cc)	797
Compression ratio	9.2:1
Valve timing (2mm valve clearance, ± 2.5-degrees) intake opening	16°BTDC
Intake closing	44°ABDC
Exhaust opening	56°ABDC
Exhaust closing	4°ATDC
Horsepower	55 at 7000rpm
Left carburetor	Bing 64/32/13 (64/32/201 from 1978)
Right carburetor	Bing 64/32/14 (64/32/202 from 1978)
Main jet	145 (135 from 1978)
Needle jet	2.66
Jet needle no.	46-241
Needle position	3
Idle jet	50
Sparkplugs	Bosch W200 T30, Champion N7Y, Beru 200/14/3A
Ignition timing	9 deg BTDC
Points gap	0.35-0.40mm
First gear	4.40:1
Second gear	2.86:1
Third gear	2.07:1
Fourth gear	1.67:1
Fifth gear	1.50:1
Final drive	10:32
Overall width	746mm
Seat height	810mm
Overall length	2180mm
Wheelbase	1465mm
Weight including oil and fuel	215kg
Top speed	182km/h (113mph)

R100S

Year	1977-80
Bore (mm)	94
Stroke (mm)	70.6
Capacity (cc)	980
Compression ratio	9.5:1 (8.2:1 US)
Valve timing (2mm valve clearance, ± 2.5-degrees) intake opening	10 BTDC (16 BTDC from 1978)
Intake closing	50 ABDC (44 ABDC from 1978)
Exhaust opening	50 BBDC (56 BBDC from 1978)
Exhaust closing	10 ATDC (4 ATDC from 1978)
Horsepower	65 at 6600rpm (70 at 7250rpm)
Left carburetor	Bing 94/40/103 (94/40/105 from 1979)
Right carburetor	Bing 94/40/104 (94/40/106 from 1979)
Main jet	170
Needle jet	2.66 (2.68 from 1979)
Jet needle no.	46-341
Needle position	3
Idle jet	45
Sparkplugs	Bosch W200 T30, Champion N7Y, Beru 200/14/3A
Ignition timing	9 deg BTDC
Points gap	0.35-0.40mm
First gear	4.40:1
Second gear	2.86:1
Third gear	2.07:1
Fourth gear	1.67:1
Fifth gear	1.50:1
Final drive	11:32
Overall width	746mm
Seat height	810mm
Overall length	2180mm
Wheelbase	1465mm
Weight including oil and fuel	220kg
Top speed	Over 200km/h (124mph)

R100RS

Year	1977-80
Bore (mm)	94
Stroke (mm)	70.6
Capacity (cc)	980
Compression ratio	9.5:1 (8.2:1 US)
Valve timing (2mm valve clearance, ± 2.5-degrees) intake opening	10 BTDC (16 BTDC from 1978)
Intake closing	50 ABDC (44 ABDC from 1978)
Exhaust opening	50 BBDC (56 BBDC from 1978)
Exhaust closing	10 ATDC (4 ATDC from 1978)
Horsepower	70 at 7250rpm
Left carburetor	Bing 94/40/105
Right carburetor	Bing 94/40/106
Main jet	170
Needle jet	2.68
Jet needle no.	46-341
Needle position	2
Idle jet	45
Sparkplugs	Bosch W200 T30 Champion N7Y Beru 200/14/3A
Ignition timing	9 deg BTDC
Points gap	0.35-0.40mm
First gear	4.40:1
Second gear	2.86:1
Third gear	2.07:1
Fourth gear	1.67:1
Fifth gear	1.50:1
Final drive	11:33
Overall width	746mm
Seat height	810mm
Overall length	2180mm
Wheelbase	1465mm
Weight including oil and fuel	230kg
Top speed	Over 200km/h (124mph)

R100T

Year	1979-80
Bore (mm)	94
Stroke (mm)	70.6
Capacity (cc)	980
Compression ratio	9.5:1 (8.2:1 US)
Valve timing (2mm valve clearance, ± 2.5-degrees) intake opening	16°BTDC
Intake closing	44°ABDC
Exhaust opening	56°ABDC
Exhaust closing	4°ATDC
Horsepower	65 at 6600rpm
Left carburetor	Bing 94/40/103
Right carburetor	Bing 94/40/104
Main jet	170
Needle jet	2.66
Jet needle no.	46-341
Needle position	2
Idle jet	45
Sparkplugs	Bosch W200 T30,

Champion N7Y, Beru 200/14/3A

Ignition timing	9 deg BTDC
Points gap	0.35-0.40mm
First gear	4.40:1
Second gear	2.86:1
Third gear	2.07:1
Fourth gear	1.67:1
Fifth gear	1.50:1
Final drive	11:33
Overall width	746mm
Seat height	810mm
Overall length	2130mm
Wheelbase	1465mm
Weight including oil and fuel	215kg
Top speed	190km/h (118mph)

R100RT

Year	1979-80
Bore (mm)	94
Stroke (mm)	70.6
Capacity (cc)	980
Compression ratio	9.5:1 (8.2:1 US)
Valve timing (2mm valve clearance, ± 2.5-degrees) intake opening	16°BTDC
Intake closing	44°ABDC
Exhaust opening	56°ABDC
Exhaust closing	4°ATDC
Horsepower	70 at 7250rpm
Left carburetor	Bing 94/40/105
Right carburetor	Bing 94/40/106
Main jet	170
Needle jet	2.68
Jet needle no.	46-341
Needle position	2
Idle jet	45
Sparkplugs	Bosch W200 T30, Champion N7Y, Beru 200/14/3A
Ignition timing	9 deg BTDC
Points gap	0.35-0.40mm
First gear	4.40:1
Second gear	2.86:1
Third gear	2.07:1
Fourth gear	1.67:1
Fifth gear	1.50:1
Final drive	11:33
Overall width	746mm
Seat height	810mm
Overall length	2130mm
Wheelbase	1465mm
Weight including oil and fuel	234kg
Top speed	190km/h (118mph)

R100

Year	1981-84
Bore (mm)	94
Stroke (mm)	70.6
Capacity (cc)	980
Compression ratio	8.2:1
Valve timing (2mm valve clearance, ± 2.5-degrees) intake opening	16°BTDC
Intake closing	44°ABDC
Exhaust opening	56°ABDC
Exhaust closing	4°ATDC
Horsepower	67 at 7000rpm
Left carburetor	Bing 94/40/111 (113 US models)
Right carburetor	Bing 94/40/112 (114 US models)
Main jet	160
Needle jet	2.66
Jet needle no.	46-341
Needle position	3 (2)
Idle jet	45
Sparkplugs	Bosch W6DC, Champion N7Y, Beru 14-6D
Ignition timing	6 deg BTDC
Points gap	Electronic Ignition
First gear	4.40:1
Second gear	2.86:1
Third gear	2.07:1
Fourth gear	1.67:1
Fifth gear	1.50:1
Final drive	11:33
Overall width	746mm
Seat height	810mm
Overall length	2210mm
Wheelbase	1465mm
Weight including oil and fuel	225kg
Top speed	190km/h (118mph)

R100CS

Year	1981-84
Bore (mm)	94
Stroke (mm)	70.6
Capacity (cc)	980
Compression ratio	9.5:1
Valve timing (2mm valve clearance, ± 2.5-degrees) intake opening	16°BTDC
Intake closing	44°ABDC
Exhaust opening	56°ABDC
Exhaust closing	4°ATDC
Horsepower	70 at 7000rpm
Left carburetor	Bing 94/40/111 (113 US models)
Right carburetor	Bing 94/40/112 (114 US models)
Main jet	160
Needle jet	2.66
Jet needle no.	46-341
Needle position	3 (2)
Idle jet	45
Sparkplugs	Bosch W5DC, Champion N6Y, Beru 14-5D
Ignition timing	6 deg BTDC
Points gap	Electronic Ignition
First gear	4.40:1
Second gear	2.86:1
Third gear	2.07:1
Fourth gear	1.67:1
Fifth gear	1.50:1
Final drive	11:33
Overall width	746mm
Seat height	810mm
Overall length	2210mm
Wheelbase	1465mm
Weight including oil and fuel	220kg
Top speed	200km/h (124mph)

R100RS

Year	1981-84
Bore (mm)	94
Stroke (mm)	70.6
Capacity (cc)	980
Compression ratio	9.5:1
Valve timing (2mm valve clearance, ± 2.5-degrees) intake opening	16°BTDC
Intake closing	44°ABDC
Exhaust opening	56°ABDC
Exhaust closing	4°ATDC
Horsepower	70 at 7250rpm
Left carburetor	Bing 94/40/111 (113 US models)
Right carburetor	Bing 94/40/112 (114 US models)
Main jet	160
Needle jet	2.66
Jet needle no.	46-341
Needle position	3 (2)
Idle jet	45
Sparkplugs	Bosch W5DC, Champion N6Y, Beru 14-5D

Ignition timing	6 deg BTDC
Points gap	Electronic Ignition
First gear	4.40:1
Second gear	2.86:1
Third gear	2.07:1
Fourth gear	1.67:1
Fifth gear	1.50:1
Final drive	11:33
Overall width	746mm
Seat height	810mm
Overall length	2210mm
Wheelbase	1465mm
Weight including oil and fuel	230kg
Top speed	190km/h (118mph)

R100RT

Year	1981-84
Bore (mm)	94
Stroke (mm)	70.6
Capacity (cc)	980
Compression ratio	9.5:1
Valve timing (2mm valve clearance, ± 2.5-degrees) intake opening	16°BTDC
Intake closing	44°ABDC
Exhaust opening	56°ABDC
Exhaust closing	4°ATDC
Horsepower	70 at 7250rpm
Left carburetor	Bing 94/40/111 (113 US models)
Right carburetor	Bing 94/40/112 (114 US models)
Main jet	160
Needle jet	2.66
Jet needle no.	46-341
Needle position	3 (2)
Idle jet	45
Sparkplugs	Bosch W5DC, Champion N6Y, Beru 14-5D
Ignition timing	6 deg BTDC
Points gap	Electronic Ignition
First gear	4.40:1
Second gear	2.86:1
Third gear	2.07:1
Fourth gear	1.67:1
Fifth gear	1.50:1
Final drive	11:33
Overall width	746mm
Seat height	810mm
Overall length	2210mm
Wheelbase	1465mm
Weight including oil and fuel	245kg
Top speed	185km/h (115mph)

R80RT

Year	1983-84
Bore (mm)	84.8
Stroke (mm)	70.6
Capacity (cc)	797
Compression ratio	8.2:1
Valve timing (2mm valve clearance, ± 2.5-degrees) intake opening	16°BTDC
Intake closing	44°ABDC
Exhaust opening	56°ABDC
Exhaust closing	4°ATDC
Horsepower	50 at 6500rpm
Left carburetor	Bing 64/32/305 (323 US)
Right carburetor	Bing 64/32/306 (324 US)
Main jet	150
Needle jet	2.66
Jet needle no.	46-241
Needle position	3
Idle jet	40
Sparkplugs	Bosch W7DC, Champion N10Y, Beru 14-7D
Ignition timing	6 deg BTDC
Points gap	Electronic Ignition
First gear	4.40:1
Second gear	2.86:1
Third gear	2.07:1
Fourth gear	1.67:1
Fifth gear	1.50:1
Final drive	11:37
Overall width	746mm
Seat height	810mm
Overall length	2210mm
Wheelbase	1465mm
Weight including oil and fuel	235kg
Top speed	161km/h (100mph)

R80RT

Year	1985-96
Bore (mm)	84.8
Stroke (mm)	70.6
Capacity (cc)	797
Compression ratio	8.2:1
Valve timing (2mm valve clearance, ± 2.5-degrees) intake opening	–
Intake closing	–
Exhaust opening	–
Exhaust closing	–
Horsepower	50 at 6500rpm
Left carburetor	Bing V64/32/353
Right carburetor	Bing V64/32/354
Main jet	–
Needle jet	–
Jet needle no.	–
Needle position	–
Idle jet	–
Sparkplugs	Bosch W7DC, Champion N9YC, Beru 14-7DU
Ignition timing	–
Points gap	Electronic Ignition
First gear	4.40:1
Second gear	2.86:1
Third gear	2.07:1
Fourth gear	1.67:1
Fifth gear	1.50:1
Final drive	11:37
Overall width	960mm
Seat height	807mm
Overall length	2175mm
Wheelbase	1447mm
Weight including oil and fuel	227kg
Top speed	170km/h (106mph)

R80

Year	1985-95
Bore (mm)	84.8
Stroke (mm)	70.6
Capacity (cc)	797
Compression ratio	8.2:1
Valve timing (2mm valve clearance, ± 2.5-degrees) intake opening	–
Intake closing	–
Exhaust opening	–
Exhaust closing	–
Horsepower	50 at 6500rpm
Left carburetor	Bing V64/32/353
Right carburetor	Bing V64/32/354
Main jet	–
Needle jet	–
Jet needle no.	–
Needle position	–
Idle jet	–
Sparkplugs	Bosch W7DC, Champion N9YC, Beru 14-7DU
Ignition timing	–
Points gap	Electronic Ignition
First gear	4.40:1
Second gear	2.86:1

Third gear	2.07:1
Fourth gear	1.67:1
Fifith gear	1.50:1
Final drive	10:32
Overall width	800mm
Seat height	807mm
Overall length	2175mm
Wheelbase	1447mm
Weight including oil and fuel	210kg
Top speed	178km/h (111mph)

R65

Year	1986-88
Bore (mm)	82
Stroke (mm)	61.5
Capacity (cc)	650
Compression ratio	8.7:1
Valve timing (2mm valve clearance, ± 2.5-degrees) intake opening	–
Intake closing	–
Exhaust opening	–
Exhaust closing	–
Horsepower	48 at 7250rpm
Left carburetor	Bing V64/32/359
Right carburetor	Bing V64/32/360
Main jet	–
Needle jet	–
Jet needle no.	–
Needle position	–
Idle jet	–
Sparkplugs	Bosch W7DC, Champion N9YC, Beru 14-7DU
Ignition timing	–
Points gap	Electronic Ignition
First gear	4.40:1
Second gear	2.86:1
Third gear	2.07:1
Fourth gear	1.67:1
Fifith gear	1.50:1
Final drive	11:37
Overall width	800mm
Seat height	807mm
Overall length	2175mm
Wheelbase	1447mm
Weight including oil and fuel	210kg
Top speed	174km/h (108mph)

R100RS

Year	1987-93
Bore (mm)	94
Stroke (mm)	70.6
Capacity (cc)	980
Compression ratio	8.45:1
Valve timing (2mm valve clearance, ± 2.5-degrees) intake opening	–
Intake closing	–
Exhaust opening	–
Exhaust closing	–
Horsepower	60 at 6500rpm
Left carburetor	Bing V64/32/363
Right carburetor	Bing V64/32/364
Main jet	–
Needle jet	–
Jet needle no.	–
Needle position	–
Idle jet	–
Sparkplugs	Bosch W7DC, Champion N9YC, Beru 14-7DU
Ignition timing	–
Points gap	Electronic Ignition
First gear	4.40:1
Second gear	2.86:1
Third gear	2.07:1
Fourth gear	1.67:1
Fifith gear	1.50:1
Final drive	11:33
Overall width	800mm
Seat height	807mm
Overall length	2175mm
Wheelbase	1447mm
Weight including oil and fuel	229kg
Top speed	185km/h (115mph)

R100RT

Year	1988-95
Bore (mm)	94
Stroke (mm)	70.6
Capacity (cc)	980
Compression ratio	8.45:1
Valve timing (2mm valve clearance, ± 2.5-degrees) intake opening	–
Intake closing	–
Exhaust opening	–
Exhaust closing	–
Horsepower	60 at 6500rpm
Left carburetor	Bing V64/32/363
Right carburetor	Bing V64/32/364
Main jet	–
Needle jet	–
Jet needle no.	–
Needle position	–
Idle jet	–
Sparkplugs	Bosch W7DC, Champion N9YC, Beru 14-7DU
Ignition timing	–
Points gap	Electronic Ignition
First gear	4.40:1
Second gear	2.86:1
Third gear	2.07:1
Fourth gear	1.67:1
Fifith gear	1.50:1
Final drive	11:33
Overall width	960mm
Seat height	807mm
Overall length	2175mm
Wheelbase	1447mm
Weight including oil and fuel	234kg
Top speed	185km/h (115mph)

R100R

Year	1992-95
Bore (mm)	94
Stroke (mm)	70.6
Capacity (cc)	980
Compression ratio	8.5:1
Valve timing (2mm valve clearance, ± 2.5-degrees) intake opening	–
Intake closing	–
Exhaust opening	–
Exhaust closing	–
Horsepower	60 at 6500rpm
Left carburetor	Bing V64/40/123
Right carburetor	Bing V64/40/124
Main jet	–
Needle jet	–
Jet needle no.	–
Needle position	–
Idle jet	–
Sparkplugs	Bosch W7DC, Champion N9YC, Beru 14-7DU
Ignition timing	–
Points gap	Electronic Ignition
First gear	4.40:1
Second gear	2.86:1
Third gear	2.07:1
Fourth gear	1.67:1
Fifith gear	1.50:1
Final drive	11:34
Overall width	1000mm
Seat height	800mm
Overall length	2210mm
Wheelbase	1495mm

Weight including oil and fuel	218kg	Intake closing	–
Top speed	181km/h (112mph)	Exhaust opening	–

R80R

Year	1992-94	Exhaust closing	–
Bore (mm)	84.8	Horsepower	50 at 6500rpm
Stroke (mm)	70.6	Left carburetor	Bing V64/32/349
Capacity (cc)	797	Right carburetor	Bing V64/32/350
Compression ratio	8.2:1	Main jet	–
		Needle jet	–
		Jet needle no.	–
		Needle position	–
		Idle jet	–
Valve timing (2mm valve clearance, ± 2.5-degrees)		Sparkplugs	Bosch W7DC, Champion N9YC, Beru 14-7DU
intake opening	–	Ignition timing	–

Points gap	Electronic Ignition
First gear	4.40:1
Second gear	2.86:1
Third gear	2.07:1
Fourth gear	1.67:1
Fifth gear	1.50:1
Final drive	10:32
Overall width	1000mm
Seat height	800mm
Overall length	2210mm
Wheelbase	1495mm
Weight including oil and fuel	217kg
Top speed	168km/h (104mph)

/5 production

Model	Dates	1969	1970	1971	1972	1973	Total
R50/5	11/69-04/73	399	2053	1737	2130	1546	7865
R60/5	09/69-04/73	666	4116	6645	6564	4730	22,721
R75/5	10/69-08/73	540	6118	10,390	12,428	8894	38,370

/6 production 1974 model year

Model	Dates	1973	1974	Total
R60/6	09/73-08/74	448	1229	1677
R60/6 US	01/74-08/74		827	827
R75/6	09/73-08/74	1203	1628	2831
R75/6 US	06/74-08/74		1097	1097
R90/6	09/73-08/74	3049	1922	4971
R90/6 US	01/74-08/74		2218	2218
R90S	09/73-08/74	986	4067	5053
R90S US	09/73-08/74		1005	1005

/6 production 1975 model year

Model	Dates	1974	1975	Total
R60/6	08/74-08/75	1575	2293	3868
R60/6 US	08/74-07/75	593	510	1103
R75/6	08/74-08/75	1198	2490	3688
R75/6 US	08/74-08/75	962	1125	2087
R90/6	08/74-08/75	984	2327	3311
R90/6 US	08/74-08/75	1802	2461	4263
R90S	08/74-09/75	1376	3299	4675
R90S US	08/74-08/75	677	1061	1738

/6 production 1976 model year

Model	Dates	1975	1976	Total
R60/6	09/75-07/76		2012	2012
R60/6 US	09/75-07/76		643	643
R75/6	09/75-07/76	1955	3351	5306
R75/6 US	09/75-07/76	1166	1412	2578
R90/6	09/75-07/76	716	2302	3018
R90/6 US	09/75-07/76	2012	1304	3316
R90S	09/75-07/76	912	2812	3724
R90S US	09/75-07/76	584	676	1260

/7 production 1977 model year

Model	Dates	1976	1977	Total
R60/7	08/76-07/77	2207	3310	5517
R60/7 US	08/76-06/77	296	111	407
R75/7	08/76-07/77	1533	2974	4507
R75/7 US	08/76-06/77	1315	159	1474
R100/7	08/76-07/77	1771	1643	3414
R100/7 US	08/76-07/77	1587	864	2451
R100S	08/76-06/77	1461	1688	3149
R100S US	08/76-06/77	841	544	1385
R100RS	08/76-07/77	1418	3741	5159
R100RS US	08/76-06/77	542	721	1263

/7 production 1978 model year

Model	Dates	1977	1978	Total
R60/7 (&T)	07/77-07/78	3035	1391	4426
R60/7 US	08/77-12/77	158		158
R75/7	08/77-05/78	107	171	278
R80/7 (&N,T)	07/77-07/78	2323	3658	5981
R80/7 US	08/77-03/78	1813	596	2409
R100/7	07/77-07/78	898	2185	3083
R100/7 US	07/77-07/78	2565	631	3196
R100S	07/77-07/78	752	3003	3755
R100S US	07/77-07/78	963	407	1370
R100RS	08/77-07/78	2395	4470	6865
R100RS US	08/77-12/77	751	341	1092
R100RS-T US	04/78-08/78		4	4

7 production 1979 and 1980 model years

Model	Dates	1978	1979	1980	Total
R60/7 (&T)	09/78-07/80	263			263
R75/7	01/79-07/79		5		5
R80/7 (&N,T)	09/78-07/80	545	2271	2278	5094
R80/7 US	09/78-07/80	103	73	173	349
R100/7	08/78-07/80	393	1553	1689	3635
R100/7 US	09/78-07/80	202	723	419	1344
R100T	11/78-07/80	58	307	31	396
R100S	09/78-07/80	224	645	1082	1951
R100S US	09/78-07/80	102	2	48	152
R100RS	08/78-07/80	704	2303	2323	5330
R100RS US	09/78-07/80	209	223	87	519
R100RS-T US	09/78-06/80	628	656	567	1851
R100RT	08/78-07/80	1029	3055	2270	6354

R100 and R80RT production 1981-84 model years

Model	Dates	1980	1981	1982	1983	1984	Total
R100CS	09/80-10/84	516	1530	1276	493	49	3864
R100CS US	09/80-9/84	126	38	4	3	3	174
R100	09/80-11/84	948	2666	2394	594	193	6795
R100 US	09/80-10/84	358	556	598	673	237	2422
R100 TIC (Police)	10/80-10/84	9	235	214	284	152	894
R100RT	08/80-10/84	1140	2910	2512	909	45	7516
R100RT US	09/80-9/84	729	1292	549	1284	291	4145
R80RT	07/82-11/84			1638	2539	986	5163
R80RT US	08/82-10/84			632	967	553	2152

R80 and R100 production 1985-90

Model	Dates	1984	1985	1986	1987	1988	1989	1990	Total
R80	09/84-01/95	497	3637	2180	1155	761	797	1702	10,729
R100RS	09/86-07/93			435	1613	860	890	337	4135
R80RT	09/84-12/95	446	3638	2382	3274	1914	2107	2287	16,048
R100RT	09/87-12/96				689	570	1181	901	3341
R100US	12/90-12/95							157	157
R80US	11/84-07/87	10	794	313	3				1120
R80RT US	11/84-04/87	10	1224	215	3				1452
R100RS US	09/87-07/92				300	298	1		599
R100RT US	09/87-12/95				402	395	2	181	980

Index